GLOBAL ORDER AND GLOBAL DISORDER

GLOBAL ORDER AND
GLOBAL DISORDER

Globalization and the Nation-State

Keith Suter

Westport, Connecticut
London

Library of Congress Cataloging-in-Publication Data

Suter, Keith.
 Global order and global disorder : globalization and the nation-state / Keith Suter.
  p. cm.
 Includes bibliographical references and index.
 ISBN 0–275–97388–3 (alk. paper)
 1. Globalization. 2. International organization. 3. State, The. 4. Non-governmental
organizations. I. Title.
JZ1318 .S88 2003
327.1—dc21   2002070863

British Library Cataloguing in Publication Data is available.

Library of Congress Catalog Card Number: 2002070863
ISBN: 0-275-97388-3

First published in 2003

Praeger Publishers, 88 Post Road West, Westport, CT 06881
An imprint of Greenwood Publishing Group, Inc.
www.praeger.com

Printed in the United States of America

The paper used in this book complies with the
Permanent Paper Standard issued by the National
Information Standards Organization (Z39.48–1984).

10 9 8 7 6 5 4 3 2 1

Contents

Preface   vii

1. Global Order and Global Disorder   1

2. The Rise of the Old World Order: The Nation-State System   17

3. The Weaknesses of the Nation-State System   31

4. The New Global Actors   67

5. The Characteristics of Globalization   115

6. Thinking About the Future: The Value of Scenario Planning   151

7. Four Worldviews on Globalization   161

8. Ready for Change   195

Selected Bibliography   199

Index   203

Preface

This book is about the end of the current world order and the rise of globalization. We are witnessing the end of what international lawyers call the Westphalian System of nation-states. The erosion of that system is manifested in, for example, the increasing influence of transnational corporations in national economies, the growing recognition by intergovernmental organizations of the need to respect human rights, and the capacity of nongovernmental organizations to draw attention to the need to protect the environment. National governments will remain in existence but they will have reduced significance. We are moving from a world with borders to one without.

This book, then, is an examination of the changing global structure. It is not an attempt to predict the shape of the new global order that is coming into being with the erosion of the nation-state. No one knows for sure where the process of globalization will take the world.

This is a very exciting time to live. The Westphalian System began three centuries ago. We are living on the hinge of history: one era is swinging closed and another is swinging open.

This book draws upon my activities in three areas. I have been involved in the work of the United Nations Association (in the UK and Australia) for over thirty years. I wrote my first book on the UN for the UN Association of Australia in 1985: *Reshaping the Global Agenda*.

Second, I belong to a variety of other nongovernmental organizations, such as The Club of Rome and the World Federalists. These, too, have been useful sources of information. The Australian Branch of the World Federalists encouraged me to write my first book on globalization in 1981 titled *A New International Order: Proposals for Making a Better World*.

Finally, I have designed and taught courses on globalization at the University of Sydney, the University of New South Wales and the Workers Education Association in Sydney. The best way to learn is to teach, and I am grateful for my contacts with students over all the years. I am pleased to note the growth of interest in the subject of globalization over time.

I am also very grateful to the team at Greenwood.

Global Order and Global Disorder

INTRODUCTION

The Nature of Globalization

The current world order is ending, but there is no clear replacement for it. The old order has been based on nation-states, or countries, with centralized national governments. The old order has worn well but now it is wearing out. The process of globalization, which is now the most important factor in world politics, is undermining the traditional order and leading to world disorder.

Globalization is defined in this book as the process by which the nation-state is eroding as the basic unit of world politics. The term includes the declining power of national governments and the reduced significance of national boundaries.

This book's approach to globalization is based on five features. First, the new era is global, rather than international. The concept "international" regards the nation-state as the basic component of world affairs: all that happens at the planetary level is a form of interaction among nation-states or national governments. That is no longer the case. There are other nonstate actors on the world stage. Most notably, these actors include transnational corporations; intergovernmental organizations, particularly the United Nations; and nongovernmental organizations, such as those for women, peace, and the environment.

Second, globalization is more than just a matter of economics (as was the concern of protesters at Seattle in 1999 and Davos, Switzerland and Melbourne, Australia in 2000 and the 2001 riot in Genoa in which a demonstrator was killed). Globalization means that global change is running ahead of the ability of governments to manage it. Economics is only a part of that process. This book also deals with other matters such as war, crime, environment, and health. Therefore, while there is an examination of the growth and impact of transnational corporations, this book takes in many other matters so as to get a fuller picture of globalization.

Third, this book does not view the process of globalization as some dark, sinister conspiracy organized by a group of transnational corporations or some group of ill-motivated individuals wishing to take over the world.[1] On the contrary, this book sees globalization more as chaos than conspiracy, with no overall guiding hand. It is a matter of "disorder" rather than "order."

Fourth, the reduction in national government power is creating a vacuum at the global level which is not being filled by any supranational organization. There is no clear replacement for the existing traditional world order—or even an agreed mechanism for creating one. Therefore, the book deals with disorder as well as order.

Finally, the process of globalization is not reversible. It is not possible to reinvent the era of nation-states. Coming to terms with the new era and seeing how we are to cope with it is necessary. Therefore, there has to be a search for a new order rather than an attempt to patch up the system of nation-states which would only waste time.

OVERVIEW OF THE BOOK

Much of the anger now evident about economic globalization is based on the resentment of being taken by surprise. However, the process of globalization has not been done in secret. Many people have been simply focusing their attention on other matters. The next section of this chapter deals with the importance of paying more attention to the underlying structural level of events—or else people will continue to be taken by surprise. Chapter 1 ends with a case study of the end of the Cold War viewed through the perspective of globalization.

The basic component of global politics has been the nation-state system. Chapter 2 looks at the evolution of that system, also called the Westphalian System, and how its logic has dominated the study of world politics. Even without the rise of global nonstate actors and forces, the Westphalian System was heading for trouble because too many nation-states exist for the system to work as in previous centuries.

Chapter 3 examines the erosion of the Westphalian System. One problem for the system has been the ending of the Europeanization of the globe, as the Westphalian structure is very much a European product. Other difficulties have included the proliferation of nation-states; the new era in which warfare is noninternational guerrilla fighting, rather than conventional international battles; and the lack of agreement among governments on how to handle the break-up of nation-states.

Chapter 4 deals with the new global actors: transnational corporations, intergovernmental organizations, and nongovernmental organizations. While the nation-state will continue to exist, it will have to reconcile itself to sharing power with these new influences.

Chapter 5 analyses the five main characteristics of globalization. These characteristics include global problems not being solved by governments acting alone, the process of global fragmentation and reconfiguration, the erosion of the distinction between domestic and foreign policies, the importance of new technology, and the reaction against globalization.

Chapter 6 looks at the technique, now increasingly popular in business, of scenario planning which enables people to look at possible futures. It is impossible to predict the future, but one should try to anticipate the future by having contingency plans.

Chapter 7 takes a part of the scenario planning technique to devise four worldviews on the future of the nation-state system and globalization.

Chapter 8 concludes the book with a call for more attention to the subject of global governance.

THE MEDIA AND GLOBALIZATION: THREE WAYS OF LOOKING AT EVENTS

Much of the current attention to globalization outside academic circles is driven by a sense of anger at being taken by surprise by what is happening. At one end of the political spectrum, some nationalistic politicians have become spokespersons for that anger; some of these politicians are Patrick Buchanan in the United States, Jorge Haider in Austria, Jean Le Pen in France, and Pauline Hanson in Australia.[2] At the other end of the political spectrum, there have been demonstrators in Seattle, Davos, and Melbourne. While these demonstrators may have had different political values, such as less xenophobia, they have been equally critical of corporate power.[3]

However, the process of globalization has not been created in secret. There has been no conspiracy of silence. It is simply that people have been looking elsewhere.

There are three ways of looking at issues: events, patterns, and structures.

"Events" are the daily blow-by-blow items that receive most of the coverage in the mass media, such as crimes and the personal activities of politicians. Almost all political reporting, particularly on television, falls into this category. Detailed reports, for example, of what the president did that day and stories about political confrontation are examples of events. Stories about foreign affairs are often based on what the secretary of state did that day. The mass media tend to focus too much on personalities and too little on policies. The emphasis is more on who will win rather than who is right.

"Patterns" are covered in television and radio documentaries as well as feature articles and opinion pieces in newspapers. The events filling television screens and front ends of the newspapers each day can be seen as part of wider range of occurrences. A documentary or feature article may, for example, trace the progress made in seeking a peace agreement in the Middle East or China's entry into the World Trade Organization. They help put the daily events into some form of perspective

At the "structural" level (which receives the least amount of attention in the public discourse), the attention is on the foundation under girding the patterns. This book is about one such foundation: the Westphalian System of nation-states. The erosion of that system is manifested in most notably the increasing influence of transnational corporations in national economies, the increasing importance of intergovernmental organizations in facilitating co-operation among governments on common problems, and the capacity of non-governmental organizations to draw attention to different needs, for example protecting the environment.

REPORTING GLOBALIZATION

Until the recent backlash against globalization, there was little media cov-erage of it. First, globalization was seen as too detached from the lives of the consumers of the media. At the level of events, it appeared in such matters as the involvement of the United States in UN treaties, conferences, and peace-keeping operations. Even now much of the media coverage is still limited to the level of events and particular aspects of the impact of economic globaliza-tion, including the use of violence in anti-globalization demonstrations.

Second, most consumers in developed countries do not want to devote much time to the task of watching, listening to, or reading about serious world affairs. Instead, their preference is for sport, sex, scandal, and entertainment. This sounds very cynical but it is illustrated by the popularity of MTV over PBS television programs and the popularity of late night comedy programs over serious current affairs discussions. Even these latter programs have to be based on current events of concern, rather than the underlying structural matters relating to globalization.

Third, the media bombard consumers with so much information on events that they may feel confused about what is happening. There is an emphasis on instant reporting over more reflective reporting, which could help consumers put the events in context. In other words, news programs tend to go for break-ing stories in the desire to be first with the news. (I broadcast on a radio station in Sydney that prides itself on being "first, fast and factual.") However, what is disturbing is the way that television and radio presenters (let alone the con-sumers) have no sense of a larger pattern into which the events they are so breathlessly reporting may be forming.

Finally, the nature of reporting has changed so that it is more tabloid: there is a concern with emotions rather than facts. For example, in December 1988, a Pan Am aircraft was destroyed by a bomb over Scotland. Ms. Georgia Nucci, mother of one of the victims, later complained that within two minutes of discovering herself to be one of the relatives, she was "swamped by hordes of journalists" who invaded her privacy and asked her "How do you feel?"[4] Tab-loid reporting means that consumers may learn about the anger of people who see themselves as losers in the process of globalization but not necessarily learn much about the process itself or what might be done about it. The anger itself is reported, rather than some suggestions for action.

To conclude, these four factors help explain why the process of globalization has received so little coherent treatment in the media. This book deals with the underlying structural issues of globalization. Further, the focus is on the declining role of the nation-state, rather than events such as a factory closure or demonstration by a group of unemployed workers.

GLOBALIZATION AND THE END OF COLD WAR: THE END OF THE U.S.S.R.

To lose one's best friend is a tragedy; to lose one's worst enemy is a catastrophe. The disappearance of the U.S.S.R. deprived the United States and its allies of their central foreign policy theme. Life will not be the same without the U.S.S.R. The post–Cold War world is an uncertain place. For almost half a century, it was the defining global political event. The Cold War simplified issues: a decision for most national governments on any foreign problem was made in the context of how that would affect the relationship with the United States or U.S.S.R. and help the aims of either country.

This section is a case study of how the Cold War may be viewed through the prism of globalization. Governments have been slow to recognize the process of globalization. This is partly due to the way in which they were too focused on the Cold War. While the two super powers and their respective allies were so busy running the arms race, a new global order began to emerge. Globalization has been particularly influenced by three groups of nonstate actors: transnational corporations, hence the importance of trade and finance; intergovernmental organizations, including the UN and others which have facilitated greater economic and social cooperation despite the Cold War; and nongovernmental organizations, which have sought to change government policy and have facilitated greater people-to-people contacts across national lines.

TRADE AND FINANCE

Transnational corporations are helping to create a new global trade and financial order. In the context of the Cold War, five trends are worth noting.

The U.S.S.R. and the Global Consumer Culture

There is a new global consumer culture. The citizens of the U.S.S.R. may have been militarily loyal to Moscow, but their hearts were in Hollywood. Hollywood makes the best dreams.

The United States made a major mistake in the mid-1940s in implementing its policy of containment. It opposed the U.S.S.R. on that country's own grounds rather than on its own. A centrally planned economy can make weapons, but it has much more difficulty in making consumer goods. Thus, a country like the U.S.S.R. is itself the market for weapons and knows what it wants. However, its citizens are the market for consumer items, and a government committee of old men living a comparatively luxurious and isolated existence in Moscow cannot easily ascertain the tastes of the ordinary person. Therefore, the U.S.S.R. was able to keep in the arms race—even though the United States overestimated the U.S.S.R.'s strength.[5] However, matching the U.S. production of consumer goods was not possible. While the U.S.S.R. could put people into space, it could not put consumer goods on shop shelves.

Western Cold War politicians saw the arms race as the key component of the Cold War. But they ignored the everyday basics of life. Few predicted the collapse of the U.S.S.R. from within.[6] Although Soviet citizens were yearning for the so-called good things of life, they recognized that their system could not produce Coke, Big Macs, and Madonna. Thus, while President Reagan in the early 1980s regarded the U.S.S.R. as the "evil empire," transnational corporations saw Soviet citizens as potential customers. Soviet citizens were disturbed by such presidential rhetoric but still yearned for the American way of life.

Russia's greatest writer in the twentieth century, Aleksandr Solzhenitsyn, provides an example of the impact of the consumer culture. Seeing himself as a conscience during the Communist era, he was a critic of the regime.[7] Solzhenitsyn was eventually expelled from the U.S.S.R. in 1974 and lived in exile in Vermont. In 1989, with the Soviet regime in trouble, Solzhenitsyn insisted that his books had to be available at book stores in the U.S.S.R. before he would return home. In 1994, he returned home for the first time in two decades. The Soviet regime had gone. Although his books were in the book stores, few copies were being sold. Instead, many consumers were now purchasing the books on sports, sex, romance, and entertainment that were available from the West. They did not want to read about the suffering under communism—they wanted escape from it.

Information Technology

In 1986, I raised the issue of what modern technology would do to the U.S.S.R., and I predicted that Moscow would have increasing difficulty in controlling its citizens (though I did not forecast as dramatic an end to the U.S.S.R. as in fact took place).[8] In essence, the U.S.S.R. was a country that had specialized in basic tasks, such as feeding its own people, and lived off an economy based on agriculture, oil, and mining. Many of its best brains had gone into the defense industry. Even this relatively unsophisticated economy was having problems catering to its people.

However, the U.S.S.R.'s problems were only just beginning because the information technology revolution meant that the key components in the economy would be research and information. Raw materials, like metal, were less important. A Western 2000 car, for example, has about as much metal in it as does a 1960 model; the difference in the two models lies in the information as to how that metal is used.[9] But the U.S.S.R. was a society in which information was closely guarded, even to the extent that there were not telephone directories or detailed street maps.[10]

Thus, the U.S.S.R. was presented with a challenge. It could continue on in the way it was doing, and continue to slip further and further behind the Western developed countries. This in itself would be a problem as its citizens could receive Western radio broadcasts and learn about the much better life enjoyed on the other side of the iron curtain. Alternatively, the Soviet Union could decide to go into the informatics era. A good way for the latter approach is to encourage people to use computers at home so that, without extensive computer classes in the workplace, they become computer-literate on their own time and in their own way and encouraging children also to learn the intricacies of computer technology.

However, entering the computer era contained three dangers for the Soviet system. First, it would eventually enable people to get access to databases and to learn more about what was really going on in the U.S.S.R. Second, each computer was potentially a small printing press, which could erode the government's control over the printed word. In Poland at that time, it was even illegal for individuals to have their own duplicators. Third, linking computers to telephone lines would enable Soviet citizens to communicate around the world. They could relay stories to the outside world, as well as gain information from it. Soviet citizens would gain further information on how their material standard of living was slipping behind that of the West. The information technology revolution was only just getting underway when the U.S.S.R. disappeared, and Gorbachev was swept from power.

Transparency

Transparency is another important component of globalization. On the one hand, the Red Army could resist a NATO invasion into Eastern Europe, but it could not stop the televised transmission of *Dallas* and *Dynasty*. These television programs augmented the development of a consumer culture within Eastern Europe. They were also, for better or worse, symbols of the impact of transnational communications corporations and their creation of a new era of global transparency.

On the other hand, transparency ended the Soviet tradition of secrecy. Stalin could get away with his mass murders because they were done out of the media spotlight. Similarly, the U.S.S.R.'s first nuclear disaster in the Urals in 1957 was hidden from foreign view for about two decades.[11]

Tragedies in Gorbachev's U.S.S.R., by contrast, could not be so easily hidden from foreign view. Gorbachev had been the Soviet leader for only about a year when the April 26, 1986 Chernobyl nuclear disaster took place. It was known about overseas within hours; not only was the radiation detected, but also news of the accident was well televised (including by foreign satellite coverage—one

of the first occasions when such coverage was used). Lou Cannon, a biographer
of Ronald Reagan, recalled that Gorbachev first used the traditional Soviet
technique of delay. When he did finally comment on the crisis on May 14, he
blamed the media coverage on an unrestrained anti-Soviet propaganda campaign. Cannon said that Soviet citizens learned more about what was happening
in the critical days after the Chernobyl explosion from the Voice of America
and the BBC than from their own government. Western Europeans were also
critical of Gorbachev's inaction, and he lost a great deal of the public sympathy
he had acquired during his first year in office. The disaster had a profound
impact on Gorbachev.[12] From that point on, natural disasters and human-made
calamities would be reported promptly in the Soviet media.[13]

Incidentally, Gorbachev also had the flair for making television work for him.
Unlike all previous Soviet leaders, he had the ability to use U.S. television to
reach directly into American homes, thereby reducing fears about Soviet lead-
ers held since the Russian Revolution in 1917. Reagan also was normally very
good at staging an event (and upstaging the other leaders appearing with him).
However, in December 1987, Gorbachev mounted his own charm offensive
during his visit to the United States by conducting himself as if he were an
American politician, much to the consternation of the Secret Service and the
KGB. Wherever he went, crowds lined the streets to applaud him. Television,
Gorbachev's medium for popularity, also had a major role in developing the
global consumer culture.

The United States' Financial and Social Problems

The Cold War also had a severe impact on the United States. Winning the
Cold War came at great cost to the Americans. Although the nation began the
1980s as the major lending country, it ended that decade as the world's main
borrower. In the meantime, Japan became the world's largest creditor country,
and it financed a third of the U.S. national debt. President Reagan embarked
upon the largest and most expensive peacetime military expansion in U.S. history. Ironically committed to reducing national budget deficits, Reagan actually
borrowed more than all his predecessors combined. In the middle of 1985,
despite the economic recovery underway, the United States became a net debtor
internationally for the first time in 70 years. While a great achievement of the
Clinton administration was the balancing of the federal budget, there is still
the accumulated national debt to be serviced. Debt has destroyed empires in
the past. It is now a major problem for the United States.

A country is not rich because it has a large military force; it has a large
military force because it is rich and so can afford that force. Paul Kennedy in
his *Rise and Fall of Great Powers* examined the rise and fall of major European
nation-states since 1500.[14] Starting out small and efficient, each nation-state
became big, overly ambitious, and imperially over-stretched; each acquired too
many foreign commitments. The United Kingdom, was the most recent coun-

try to succumb to this cycle. Kennedy argued that the United States was going the same way.

A country in debt has limitations on how it may act. Creditors may require it to carry out certain tasks, such as working off the debt, so that it cannot embark upon foreign adventures. Indebted Third World countries are very vulnerable to pressure from international financial institutions that insist on economic restructuring, and the United States is not at this level of vulnerability. Even so, some U.S. business people have argued that their country should have left the arms race sooner and started rebuilding itself economically and socially.[15] The lack of firm structure is reflected partly in the situation of medical insurance. Some 44 million Americans, 16 percent of the population, totally lack insurance cover for the cost of medical care services; further, it is estimated that 50 million more are grossly underinsured.[16]

There is no automatic trade-off between reduced military expenditure and increased social welfare expenditure. There was no guarantee that reduced military expenditure in the United States would be converted into increased social welfare expenditure; the reduction could have been manifested, for example, as a tax cut. But a continued high rate of military expenditure does give an excuse to provide fewer resources to social welfare, since national security has to come first.

To sum up so far, the United States and U.S.S.R. eroded their national economies in running their arms race. The difference between Gorbachev and Reagan, is that Gorbachev recognized this danger and so took the U.S.S.R. out of the arms race while Reagan left office still blind to it.[17]

Looking Beyond the Cold War

The major factors that affect a person's life are rarely on the front pages of a newspaper. The front pages or television headlines deal with what I've defined as events rather than structures. Here are the experiences of two people who encouraged governments to look beyond the Cold War and address structures.

Peter Schwartz, one of the world's leading futurists, is the president of Global Business Network, based in California. His organization develops scenarios. These are a tool for ordering perceptions about alternative future environments in which decisions may be played out. These are not extrapolations from the present but are ways of thinking about how the future may be different from the present. Chapter 6 of this book uses the scenario technique to think about the future of global governance.

Schwartz has given up trying to advise the U.S. government and politicians.[18] An initial disheartening experience occurred when he was with the Stanford Research Institute (SRI) in the 1970s. SRI did scenarios for the Department of Transportation that looked at the failure to build enough highways and public transportation. Cities could end up with massive gridlocks. The project was singled out by Senator William Proxmire, a critic of U.S. government expenditure, as a waste of money because no one would be stupid enough to allow those traffic problems to occur. Politicians such as Proxmire were unwilling to "think about the unthinkable."[19]

The Cold War provided another disheartening experience for Schwartz. During the early 1980s, official U.S. thinking was based on some form of nuclear war: either a "limited" nuclear war or an all-out World War III which would destroy much of the planet.[20] In his meetings with politicians, Schwartz found that they never asked themselves what would happen if the U.S.S.R. simply surrendered without a shot being fired. When Gorbachev came to office in 1985, he in fact set about reforming the U.S.S.R. via "perestroika" (restructuring) and "glasnost" (openness). He had to reduce military expenditure and withdraw the U.S.S.R. from Afghanistan. However, U.S. politicians had no post-Cold War strategy with which to cope with a Soviet surrender, so they have been of little assistance to Moscow in the post–Cold War era. They had failed to think about the unthinkable: a victory without a war.

The United States spent 45 years (1945–1990) worrying about the power of Moscow and its potential threat to the rest of the world. Now the nation is worried that Russia does not have enough power to maintain order, such as combating organized crime. The United States had plans for war but not for peace. Unable to look beyond the end of the Cold War, the nation could not even envisage a comparatively peaceful settlement to it.

Jean-Jacques Servan-Schreiber in 1981 wrote about the coming impact of information technology.[21] He argued that this technology was of greater importance than the then current Cold War. Two decades later, his claim has been vindicated. In the meantime, however, much effort was wasted by the super powers and their allies in waging the Cold War. Indeed, part of Servan-Schreiber's agenda has still not been realized. He argued that the Third World should be brought into a technological partnership with developed countries so that more of humanity would be mobilized in the world's economic and social development. This would require a transfer of technology, but he did not know how Western knowledge could be transferred to the developing countries. Currently, many people are still living in desperate circumstances. Once again, the politicians were focused on immediate military matters and not the long-term economic and social ones.

To sum up, these two authors provided warnings about excessive concentration on the Cold War. Both also provided reasons for why the United States and other nations should look beyond that impasse. Although neither author dealt explicitly with globalization, features of the trend tacitly informed their ways of looking at world affairs.

INTERGOVERNMENTAL COOPERATION

Despite the Cold War, life had to go on. There were diseases to combat, trade to facilitate, treaties to negotiate, and scientific research to conduct. Thus, while the United States and U.S.S.R., together with their respective allies, were opposed in military terms, civilian members of the countries could work together on cooperative projects.

This is called functional cooperation. Functionalism, according to the political scientist David Mitrany, means that it is better initially to get cooperation on specific economic and social tasks than to work directly on political unity.[22] By this means, countries and individuals can gradually see the benefits of mutual cooperation and create a sustained ethos of it. This is done out of the public eye, with little publicity and political controversy.

Until the expansion, in the early 1990s, of the United Nations' peacekeeping work, at least 80 percent of the institution's finance and staff were devoted to functional cooperation, mainly through the specialized agencies. Although the Cold War was underway, the United States and U.S.S.R. along with their respective allies were working together on various projects. For example, small pox was eradicated by the World Health Organization; based on a Soviet proposal, the work was headed by an American. In addition, the International Telecommunications Union (ITU) oversaw the creation of the global telephone dialing service based on numbers which led to ISD (international subscriber dialing) and also oversaw the conference process by which radio and television air waves were apportioned out. Further, the International Maritime Organization created a common bill of lading for merchant marine vessels, and the World Meteorological Organization created a global network for exchanging data on weather patterns.

These were all unexciting developments, at least compared with the mass media's interest in war and the arms race. Too easily taken for granted, these cooperative ventures provided benefits, which have had lasting significance. The Cold War has come and gone, but the contribution of the less glamorous, functional cooperation remains. Indeed, there are now far more opportunities to trade across national lines or to telephone across them.

NONGOVERNMENTAL ACTIVITIES

Nongovernmental organizations (NGOs) also cut across national borders. Citizens' diplomacy enabled U.S. and Soviet citizens, such as those in peace groups, to meet and discuss the Cold War together with ways of ending it. They focused on what united humankind, rather than what divided it. NGOs in other walks of life enabled citizens to discuss, for example, scientific and cultural matters.

There was never a Cold War at the South Pole; scientists either had to cooperate together or would have frozen separately.[23] The 1959 basic Antarctic Treaty, one of the most effective treaties in world history, was written at a very difficult time in international politics. The Cold War was underway, and it is amazing that anything was written at all. At one point of international tension

in 1962, Australia broke off diplomatic relations with the U.S.S.R. Coincidentally on that day in the Antarctic, the Red Flag was hoisted over a new Soviet
base on the Australian Antarctic Territory. Although politicians were squab-
bling in Canberra, the scientists in Antarctica were not. Additionally, the Antarctic is the only continent where scientists have control over the military.
While the continent is demilitarized, the best equipped personnel for transport
over rough terrains are in fact the military forces of the various countries
conducting scientific research. The military do the work under the overall direction of scientists.

NGOs are the most important way of mobilizing public opinion and focusing attention on a problem. The 1972 UN Conference on the Environment
arose largely from the way in which NGOs argued that there was an environmental crisis; the Club of Rome, for example, reported on the "limits to
growth" in the biggest selling environment book in history.[24] NGOs acted—
and governments re-acted. Similarly, by publicizing the Brundtland Report on
the environment and development, NGOs encouraged governments and the
UN to create the 1992 Conference on Environment and Development
(UNCED).[25]

NGOs are then a growing force in global politics.[26] Adept at attracting media
coverage, these organizations appeal to people who are disenchanted with the
usual party political process, providing vision and continuity which outlasts
the short-term perspective of governments.

"People power" within Eastern Europe also helped to end the Cold War.
Ordinary people were suddenly given the opportunity to change the flow of
political events, especially when their work was publicized by the global mass
media.

For example, journalist Robert Cullen traveled extensively in Eastern Europe
as the Soviet bloc crumbled. He recalled the role of the Reverend Laszlo Tokes
in galvanizing public opinion against the Ceausescu regime in Romania.[27] Tokes
and his congregation were in the Hungarian minority in western Romania
(Transylvania). The discipline of the Warsaw Pact had for years stifled Hungarian resentment not only over the 1918 loss of Transylvania at the end of
World War I, but also over the mistreatment of the Hungarian minority in
Romania by its regime. But as "glasnost" lifted limits on political expression,
the fate of Transylvania became a major issue in Hungary. When word of
Tokes's plight leaked out to Hungary, a Hungarian television crew filmed an
interview with him in July 1989. He spoke of his own situation and, more
generally, of repression in Romania. The interview also made its way to Radio
Free Europe, the BBC, and other Western radio stations that transmitted to
Romania. Foreign broadcasts over Romania's borders, bypassing the state media, played a major role in the Romanian revolution because ordinary people
could hear about how others were rebelling against the regime. The Ceausescu
regime was not invincible.[28]

THE COLD WAR BECAME IRRELEVANT

Thus, there was a growing sense that the Cold War was irrelevant. While some governmental relations between the United States and U.S.S.R. froze, the chill did not reach all areas of the lives of civilians.

Along with the growing importance of the new global actors, notably transnational corporations, nongovernmental organizations, and the UN, a new global agenda also emerged. For example, the national security state that emerged at the outset of the Cold War had a narrow, military-dominated perception of national security.[29] A broader definition of this assurance of security has been pioneered by Lester Brown and his colleagues at the Worldwatch Institute in Washington, D.C. They have argued that national security should also include environmental concerns: the erosion of soils, the deterioration of the earth's basic biological systems, and the depletion of oil reserves all threaten the national security of countries. Ecological stresses and resource scarcities have already given rise to economic stresses including inflation, unemployment, capital scarcity, and monetary instability. Ultimately, these economic stresses will translate into social unrest and political instability.[30] Similarly, Norman Myers has argued that whereas the years 1945–1990 were dominated by the Cold War, coming decades will be dominated by environmentally based conflicts.[31]

Of course, military expendituredoes little to help protect the environment. During the Cold War, defense expenditure diverted money from the renewal of natural resources. Indeed, some military activities have actually undermined the environment: nuclear weapon testing; the deployment of land mines; the destruction of the oil rigs in the 1991 Gulf War; and the 2000 sinking of the Russian nuclear submarine, "The Kursk."

To conclude, the Cold War was overtaken by other events and became an expensive irrelevance, especially given the increase in nuclear arsenals.[32] In May 1994, the former Cold War enemies had their first major joint war game exercise ("RUKUS 94") involving naval personnel from Russia, the United Kingdom and United States.[33] In the meantime, out of the glare of mass media attention, the world in recent decades has been undergoing a significant change: the erosion of the basis of the present system of nation-states and the rise of globalization.

NOTES

1. For example: Laurence Shoup and William Minter, *Imperial Brains Trust: The Council on Foreign Relations and United States Foreign Policy.* New York: Monthly Review Press, 1977; Holly Sklar (ed.), *Trilateralism: The Trilateral Commission and Elite Planning for World Management.* Boston: South End Press, 1980.

2. See: Keith Suter, "Politics With a Dash of Vinegar," *The World Today* (London), July 1998.

3. Keith Suter, "Globalization and Protest: People Power," *The World Today* (London), October 2000, pp. 12–14.

4. Georgia Nucci, "Reporting Death," (letter) *Time* magazine, March 27, 1989, p. 9.

5. Anne Hessing Cahn and John Prados, "Team B: The Trillion Dollar Experiment," *Bulletin of Atomic Scientists* (Chicago), April 1993, pp. 23–31.

6. A good piece of predictive writing was a novel by Donald James, *The Fall of the Russian Empire*. London: Granada, 1982.

7. Aleksandr Solzhenitsyn (translated by Alexis Klimoff and Michael Nicholson), *Invisible Allies*. London: Harvill, 1997.

8. Keith Suter, *Reshaping the Global Agenda: The United Nations at Forty*. Sydney: United Nations Association of Australia, 1986, pp. 96–99.

9. See: Paul Hawken et al., *Natural Capitalism: The Next Industrial Revolution*. London: Earthscan, 1999, pp. 21–47.

10. See Hedrick Smith, *The Russians*. London: Sphere, 1976, pp. 455–456.

11. Zhores Medvedev, *Nuclear Disaster in the Urals*. New York: Norton, 1979.

12. Lou Cannon, *President Reagan: The Role of a Lifetime*. New York: Simon & Schuster, 1991, pp. 756–757.

13. Coincidentally, I was in Moscow in early December 1998, at the time of a major earthquake in the southern U.S.S.R., and Gorbachev's policy of transparency was much in evidence: we learned about the disaster very quickly as well as the difficulties the Soviet authorities were having in the disaster relief.

14. Paul Kennedy, *The Rise and Fall of Great Powers*. London: Fontana, 1989.

15. Harold Willens, *The Trimtab Factor*. New York: Morrow, 1984.

16. Victor Sidel, "Working Together for Health and Human Rights," *Medicine, Conflict and Survival* (London), October 2000, p. 357.

17. For some ideas on how the United States could have been rebuilt at the end of the Cold War, see Joseph Romm, *The Once and Future Superpower*. New York: Morrow, 1992.

18. Peter Schwartz, *The Art of the Long View: Planning for the Future in an Uncertain World*. New York: Doubleday, 1991, pp. 36–37.

19. The phrase "thinking about the unthinkable" was popularized by another pioneer in scenario planning, Herman Kahn, who applied it to nuclear warfare. See his *On Escalation: Metaphors and Scenarios* (New York: Hudson Institute, 1965).

20. See Robert Aldridge *First Strike! The Pentagon's Strategy for Nuclear War*. London: Pluto, 1983; Robert Scheer, *With Enough Shovels: Reagan, Bush and Nuclear War*. New York: Random House, 1982.

21. Jean-Jacques Servan-Schreiber, *The World Challenge*. London: Collins, 1981.

22. David Mitrany, *The Functional Theory of Politics*. London: Martin Robertson, 1975.

23. See: Keith Suter, *Antarctica: Private Property or Public Heritage?* London: Zed, 1991.

24. Dennis Meadows et al., *The Limits to Growth*. New York: Universe Books, 1972.

25. World Commission on Environment and Development, *Our Common Future*. Oxford: Oxford University Press, 1987.

26. See Peter Willetts (ed.), *The Conscience of the World: The Influence of Non-Governmental Organizations in the UN System*. London: Hurst, 1996.

27. Robert Cullen, *Twilight of Empire: Inside the Crumbling Soviet Bloc*. London: The Bodley Head, 1991, pp. 77–78.

28. During the 1990 attempted coup against him, Gorbachev also benefited from foreign radio broadcasts. Detained in his dacha in the Crimea, he was still able to follow, via BBC radio and Voice of America, the resistance of Boris Yeltsin and others in Moscow to the coup.

29. See Daniel Yergin, *Shattered Peace: The Origins of the Cold War and the National Security State.* London: Penguin, 1977.

30. Lester Brown, *Building a Sustainable Society.* New York: Norton, 1981, p. 362.

31. Norman Myers, *Ultimate Security: The Environmental Basis of Political Stability.* London: Norton, 1993.

32. See Keith Suter, "How the Cold War Became an Expensive Irrelevance." In *Why the Cold War Ended: A Range of Interpretations,* ed. Ralph Summy and Michael Salla. Westport, CT: Greenwood Press, 1995, pp. 187–203.

33. Leslie Sim, "The 1994 Russian-UK-US Naval War Game (RUKUS 94): Important Considerations for Multinational Naval Operations," *Journal of the Royal United Services Institute* (London), October 1994, pp. 19–22, 56.

2

The Rise of the Old World Order: The Nation-State System

INTRODUCTION

The nation-state is the basic component of the old world order. The old world order is also called the Westphalian System, and it is named after the Westphalian peace process of 1648. The Westphalian System has worn well. But it is now wearing out.

No one in Europe in 1648 suddenly realized that he or she was now living in a new era. Everyday life remained harsh. There were plagues and poverty; that the peace at the end of the Thirty Years War would last was not guaranteed. Some of the components of the Westphalian System were in place before the key year of 1648, and many of them would arrive later.

Within the context of the globalization process, the world is moving into a post-Westphalian era, with the new process creeping up on nation-states. It is not possible suddenly to declare that the Westphalian System has ended and that a new global system has taken its place. People living through such a momentous global change are the least equipped to detect the full extent of that change; later historians will have to do that. All that can now be done is to identify some of the features of the change.

This chapter deals with two aspects of the Westphalian System. The first is an overview of how the system was created and why it was so different from the previous prevailing order in Europe. The second is an examination of the four ambiguities inherent in the Westphalian System: nation, state, sovereignty, and self-determination are all well known yet also unclear terms.

THE WESTPHALIAN SYSTEM: THE TREATY OF WESTPHALIA

The Westphalian System takes its name from the Treaty (or Peace) of Westphalia of 1648. Like the dating of the beginning and end of all eras, the precision of the date is somewhat ambiguous. However, it is necessary to give some sort of date as the beginning of the era, and so it might as well be 1648. Ian Brown-lie, QC of Cambridge University, pointed out that while it is absurd to think that everything started in 1648, it is reasonable to assume that by the time of the Peace of Westphalia, the system was already in being.[1] A simple test was to note both the extensive political reach of the arrangements of the West-phalian phase of state relations and also their long-standing role as important territorial settlements.

The Treaty of Westphalia marked the effective end of the legal and political domination by the Catholic Church of much of Western Europe. Christianity began as a persecuted, minor religion on the fringe of the Roman Empire.[2] Around the year 300, Emperor Constantine converted to Christianity and made it the official religion of the empire.[3] Since Christianity had become a major force in his empire, he decided to absorb it into his system of governance. Over the subsequent centuries, Christian officials increased their power so that they provided much of the legal, political, and bureaucratic underpinning of the empire. The Church had its own language (Latin), officials, and places of train-ing; its staff were mobile across Europe. For about a thousand years, the Church was the closest structure that Europe, or the rest of the world, has ever had to a regional government; the European Union is still a long way from having the power of the medieval Church.

However, the official Church power was not completely absolute. Even at the time of Constantine, rival groups of Christians disputed about matters of faith. As the centuries rolled by, there were often dissidents protesting against some of the Catholic teachings or the behavior of the clerics. But these protests were usually brutally suppressed.

By the sixteenth century, however, Rome was caught between two forces. First, there were renewed criticisms of the corruption within the Church, which this time caught the popular mood. On October 31, 1517, Martin Luther nailed a paper of Ninety-Five Theses to the door of the Castle Church in that town. Professor of theology in the Saxon University of Wittenberg, he attacked the practice of selling indulgences. These documents offered commutation of pen-ance for money payments; in other words, if people gave money to the Church, they or their dead relatives would be spared some of the punishment in hell. G.R. Elton of Cambridge University has pointed out that Luther's theses were not the first he had offered for public disputation, or even necessarily revolu-tionary doctrines.[4] Nevertheless, October 31 continues to be celebrated in the Lutheran countries as the anniversary of the Reformation. The controversy over indulgences brought together the person and the occasion: It signaled the end of the medieval Church.

Second, secular rulers were getting restless about being subservient to Church influence, especially because the center of that influence was so far away. For example, as the British historians Heard and Tull have pointed out, the Reformation in England began as a political movement, rather than a theo-logical one.[5] The question of England's loyalty to the Catholic Church arose through the anxiety of Henry VIII over the royal succession. In 1527, Henry wanted to divorce his first wife; this was opposed by Rome, which did not approve of the principle of divorce. This changed Henry's mind about Rome, to which he had previously been sympathetic in the face of the problems being caused by Luther and the other Protestants. In fact, Henry had written a book in 1521 attacking Luther and had been rewarded by the Pope with the title 'Defender of the Faith.' Now Henry decided that it was wrong for an Italian Pope to interfere in English affairs. Throughout the 1530s, Henry gradually severed the links with Rome. By 1540, the first stage of the Reformation in England was complete. During Henry's lifetime, very little altered in the doctrines of the Anglican Church; the significant change was that the king had the power to alter the doctrines at any time. This enabled the sweeping changes that took place later in the century. Henry VIII declared himself to both head of State and head of the Church—a much greater dominance of the Church by the monarch than had ever been allowed by Rome in medieval society.

Henry's daughter Elizabeth I (1533—1603), who was Queen from 1558–1603, consolidated the Crown's power in what was called the Elizabethan Settlement. The Church of England was a State Church under the Queen as Supreme Governor. Only members of the Church could hold public office. There was uniformity of worship strictly in accordance with a government-approved prayer book. Bishops were to be appointed by the Queen. Clergy were to be ordained and licensed by bishops.

The Catholic Church, starting in the 1540s, embarked upon the Counter-Reformation to check the popularity of the Protestant movements throughout Europe. The ensuing disputes were not a clear-cut struggle between Protestants and Rome because some Catholic regions also liked the idea of greater autonomy from Rome. Meanwhile, the Protestants were united in their dislike of Rome but often divided over other issues, such as split loyalties between Luther and Calvin, based in Geneva.

These disputes reached a crescendo in Germany where the Thirty Years War began in 1618. This was the last of Europe's major religious wars. The people who took part in it were fighting not only for their own form of Christianity, but also for greater freedom and independence in the way they were governed. Much of the fighting was done within Germany's boundaries by foreign armies. By 1648, there was a sense of exhaustion. As a result of the war—and compounded by plague—the population within the German territories fell from 17 million to 10 million, with the deaths exceeding the 5.5 million German lives lost in World War II.

Robert Johansen of Notre Dame University has claimed that the significance of the Westphalian treaty stood in sharp contrast to the political organization of the Middle Ages before the religious wars began.[6] Medieval society was hierarchically organized and subject to the authority of the Pope and the Holy Roman Empire. The Roman Catholic Church and its appointed representatives exercised centralized authority across the territorial boundaries of Western

Europe. Although local, territorially based secular entities had some power, this was subject to the ultimate authority of the Pope and Emperor, who claimed to rule from God. This system gradually changed as authority, power, wealth, and loyalties coalesced to a state level. The Westphalian peace process acknowledged the development of independent, secular, sovereign nation-states no longer subject to the centralized authority of the Pope or Emperor.

The 1791 Bill of Rights to the 1787 U.S. Constitution took this process of secularization a step further. In Amendment 1, the Bill provides for the separation of church and state, so that the United States is a secular state with no established religion. This eliminated the risk of religiously based wars in the country. By the same token, it also set the church free from the iron grip of the state and enabled religious freedom to flourish. Church people were free to speak out against the state.

THE CHARACTERISTICS OF THE NATION-STATE

Manufacturing a Nation-State

The creation of nation-states was a deliberate effort. This has involved five developments: national consolidation of power, creation of a national sense of loyalty, erosion of natural law to which national rulers were accountable, creation of a system of national laws, and the creation of the concept of national, sovereign equality of all nation-states. The five developments ran together and reinforced one another. The following analysis is not in any order of priority; rather, it is an examination of the same process from five perspectives.

Consolidating Power

Rulers had to consolidate themselves against domestic and foreign forces. Historian Paul Kennedy noted that the seventeenth-century monarchies emerged from and then subdued a patchwork quilt of local baronies, dukedoms, principalities, free cities, and other localized authorities such as those at Burgundy, Aragon, and Navarre.[7] While they consolidated power internally, the nation-states also asserted themselves against transnational institutions like the papacy, monastic and knightly orders, and the Hanseatic League, the last being in many ways a sort of early transnational corporation based in the present northern Germany and mainly influential in the late fourteenth and fifteenth centuries.

Creating a National Sense of Loyalty

The governments had to manufacture loyalty to the nation-state. Paul Kennedy has written that each state evolved symbols (flag, anthem, historical figures and events, special holidays) to reinforce consciousness of national identity.[8] Schoolchildren studied some subjects, such as history, with a particular national focus. The national language steadily encroached upon such regional tongues as Breton, Welsh, and Catalan, though the resistance was often deep and determined.

Technology had a role to play in this evolution, particularly the invention of the printing press. James Burke and Robert Ornstein have recounted the importance of printing for state-building.[9] One impact was the advantage it gave to Martin Luther to spread his Reformation message across the German dukedoms. Another was the standardization of language so that, for example, the London dialect became English and Dante's Tuscan dialect became the official Italian. Third, religious books, such as prayer books, became more nationally focused and regulated by national governments as a form of guiding, if not controlling, what their respective citizens were thinking.

British political scientist William Wallace has said that state-building became an accelerating process.[10] As national governments required more and more from their citizens, they had to whip up even more of a sense of national unity. Nationhood and national identity represent necessary myths that underpinned foreign policy. They constituted the distinction between the national community, which the government represented abroad, and the foreigners with whom it dealt. These concepts legitimated the actions of government in defense of the "national" interest. As states increased the demands made upon their citizens in the form of taxes and contributions to the national economy and military service, they reinforced the symbols and myths of national solidarity. States emphasized their claim to national sovereignty; they sought to strengthen the bonds of loyalty which mobilized the population to work or fight in support of supposedly national aims.

Erosion of the Natural Law

Simultaneously, natural law eroded. While the Catholic Church had claimed to rule from a divine mandate, Hedley Bull has noted that human reason replaced the theological principles, which saw a divine force in the universe creating a uniform sense of justice and morality.[11] Natural law had proclaimed that rights and duties were attached to human beings as such and existed by nature throughout the world as a whole, whatever secular convention decreed at particular times and in particular places. However, the Treaty of Westphalia ended the medieval idea that a universal religious authority acted as the final arbiter in all things.

The natural law had also been a unifying factor in that it gave Western Europe a standard system of morality. A person living in England or Upper Saxony, for example, lived under similar laws for murder, robbery, and rape. Thus, the end of the natural law meant that medieval Europe's Christendom had gone; the sense that all localities lived within a wider context of a universal

Christian society was over. From now on, states would make their own rules and there would be different laws from one state to another.

Rise of Positivism

Positivism replaced the natural law. Positive law was created by the national sovereign whether king, president, parliament, or congress. The nation-state was bound only by the laws it created or international treaties it agreed to accept. In theological terms, then, positivism ended the idea that rulers were ultimately accountable to God. Rulers themselves were at liberty to do what they decided was best for their countries. In international law terms, states could not be forced to accept any international treaty they did not like.[12]

Sovereignty

With the erosion of natural law and the growth of positivism, the concept of sovereignty evolved. The political basis of this concept grew out of the turmoil in the sixteenth and seventeenth centuries. Thomas Hobbes, for example, wrote in *Leviathan* about the need to have a strong central ruler.[13] Having lived through the English Civil War of the 1640s, Hobbes wrote his book in 1651, with the recollection of the civil violence firmly in his mind. The strong central ruler would make the laws and enforce them. After the American and French Revolutions in the late eighteenth century, this absolutism was toned down to make rulers more accountable to the people. Thus, "popular sovereignty" referred to the ruler interpreting the wishes of the people (all of whom, incidentally, were property-owning, white adult males).

In international law terms, the shift from Hobbesian sovereignty to popular sovereignty had, in one sense, little significance: The property-owning, white adult males were self-governed in their own country and had no need to take any notice of property-owning, white adult males in other countries. Similarly, people within the national borders had no recourse to a higher law outside their country if they disapproved of a government policy or were being victimized by it. For example, as soon as Hitler came to power in 1933 he started violating Jewish human rights. While other governments may have disapproved of his actions, no formal complaints were made because Hitler's policies were seen as an internal German matter.[14]

Thus, all nation-states are equal in international law. In November 1991, Javier Perez de Cuellar, on the eve of his retirement as UN Secretary-General, gave an address at the University of Florence on sovereignty and international responsibility. He set out the following as elements of sovereign equality:

- States are juridical equals.
- Each state enjoys the rights inherent in full sovereignty.
- Each state has the duty to respect the personality of other states.

- The territorial integrity and political independence of the state are inviolable.
- Each state has the right freely to choose and develop its political, social, economic and cultural systems.
- Each state has the duty to comply fully and in good faith with its international obligations and to live in peace with other states.[15]

To sum up, international lawyer Richard Falk has pointed out that the logic of Westphalia established the state system as the basis of world order.[16] Enjoying exclusive control over their internal affairs, national governments also were the exclusive formal actors at the international level. Sovereign status was the essential ingredient of formal participation in international society. Out of this basic Westphalian premise arose many fundamental doctrines of international law: domestic jurisdiction, the sovereign equality of states, diplomatic and sovereign immunity, the doctrine of nonintervention, and the doctrine of recognition of new states and governments.

THE AMBIGUITIES OF THE WESTPHALIAN SYSTEM

The Westphalian System had problems from the outset. These were derived from the ambiguities in four basic concepts. The Westphalian System is based on the assumption (or more likely, the hope) that the boundaries of nations should coincide with the boundaries of states. The first two ambiguities were based on this defective assumption. The second two ambiguities were derived from legal and political control, sovereignty and self-determination.

NATION

The nation in the Westphalian System is taken to refer to a group of people who see themselves as a particular group.

The application of the definition, however, is often difficult. On the one hand, there is certainly something that provides a common bond. For instance, a tune—which is not necessarily the official national anthem—can bond a group of people. *Waltzing Matilda*, a pleasant piece of music for most of the world's population who may hear it as at the 2000 Sydney Olympics, is for Australians a special tune; they need only to hear a few bars to become misty-eyed, especially if overseas at the time. Much the same can be said for other musical items such as *Jerusalem* for the English and *Egypt's Our Mother*. The element of self-definition is reinforced by reference to geography, language, hostility to neighbors, and history.

On the other hand, however, the people encompassed by nation are an unclear group. First, members of nations move around the globe. The British nation runs into hundreds of millions of people, with members in countries like the United States, Canada, South Africa, Australia, and New Zealand. Much the same can be said about the Irish, French, and Indians. For hundreds of years, people from these nations have been moving overseas to take up positions as traders, administrators, clerks, educators, soldiers, health practitioners, and religious missionaries. Married and settled down, they produce children who have two sets of loyalty (and often two passports). Sterling Seagrave has written about the 55 million overseas Chinese who have long played extremely powerful roles in the development of such countries as Singapore, Indonesia, Malaysia, Thailand, Vietnam, and the Philippines.[17] Finally, there is now a problem for the Russian officials who in the days of the U.S.S.R. were transferred to the southern part of that republic. These areas, including Turkmenistan, Uzbekistan, Tajikistan, and Kirgizstan, are now independent nation-states. Having married local people, the officials have few relatives to return to in Russia although the new governments would like them out of their territories.

In addition, there is the problem of how nationality is acquired. There is no single agreed upon way of acquiring citizenship. Sussex University's Mary Kaldor has pointed out how concepts of citizenship have varied.[18] Historians often distinguish between Western and Eastern European nationalism, in particular, the French and German variants of citizenship.[19] In France, the citizens are the inhabitants of French territory. There is a notion that being French is associated with that language and culture. But these attributes can be acquired; immigrants and minorities can assimilate. By contrast, the German notion of citizenship is ethnic. Thus, a person of German descent living in, say, Russia could more easily acquire German citizenship than a German-born Turkish "guest-worker" whose parents had lived in the country since World War II. In 2000, the German government began to relax its policies because of the need to attract more information-technology workers, such as from India, to make up for the shortage of native workers.

U.S. citizenship is acquired by residence in the country and government criteria, nowadays usually based on the applicant's skills or the number of relatives already present in the country. At the other end of the spectrum, being a Japanese citizen means that a person has to be born of parents whose own parents were Japanese. This explains why Japanese-Koreans whose families have been residents in Japan for a century still do not have Japanese citizenship.

Third, there is the much narrower definition of a nation from the Boston-based nongovernmental organization Cultural Survival, a human rights group concerned with the protection of indigenous peoples.[20] Thus, a nation is a group of people with a strong cultural and political identity that is both self-defined and acknowledged by others. Nations are those groups that have exercised political control over their destinies at some point in the past and still see such control as a possible future strategy.

Cultural Survival has listed some facts about the world's "nations":

Number of nations in the world: 5,000

Number of nation peoples in the world: 600 million

Percentage of the world's population that are nation people: slightly more than 10
   percent

Percentage of the earth's surface area and resources than can be legitimately claimed
   by nations: 25–40 percent

Number of nations in the US: 300+

Number of nations in Nigeria: 450

Number of nations in Indonesia: 300[21]

Finally, former senior UN public servant Brian Urquhart, estimated in 1992
that out of the 170 states at that time, only 30 had no ethnic problems at all.
He also estimated that in Africa about a thousand ethnic groups were "stuffed
into artificial envelopes of 50 nation-states, many of which are now coming
apart."[22]

STATE

A "state" is an organization for governing a set piece of the earth's surface.
The most obvious ambiguity that arises with both nation and state is that the
two rarely coincide. In contemporary terms, the most expedient way to solve
this problem has been, tragically, by ethnic cleansing, killing or in other ways
removing the other ethnic groups in a state's jurisdiction.

A second ambiguity results from the changing boundaries that may characterize a state. One example concerns Germany, whose borders have been in
flux for centuries. The guide book for the permanent historical exhibition in
the Berlin Reichstag throughout most of the 1980s had a series of colored maps
giving details of the borders.[23] However, the map has since changed because
the boundaries changed again in 1989. (The Reichstag also switched from being
a major museum back to being the national parliament.) Poland also provides
an example of a state with changing borders. Geographically in the center of
Europe, Poland had borders that moved westward into Eastern Germany as a
result of Soviet pressure in the Allied negotiations in 1945; but the country
was referred to as being part of Eastern Europe during the Cold War. Under
the pressures of World War II and then the Soviet Union, Ruthenia (or Car-
pathian Russia) was another state to experience very uncertain borders. Felix
Man, one of the pioneers of photojournalism, visited Ruthenia in the 1930s;
his photographs record a long-lost era in which Ruthenia, with Uzhorod as its
capital, had been part of the Hungarian Monarchy.[24] In 1920, when Czechoslovakia was created, the country became a province of Czechoslovakia. Under
pressure from Hitler, it was given back to Hungary in 1938. After World War
II, it was annexed by the then U.S.S.R. to become part of the Soviet Ukraine.
Australian anthropologist Bill Neville used Ruthenia's experience as the basis
of a joke.[25] When a person dies and goes to heaven, he explains to St. Peter: "I
am Hungarian. I was born in the Austro-Hungarian Empire; I lived for a time
in Czechoslovakia; then I was in Hungary. Later I was in the Soviet Union and

I died in the Ukraine." St Peter marvels at the amount of traveling the person has done. The dead man replies, "On the contrary, this is the first journey out of my village." Within a generation, a citizen in the Ruthenia area would have had three very different nationalities.

There is nothing definite or preordained about boundaries. For example, the United States could have remained huddled east of the Mississippi after the War of Independence; President Jefferson in 1802 could have foregone the opportunity to acquire "Louisiana"; the British could have moved south into present day Washington state thereby making Canada an even larger country.[26]

SOVEREIGNTY

Sovereignty, in this book's context, presents three problems. First, what, in practical terms, does "sovereignty" actually mean? Right from the outset of the Westphalian System, nation-states did not have solitary existences; they had to interact with other nation-states for trade, defense pacts, temporary wartime alliances and other societal necessities.[27] Thus, the practical meaning of sovereignty was always less than the grand claim of some form of national independence. British political scientist Alan James argued that sovereignty means constitutional independence; when states refer to themselves as sovereign, they mean that, in terms of their individual constitutional schemes, they are all independent of any larger units of a like kind.[28] Therefore, a state may in law be independent but not in reality.

Since 1648, people have forfeited portions of their national sovereignty in order to acquire the benefits arising out of a cooperative relationship with other people. This trend accelerated during the twentieth century. The former British Foreign Secretary Sir Geoffrey Howe argued in 1990 that as an individual has property which can be used in a variety of ways including direct ownership, sub-ownership, leases, licenses etc., a national government can use sovereignty in different ways.[29] In a thousand different ways and circumstances, sovereignty may be seen as divisible and exploitable in the interests of its respective nation-state. However, my concern is with how far a country can trade off its sovereignty before losing that sovereignty entirely. Constitutional independence is being surrendered in the interests of, for example, greater British cooperation within the European Union.

In addition, no central institution for according recognition of national sovereignty exists. Each nation-state has the right to recognize, or not recognize, the existence of an entity calling itself a nation-state or national government. Indeed, there is not even an agreed process about how national governments are to accord recognition; the two rival doctrines are the constitutive and the declaratory. According to the former doctrine championed by the United States, a new state becomes so only through its recognition by other states On the other hand, the latter championed by the United Kingdom, considers statehood to be only a declaration of an existing fact.[30] While the constitutive doctrine is open to political considerations because the act of recognition involves friendliness or hostility, the declaratory doctrine is simply based on a statement of fact. The latter can have unpleasant domestic political consequences if the government's act of recognizing a new state offends some of its own citizens. For example, the United States recognized Taiwan as the governing authority of China between 1949 and 1972 in what was known as the China lobby, while other countries more realistically recognized Peking/Beijing as the government.

SELF-DETERMINATION

The problem of self-determination reveals another set of ambiguities. Elie Kedourie pointed out that the idea of national self-determination assumed that the world was composed of separate, identifiable nations which meant that each of these entities were entitled to form a sovereign state.[31] The world not being what this theory assumed it to be, conforming reality to the theory must involve endless upheaval and disorder. National self-determination was thus a principle of disorder, not of order.

The concept of national self-determination has been around for thousands of years. One of the first leaders of a movement for self-determination was Moses leading the Hebrews out of Egypt. George Washington and his colleagues in the 1770s would also come into that category and around 1940–1970 Ho Chi Minh in Vietnam.

During the twentieth century, there were three phases of self-determination. The first phase was at the end of World War I when U.S. President Woodrow Wilson advocated the breaking up of the central European multiethnic empires into a series of homogenous, democratic nation-states, where people could choose, via referenda (plebiscites), where they wished to live. Wilson claimed that unrest within the minority populations, such as the assassination in Sarajevo of Archduke Franz Ferdinand by the Austrian Serb Gavrilo Princip on June 28, 1914, had contributed to the onset of World War I Therefore, he argued, special attention ought to be given to protecting minority populations, especially by letting them have their own countries. The League of Nations was created partly to deal with the problems of self-determination of nationalities. For example, the League gave minorities within the former Austro-Hungarian territories special rights including the right to petition the organization with human rights complaints.

Nations and states could not always be made to coincide in all the boundary redrawing after World War I. States were not homogenous. Allen Dulles, later head of the Central Intelligence Agency, worked as part of the U.S. delegation redrawing the maps of Eastern Europe at the 1919 World War I Peace Conference. He was on the Czechoslovak Boundary Commission, along with a fellow American and a Frenchman; none of them had any detailed knowledge of Eastern European history. Wanting to make the new nation-state of Czechoslovakia a geographically viable one, they included a considerable piece of

German-speaking territory known as the Sudetenland in addition to Bohemia and Moravia. Although the Czechs constituted a minority there, it seemed to Dulles and his two colleagues that the Sudetenland gave Bohemia and its capital Prague "a hinterland where any future German attack could be held."[32] He admitted later that "I sometimes wonder whether we weren't a little too free in drawing up the boundaries." Ironically, Adolf Hitler created the Munich crisis in 1938 over the Sudetenland. Using the alleged mistreatment of Germans in Czechoslovakia as an excuse to gain control over more territory, he originally took over the western end of that territory via the 1938 Munich Agreement and later all of it. In September 1939, Hitler used that excuse again to get control of Poland's northern coast, this time provoking the United Kingdom and France into war to protect Polish territorial integrity.

The second phase of self-determination took place after World War II with the break up of the European empires in Africa, Asia, and the Pacific. This was one of the major developments of the twentieth century: that millennium ended with almost all empires ended, thereby reversing a process begun half a century earlier. Those empires remaining include the Gibraltar and the Falklands/Malvinas islands as well as the Pitcairn Islands in the South Pacific, the latter being the only remaining Pacific Ocean colony of the United Kingdom and containing 54 people and the wreck of the ship *HMS Bounty;* these are isolated, small communities whose people preferred the status quo.

The third phase is now under way, with groups of people wishing to leave existing nation-states and form their own nation-states. Both of these developments are examined in the next chapter.

To sum up, right from the outset, there were some ambiguities in the Westphalian System to say the least. For awhile, the system proved to be very resilient. However, the problems in recent decades have forced change.

NOTES

1. Ian Brownlie, "The Expansion of International Society: The Consequences for the Law of Nations." In Hedley Bull and Adam Watson (eds.), *The Expansion of International Society.* Oxford: Clarendon, 1985, p. 358.

2. See F.F. Bruce, *The Spreading Flame: The Rise and Progress of Christianity from its First Beginnings to the Conversion of the English.* London: Paternoster Press, 1970.

3. See Michael Grant, *The Emperor Constantine.* London: Weidenfeld and Nicolson, 1993.

4. G.R. Elton, *Reformation Europe: 1517–1559.* London: Fontana, 1969, p. 15.

5. Nigel Heard and G.K. Tull, *The Beginning of European Supremacy.* London: Blandford, 1969, pp. 75–76.

6. Robert Johansen, *The National Interest and the Human Interest: An Analysis of US Foreign Policy.* Princeton: Princeton University Press, 1980, p. 15.

7. Paul Kennedy, *Preparing for the Twenty-First Century.* London: HarperCollins, 1993, p. 123.

8. Ibid., p. 124.

9. James Burke and Robert Ornstein, *The Axemaker's Gift.* New York: Grosset/ Putnam, 1995, pp. 122–129.

10. William Wallace, "Foreign Policy and the National Identity in the United Kingdom," *International Affairs* (London), December 1991, p. 66.

11. Hedley Bull, "The Emergence of a Universal International Society," in supra note 1, p. 119.

12. Natural law did not die out entirely, and it made a mild reappearance in the twentieth century (though usually without the explicit theological overtones) in the international protection of human rights; see Frederick Nolde, *Free and Equal: Human Rights in Ecumenical Perspective.* Geneva: World Council of Churches, 1968; Nehemiah Robinson, *The Universal Declaration of Human Rights.* New York: World Jewish Congress, 1958.

13. Thomas Hobbes, *Leviathan.* Cambridge: Cambridge University Press, 1991 (originally 1651).

14. See Arthur Morse, *While Six Million Died.* London: Secker & Warburg, 1968.

15. "Perez de Cuellar Discusses Sovereignty and International Responsibility," *The Review of the International Commission of Jurists* (Geneva), December 1991, p. 24.

16. Richard Falk, *This Endangered Planet.* New York: Vintage, 1972, p. 230. Also see Richard Falk, Friedrich Kratochwil, and Saul Mendlovitz (eds.), *International Law: A Contemporary Perspective.* Boulder, CO: Westview Press, 1985.

17. Sterling Seagrave, *Lords of the Rim.* New York: Putnam, 1995.

18. Mary Kaldor, "The New Nationalism in Europe," *Peace Review* (San Francisco), Summer 1993, p. 248.

19. The Council of Europe has started to address this problem, via the 1997 European Convention on Nationality, which is the beginning of harmonizing the different European approaches to the acquisition of citizenship. See Ryszard Piotrowicz, "One Nation or Two? New Developments in Citizenship Law," *The Australian Law Journal,* September 1998, pp. 673–676.

20. "A World of Nations," *Annual Report.* Boston: Cultural Survival, 1989, p. 4.

21. Ibid., p. 4.

22. Brian Urquhart, "The United Nations in 1992: Problems and Opportunities," *International Affairs* (London), April 1992, p. 313.

23. *Questions on German History: Ideas, Forces, Decisions from 1800 to the Present—Historical Exhibition in the Berlin Reichstag,* Bonn: German Bundestag Press and Information Centre, 1984.

24. Felix Man, *Man With Camera.* London: Secker & Warburg, 1983, pp. 99–106.

25. Bill Neville, "Treaties, Then and Now," *National Outlook* (Sydney), December 1994, p. 32.

26. These speculations are raised in Geoffrey Ward, *The West: An Illustrated History.* London: Weidenfeld & Nicolson, 1996, pp. 37–53.

27. See Uri Ra'anan et al. (eds.), *State and Nation in Multi-Ethnic Societies: The Breakup of Multinational States.* Manchester: Manchester University Press, 1991.

28. Alan James, "The Equality of States: Contemporary Manifestations of an Ancient Doctrine," *Review of International Studies* (Cambridge), October 1992, p. 380.

29. Geoffrey Howe, "Sovereignty and Interdependence: Britain's Place in the World," *International Affairs* (London), October 1990, p. 675.

30. See J.L. Brierly, *The Law of Nations.* Oxford: Clarendon Press, 1963, pp. 137–143.

31. Elie Kedourie, "A New International Disorder," in supra note 1, pp. 348–349. Hedley Bull and Adam Watson (eds.), *The Expansion of International Society.* Oxford: Clarendon, 1985, pp. 348–349.

32. Leonard Mosley, *Dulles: A Biography of Eleanor, Allen and John Foster and Their Family Network.* London: Hodder & Stoughton, 1978, p. 61.

3

The Weaknesses of the Nation-State System

INTRODUCTION

The Westphalian System is running into problems. The nation-state, according to this chapter, is being assailed in three ways. First, the high point of the Westphalian System was a two-level world, nation-states and their colonies. The era of the Europeanization of the globe has now ended. While almost all the colonies have become independent, many are having problems coping with the nation-state system, including the concept of self-determination. Meanwhile, other nation-states are also having problems coping with the legacy of empire, such as compensation for indigenous peoples.

Second, the present craft of diplomacy, which evolved in the early stages of the Westphalian System to accommodate the clique of nation-states, cannot easily absorb a far larger number of nation-states of differing sizes. Yet the legal principle of the sovereign equality of nation-states assures that, in theory at least, all states have to be accorded equal status.

Finally, the era of conventional warfare arrived with the nation-states system. For three centuries, the main mode of fighting was conventional and international warfare. That mode of warfare is being replaced by a new era in which warfare is guerrilla and internal. Instead of military forces enabling one state to attack or defend another, the forces are having to be used to maintain national governments in power and to put down dissident secessionist movements. Despite secession being such a major factor for the Westphalian System, there is a lack of both consistent international law and government practice about it. Meanwhile, the attacks of September 11, 2001, have been a reminder of the international community's failure to deal with "terrorism."

ENDING THE EUROPEANIZATION OF THE GLOBE

The Westphalian System is one of Europe's main impacts on the globe. This is closely linked with another development of similar vintage—colonialism. The European empires have now all largely been wound up and converted into components of the Westphalian System. But that system is having difficulty coping with all these changes.

THE RISE AND FALL OF EUROPEAN EMPIRES

The world's most ambitious colonial phase began around AD 1490, when Europeans started sailing to all parts of the globe. Searching for gold, silver, spices, and other commodities, they also took their religion with them. So the exploitation of Africa was done to create a triangular trade: European manu-factured goods were used to buy African slaves from Arab slave traders; the slaves, over 11 million people, were shipped across the Atlantic to work on sugar, cotton, and tobacco plantations; and the produce was shipped to Europe. In addition, land in the Americas was taken over by people wishing to escape religious persecution in Europe.

Despite the various motives for colonization, the overall effect was that thriving, original civilizations were destroyed while European citizens and val-ues were imposed. Colonialism not only destroyed indigenous civilizations, but also transported rivalries among colonial powers to other parts of the globe. The victims of colonialism were drawn into struggles about which they knew nothing. They were recruited to fight for European causes; for example, the Indian forces who provided so much assistance to the U.K. in World Wars I and II (indeed the Indian Army in World War II was the largest volunteer army ever raised in the history of warfare).

Colonialism had its critics even at the height of imperialism a century ago. People argued that it was wrong for one state to dominate another. This criti-cism grew much louder in World War I, partly because of competing colonial ambitions among the European countries. The Allied countries and the Asso-ciated Powers (led by the United States) agreed that—for one of the few times in history—the victor states should not take over the territories of the defeated states but that these territories should be held in trust to be put on the road to independence. This work was overseen by the League of Nations.

At the end of World War II, the same agreement was made under the aegis of the United Nations, which replaced the League. Australia, for example, had acquired German New Guinea as a League Mandate territory, and the acqui-sition became a UN Trust territory. Australia administered it with its own colony of Papua. In 1975, the nation-state of Papua New Guinea received its independence. Not only were there Trust territories of the defeated states to be administered and given independence, but also the Allied states had their own extensive colonies to be freed.

THE SECOND PHASE OF SELF-DETERMINATION

The world since 1945 has been transformed. In that year, the UN had 51 members; now it has 191, with East Timor becoming the newest member in 2002. Most of this growth has come from the winding up of empires.

This transformation is one of the greatest changes in the twentieth century and has come about for four reasons. First, colonial peoples rebelled against their masters. Japan's entry into World War II by defeating Western states, especially capturing Singapore, showed that Europeans were not always destined to win. Although Japan lost the war, its example stayed in the minds of people. They had seen a non-European state at least initially defeat the world's greatest state. White people, thus, were not invincible and were not necessarily destined to govern the world.

Second, the new global communications revolution meant that ideas about resisting colonialism could be broadcast around the world. India's nonviolent resistance to the British received much coverage in the United States; the latter had worked with the United Kingdom in ending German and Japanese aggression but now found itself linked with an old-style colonial power. The United States did not want to be associated with the old-fashioned imperial powers. India's independence in 1947 created a precedent for other colonies.

Third, colonial powers had been weakened by the fighting among themselves. The United Kingdom, for example, emerged from World War II heavily in debt and unable to maintain the large military force required to put down colonial rebellions. But the United States, which had finished the war as the world's richest country, was not only unwilling to provide money to maintain old European empires, but also ambitious for a new world order based on its own economic and military power.

Finally, the temper of the times had changed. Even in Europe, there was less enthusiasm for maintaining the burden of empire. Economists argued that the money to be made from colonies had already been made and that continued imperialism would be a financial burden. The high point of colonial exploitation was based on an industrial system that required large amounts of raw materials; the material-intensive era of industrialization has now gone. Meanwhile, developed countries had become more self-sufficient with food and so required less of it imported. The initial motivation for imperialism was to make as much as money as possible in as little time as possible—and with little regard for the colonial peoples. Now empires were described as ways of introducing civilization to people, a cultural change that would require schools, roads, hospitals, and far more money than that made by holding onto an empire.

Thus, the European powers started withdrawing from their empires. The process was as untidy as the original one of creating them. Alastair Horne's biography of the British prime minister Harold Macmillan, who held office from 1957–1963, contains a conversation between the prime minister and Sir James Robertson who had spent all of his working life in the British Colonial Service.[1] Macmillan asked if the people in the colonies were ready for the independence that the British government was then giving them. Sir James replied that they were not. Then why not delay the process? Sir James said that the colonies ideally should have another two decades to be prepared for independence. But this would not work because the people to be trained for eventual rule would be campaigning immediately for independence and would have to be imprisoned. Therefore, instead of two decades of brutal repression, it was better for the United Kingdom to leave as quickly as possible. Sir James was correct with his prediction: Many of the systems of national governance installed by the British government failed within years of the colonies becoming independent. For example, almost every former British colony in Africa has fallen into chaos.

The UN itself is a good example of how attitudes have changed. Its initial membership derived largely from developed countries. In addition to the white-minority racist regime in South Africa, it had only two other African member-nations in 1945, Ethiopia and Liberia. As the empires ended, one of the first acts of new countries was to join the UN. By 1960, only 15 years after the process began, the UN General Assembly adopted a nonbinding resolution calling for the end of the remaining empires; the resolution was called the Declaration on the Granting of Independence to Colonial Countries and Peoples.[2]

Now the formal process of decolonization is almost complete. Most of the territories that are left in some form of colonial status have very small populations. The world now has the smallest number of people, as a percentage of total population, in recorded history under colonial rule. East Timor in 2002 became the latest member to join the UN. One of the first European colonies, East Timor had been controlled by Portugal for over four hundred years.[3] Although Indonesia invaded the colony in 1975, the people fought back and, under the UN Transitional Administration, they were prepared for full independence.[4]

To conclude, the liberation of most of Europe's colonies has generated a flood of nation-states. The second phase of this century's self-determination era has almost ended.

But a new phase has opened up: the self-determination of groups of people within independent nation-states. In the case of Africa, for example, this has taken the form of disputes over boundaries because the national borders rarely coincided with tribal ones.

Meanwhile, as examined below, some developed countries have campaigns for essentially bringing about "internal decolonization." This phrase refers to the states allegedly having their own forms of internal colonization, the poor treatment of the original inhabitants. Some nations have difficulty in reconciling themselves to the states in which they are living.

THE THIRD PHASE OF SELF-DETERMINATION

After independence, the new Asian and African nation-states took on the attributes of European diplomacy. But the Westphalian System has been a large burden for them, especially the African states. Elie Kedourie commented that the policy of decolonization led to the setting up of European-style parliamentary regimes, the workings of which necessarily fell into the hands of

European-educated Africans.[5] The governments, whatever the paper checks and balances, often became engines of oppression, all the more efficient for being endowed with westernized bureaucratic devices through which the life of the ruled could be interfered with and controlled. The new rulers also had a very precarious tenure because there was little or no relation between these new institutions of government and the traditional African society of which these new rulers suddenly found themselves in control. This traditional society was a fragmented one, in which tribal loyalties and preferences ruled supreme. Decolonization, therefore, did not bring peace to Africa, and instead increased the burden of insecurity and oppression, which the African peoples carry.

As African decolonization got underway in the late 1950s, there was a basic problem to be confronted: Where were the boundaries of the new states to be drawn? Africa before colonization had contained hundreds of tribes. Then the European imperial process divided people into a patchwork of colonies, often splitting tribes into separate nationalities. Rivers in Africa, for example, formed highways, so people of the same tribe lived on either side of them. When the European map-makers appeared, they often used rivers as dividing lines on their maps; consequently, a tribe was split up into different empires. A system of tribes was therefore divided up into colonies. For example, veteran African reporter Karl Maier has written about Nigeria, the largest failed state in the world which the British had put together without much thought in 1914 from a collection of very different ethnic groups.[6] Nigeria now has 100 million people who speak 250 different languages. While the country is immensely wealthy, the wealth has been squandered or stolen by the elite since independence. It was also the site in 1967–1970 of one of the continent's worst civil wars in the twentieth century.

The decolonization process was haphazard and uncoordinated. It varied from one imperial power to another, with differing participation from the peoples about to become decolonized. In 1884–1885, there was a conference in Berlin to divide up some of the remainder of Africa, and so reduce the risk of European territorial competition as well as potential conflict.[7] This synchronized the latter end of the imperial process in Africa. But there was no synchronization at all in the decolonization process, the colonies became independent at various times and in different ways.

The decolonization process was based upon acceptance of the imperial boundaries. International lawyers Milan Sahovic and William Bishop said that most African and Asian countries declared themselves in favor of the principle of *uti possidetis*, which was applied in Latin America in the nineteenth century during the liberation of the former Spanish colonies.[8] The principle provided that boundaries among Latin American states should correspond to the administrative boundaries existing among different parts of the Spanish colonial empire. While the colonies eventually became independent, the old tribal boundaries were not revived. Consequently, Africa has had tribal problems as people come to terms with the new set of dividing lines.[9]

Since there was no easy way to bring about decolonization, the latter half of the twentieth century contained examples of the risks associated with the major alternatives. One alternative was to stick with *uti possidetis* and try to make the new nation-state succeed. Nigeria is an example of how that could fail. The other alternative was to redraw the boundaries on the eve of independence. The division of the Indian sub-continent in 1947 was an example of this. Because the new nation-state of Pakistan was to be a Muslim state, about eight million Muslims fled from India into Pakistan while as many Hindus and Sikhs fled from Pakistan into India. About half a million people were killed. Kashmir is still divided between India and Pakistan; their soldiers are killed regularly in border skirmishes. Therefore, there were no easy answers to how the decolonization process should have been carried out.

THE CONTINUING STRUGGLE FOR SELF-DETERMINATION

The UN estimates that there are 300 million indigenous people in at least 5,000 groups spread across the world in more than 70 countries. It has taken decades for international organizations to recognize their plight.[10] In the 1920s, American Indians approached the League of Nations. While their visit to Geneva attracted considerable attention, there were no tangible results. In the early years of the UN, indigenous representatives made sporadic appeals to the world organization. Again, there was no specific reaction.

The turning point came in 1970 when a UN body, the Sub-Commission on the Prevention of Discrimination and Protection of Minorities, recommended that the plight of indigenous peoples be studied. The British expert on the Sub-Commission at that time (Peter Calvocoressi of the University of Sussex) told me at the time that the Sub-Commission had been unclear as to how to conduct the "protection of minorities" side of its mandate. This was very much a task carried over in 1945 from the League of Nations. But there were concerns that according minority populations any special rights could inflame the passions of the majority population in their countries and so lead to ethnic tensions.

Additionally, the League's pioneering work in the protection of minorities was limited solely to the minorities in the former Austro-Hungarian countries. Such groups had the right to complain to the League, a right which is only now slowly being accepted by national governments in the UN's human rights work.[11] This helps explain why the American Indians got no help from the League even though the United States was one of the victors in World War I. Additionally, Italy was not bound by a Minorities Treaty because the country had been an Ally in World War I. Therefore, Italy's Yugoslav minority together with its smaller German-speaking minorities, rather over 500,000 and 200,000, respectively, were condemned to ruthless Italianization under the Fascists. In short, the League's sophisticated system for protecting minority populations was only imposed on the defeated countries of World War I.

By 1970, the temper of the times had begun to change: The civil rights movements in the United States and elsewhere meant that some governments were willing to give a grudging acceptance to intergovernmental consideration of minority problems. The UN machinery for the international protection of human rights is slowly coming up to the level of sophistication imposed by the League on the defeated Austro-Hungarian empire for the protection of minorities. Indigenous people are able to make some use of the UN system.

Additionally, indigenous people and human rights nongovernmental organizations (NGOs) have noted that, thanks partly to the communications revolution, indigenous though diverse people face similar problems.[12] The UN reported that under the march of colonialism, the spread of nonindigenous religions, and the relentless pace of development as well as modernization, indigenous groups have not only seen their traditional cultures eroded, but also their land-holdings confiscated or signed away as part of the economic coercion upon them.[13] This legacy has helped to make indigenous peoples some of the most disadvantaged on the earth. For example, most of India's tribal peoples live below the poverty line; the life expectancy of indigenous peoples in northern Russia is 18 years less than the national average; and unemployment among Australia's Indigenous Peoples is five times the national average.

But indigenous peoples are active in the pursuit of their human rights. First, the groups that have managed to survive will not now perish; their numbers are slowly increasing. Governments now grudgingly accept that they have a responsibility to take care of indigenous peoples. There is a clear trend among developed countries towards acceptance: that indigenous peoples require cultural autonomy; that they exercise self-government in respect to important local or regional matters; and that they participate significantly in management of territories, land/sea resources, as well as negotiation forums to decide the terms of these matters with national governments.

Second, indigenous peoples are learning the strength of networking. For example, the Inuit (wrongly called Eskimos) who live in northern Russia, Canada, and Scandinavia are sharing their experiences, which include how to lobby their governments and how to mobilize the mass media. In the United States, 600 First Nation lawyers now work for their people and they have also have had their first senator elected.[14]

Finally, compensation has become an important rallying point for grievances. This can be seen in a variety of ways. Indigenous peoples are seeking economic compensation. For example, while the annual market of pharmaceutical products derived from medicinal plants discovered by indigenous peoples exceeds $43 billion U.S. dollars, the profits are rarely shared with the discoverers. However, the relevant indigenous people are campaigning for their royalty payments.

Nauru, a former League of Nations Mandate which became independent in 1968, complained about Australia to the International Court of Justice in 1992. Nauru wanted compensation from Australia over the devastation caused by phosphate mining while Australia was running the Mandate/Trust Territory before 1968. Australia settled out of court by giving $107 million compensation in its dollars in August 1993. It will be interesting to see if this case stimulates other countries to claim compensation.

Australia has had its own compensation dispute against the United Kingdom over the latter's nuclear tests in Australia, though the conflict did not need go to the International Court of Justice.[15] With the agreement of the Australian government, Britain had tested nuclear devices on Australian soil in the 1950s. Although the United Kingdom claimed to have cleaned up the sites, this was later disputed. The diplomatic wrangling went on during the 1980s. The United Kingdom was not only obstinate about paying compensation to Australia for the clean-up, but also worried about compensation claims from former service personnel who claimed ill health from exposure to the tests. Any hint of accepting liability for the tests in Australia might somehow boost the case of veterans suing the British government. Also, as a former imperial power, the United Kingdom was wary of creating precedents for other issues. Indigenous peoples, aided by skilful lawyers, in former British colonies could try to sue the United Kingdom government for the damage done during colonialism. Liability for damages is also a matter of concern to the other former European colonial powers.[16]

In summary, the empires have largely gone, but there will continue to be problems. Difficulties arising from the creation and dissolution of empires will persist for many years to come.

DIPLOMACY

Diplomacy and the Westphalian System

The roots of diplomacy are much older than the Westphalian System. For over two thousand years, diplomatists (as they prefer to be called) have had a special protected status as representatives of their rulers in other lands.[17] The Westphalian System built upon those old traditions developed the process of conference diplomacy, such as the 1815 Congress of Vienna and the subsequent European "balance of power" system. It laid down the rules, which have existed largely not amended well into the twentieth century.[18]

Diplomatists have, until recent decades, tended to be recruited from the elite families of their countries since these were in the best position to assess intuitively how their rulers might react to particular proposals; communications were often difficult so that diplomatists had to have a great deal of discretion.[19] Therefore, until recent decades European diplomatists were white males drawn from the upper class of their societies who were knowledgeable in French.

The diplomatic process was a straightforward one. The Berlin Conference of 1884–1885 provides a good example. The meeting brought together representatives of 14 states, roughly all the main states of Europe except Switzerland. The conference divided up much of Africa into so-called spheres of influence, the first time this phrase had been used in international conference diplomacy. The historian David Thomson has pointed out that it was agreed that any power which effectively occupied African territory and duly notified the other powers could thereby establish possession of it.[20] This gave the signal for the rapid, straightforward partition of the rest of noncolonized Africa among the colonial powers, inaugurating a more orderly form of colonialism. A compact among the powers to pursue the further partition of Africa as amicably as possible, the treaty also was an attempt to separate colonial competition from European rivalries. The diplomatists at the Berlin Conference shared many assumptions. While they may have disagreed over which country should get what territory, they all agreed that white people had the responsibility to take European civilization into Africa for the benefit of the natives (and of course their own states).

Diplomacy is now much more complicated and more protracted.[21] The Berlin Conference split up Africa in only a few months, while the new UN law of the sea treaty took 12 years to negotiate. Even so, the United States suddenly decided to boycott the treaty. Thus, it took another 12 years for the treaty to come into effect in November 1994.[22] The creation of the International Criminal Court through the 1998 Treaty of Rome is a similar story. Although the United States was heavily involved in the negotiation process, it did not sign the 1998 treaty out of concern that it would be used for political purposes against American personnel. The outgoing Clinton Administration changed its policy and signed the treaty on December 31, 2000. However, the Bush Administration did not like the treaty. In 2002 the Bush Administration announced that it would no longer regard the United States as having signed the treaty and so it would not seek the advice and consent of the Senate for its ratification. Despite the U.S. Boycott, the Rome Treaty entered into force on July 1, 2002.

A more comical example, though not to the government of the country, arose in the April 1993 admission to the UN of a state with no name. The admission of Macedonia required the member to be "provisionally referred to for all purposes within the UN as the 'former Yugoslav Republic of Macedonia' pending settlement of the difference that has arisen over the name of the State."[23] Greece regarded the territory called Macedonia to be part of the existing Greek state; it made no claim to this other territory but insisted that the new state not use the name of Macedonia.

More Nation-States

Part of the reason for Westphalian diplomacy to be running into severe problems is that many more states are involved. The UN, the world's largest intergovernmental organization and center of multilateral diplomacy, has a membership 191), and the figure will increase as current states break up into smaller ones. There is a trend for the fragmentation of existing nation-states;

there are very few examples of successful amalgamations of existing nation-states into larger ones.

Similarly, bilateral diplomacy is also more complicated. A century ago, a diplomatist could deal, for example, with the British Government, whose views would cover those of the dominions and colonies within the British Empire; now each state has to be contacted. So in terms of sheer numbers alone diplomacy is much more difficult, especially given the doctrine of sovereign equality, whereby each state is of no higher status (in international law terms) than any other.

More Perspectives and Priorities

Additionally, there are different perspectives and priorities. African, Asian, and Latin American countries, for example, have different ways of looking at the world's problems. They have introduced their own rituals. The most notable ritual, until the early 1990s, at the UN and other major conferences included criticizing South Africa's apartheid racial policy, even if the gathering was not specifically devoted to that subject in particular or human rights in general. Even at the 1972 Stockholm UN Conference on the Human Environment, Third World delegates ensured that the Conference declaration on the environment contained in the first principle a criticism of "apartheid, racial segregation, discrimination, colonial and other forms of oppression and foreign domination."[24] This ritual was often misunderstood by commentators.[25]

The diplomatists from the Western and Eastern blocs recognized that these acts had to be performed by Third World diplomatists; if not, the omission could be regarded as a subtle hint of a policy shift of some kind. Both the diplomatists who performed the acts and those that saw them performed, mainly Western delegates, knew their importance. The acts were more than just a recitation of, say, the prayers, which are offered up at the beginning of each meeting of most Western parliaments. They were less substantive items of conference agendas, even though the media themselves regularly reported them more often than the substantive items. Indeed, they usually consumed less time than the media implied in the reporting of such events.[26]

They were part of the Third World's attempts to gradually alter the attitude of Western governments by regularly criticizing South Africa. The Third World wanted to isolate South Africa diplomatically, to use diplomatic means, rather than military ones, to reduce South Africa's international standing. This paid off in the early 1990s, with the ending of racial discrimination and the holding of free elections. With far less success, Arab states have used this method against Israel since 1973.[27]

Sovereign Equality of States

There is a discrepancy between the doctrine of sovereign equality of states and the reality of international politics. Even a century ago, of course, some states were more equal than others. But the discrepancy has become much wider in recent decades.

States vary in gross national product and population size: at one end of the spectrum, there are states like the United States, Japan, and China; at the other end, there are the micro-states in the Pacific and elsewhere that have smaller national incomes and populations than many U.S. capital cities. Fiji, for example, has a population of about 747,000 people, Western Samoa has 158,000, and Nauru has just over 10,000. About a third of the UN membership consists of nation-states with populations of less than one million inhabitants.

Incidentally, one relic of the pre-Westphalian System is still very much in operation, though naturally greatly reduced: the Vatican City (Holy See). This has a territory of 44 hectares (109 acres), a population of less than 3,000 (with few women and children), its own coinage and postal service, but no national anthem. It has a special observer status at the UN as "nonmember state permanent observer," which means that although it cannot vote it can speak at UN gatherings. The Vatican used its status to great effect in its criticism of family planning at the 1994 Cairo UN Conference on Population and Development. In 1999, a Sea Change Campaign was set up by over one hundred international groups representing women, religions, and reproductive rights; the campaign aimed to persuade the UN to downgrade the Vatican's position from nonmember state to one of a nongovernmental organization which would reduce its right to speak.[28]

However, each state has to be treated alike. According to the doctrine of sovereign equality, a visiting president of a small state is as important as a U.S. president; so all the diplomatic protocol, which has evolved over the centuries, has to apply. Additionally, some states have a limited scope for participation in diplomacy. Without the expertise required for many international conferences and projects, some states even lack the staff to sit at the delegation places at international conferences.

Improvements in Communications and Transport

One additional problem for modern diplomacy is the improvement in communications and transport. A diplomatist traveling to the 1815 Congress of Vienna took the same time to go the distance as a Roman courier would have done almost two thousand years earlier. He would have arrived with sufficient time to become refreshed and relaxed.

Since aircraft have tempted political leaders to do the negotiations in the place of diplomatists, they occasionally overdo the traveling. When President George Bush became sick at a dinner in Tokyo and vomited over the Japanese Prime Minister Kiichi Miyazawa, veteran U.S. journalist Hugh Sidey blamed the President's illness on his excessive travel.[29] Perhaps the time has come, he speculated, for all these top government officials to curtail their dashing about. Former U.S. Secretary of State Dean Rusk commented that the diplomatic service is a 500-year-old invention designed to make it unnecessary for kings, presidents, and prime ministers to be everywhere at once. Politics is now a drama of motion. The media love the exhilaration of nomadic statecraft.

U.S. economist John Kenneth Galbraith, ambassador to India in the 1960s, was also skeptical about all this traveling.[30] He saw it as "the recreational character of foreign policy," where politicians could flee from domestic turmoil; they were treated better overseas than at home. Besides the welcoming ceremonies and applause not to be expected at home, quiet, decorous, though vacuous, conversations followed which contrasted agreeably with the contentiousness so often experienced in domestic political negotiations. Communiques were issued, often written in advance, telling imaginatively of the topics under discussion and the areas of agreement. Pleasant for politicians and interesting for the mass media, the traveling also provided colorful shots of other countries. But this kind of diplomacy was of marginal use to the countries.

Complexity of the Global Agenda

Finally, the diplomatic agenda is now much longer, requiring more staff, expertise, and topics to be addressed than ever before.

Today's workload is very different from that of only a century ago. Valerie Pakenham wrote a history of the Edwardians in the British Empire.[31] She gave a description of the building containing the headquarters staff governing at least a quarter of the world at the turn of the twentieth century. In 1901, the administration of the vast United Kingdom Empire was divided among three departments of state, all housed in one massive block built around a courtyard on the south side of Downing Street, London (near the official residence of the prime minister). First, the Foreign Office was responsible for nearly all the new African protectorates that Lord Salisbury, who had held the combined posts of Prime Minister and Foreign Secretary for almost two decades, had acquired during the late 1880s and 1890s: British Central Africa (soon to be Nyasaland), British East Africa (later Kenya), Uganda, and Somaliland. Second, there was the India Office whose staff conducted relations not only with so-called British India, but also with the 600 or so nominally independent princely states and Burma, annexed by the British in 1881 after a series of "little wars." Third, compared with these two prestigious departments, the Colonial Office had always been a poor relation: a labyrinth of odd-shaped rooms with smoky chimneys and elevators that did not work. By 1900, its small staff included just over a hundred clerks who divided up the huge collection of the colonial Empire among five departments including one for the West Indies, West Africa, South Africa, Asia, and one for Canada together with Australia.

Although the empire has shrunk so that it contains just a few pieces of real estate dotted around the globe, the Foreign and Commonwealth Office (FCO) staff has increased. During the twentieth century, governments took over more and more aspects of the everyday life of their country's affairs.

Bradford University's Tom Stonier commented that the reason why governments absorbed an ever increasing share of the GNP was the feeling that they could do certain things better.[32] Thus, the local and national British government engaged in such matters as sewage disposal, the building and maintenance of roads, education, health care, and coal production. There were economies of scale in a government getting involved in this work. Building an effective sewage disposal system can be very costly. When the population density is low, each house can have its own pit or cess pool; as density builds up, this becomes less practical. If the matter were left in private hands, the wealthy areas could afford to install an effective system; but the poor could not. This would, sooner or later, lead to outbreaks of cholera, typhoid, and other infectious diseases in the poorer areas. One impact on the wealthier sector of the community would be possibility of the epidemic spilling over—that is, there would be a direct public health threat. Second, such epidemics lead to social and economic disruption as the labor force becomes unreliable and streets become unsafe among other situations.

Thus, government involvement in a country's affairs also includes trade. The modern department of foreign affairs now has to drum up foreign trade for the country's companies. This is becoming an even more important factor as economics, rather than war, become a key factor in foreign policy.

THE NEW ERA OF WARFARE

Conventional international warfare arose at the same time as the Westphalian System. The world is now moving into a new era of warfare, one characterized by less conventional fighting and more guerrilla tactics. Governments are now more concerned with maintaining the unity of the nation-state than with fighting conventional international wars. September 11, 2001, also was a reminder both of the lack of progress among governments in dealing with terrorism and the way in which no country is secure from attack, no matter how high the level of defense expenditure.

Guerrilla Warfare

The oldest form of fighting is guerrilla warfare, which has always required the least amount of training. People, including women and even children, have fought as guerrillas, usually in a part-time capacity with each person knowing the rest of the small group. The weapons have been unsophisticated and based on everyday implements, usually farming tools.

The Roman army was the exception in the early era of guerrilla warfare. It had large, organized fighting formations, professional soldiers, and distinctive uniforms. In retrospect, this army was a pioneer of modern warfare; as an ill omen, it was not always successful in its campaigns against guerrilla forces.

For about the thousand years of the European Middle Ages, little attention was given to the Roman military model. The wars of that era consisted of small battles and sieges of fortified positions, especially castles during the winter months when it was too cold for fighting out in the open fields. There were few full-time soldiers. Knights, for example, ran feudal estates as their main source of income and recruited their own workers as troops when required.

The Rise of Conventional Warfare

Then warfare changed around the seventeenth century. There is no one single explanation for the change. It was more a matter of different events influencing each other. As warfare became more than just one band of soldiers fighting another, rulers had difficulty in obtaining fighters from among their own citizens. Martin van Creveld of Hebrew University noted that rulers could no longer raise forces from their personal followers; instead, they had to create organizations separate from society at large, which would be at their exclusive disposal and whose sole function would be to fight their rulers' enemies.[33] Until 1648, those organizations consisted mostly of mercenaries. These groups were motley collections of soldiers who served under their own entrepreneur-commanders, gathered from wherever they could be found on the occasion of war and sent home whenever it was over. Hard to control, the mercenaries often inflicted more damage on the people to be defended than on the enemy. The mercenaries also ran out when the money ran out.

The creation of the nation-state system meant that the basic unit of governance shifted from a small tribal area to the nation-state, which gave rulers more people from whom taxation and conscripts could be drawn. A century later, the industrial revolution meant that industry could develop more destructive weapons. Also fighting formations could be transported over longer distances: Europeans could now fight each other over colonies in the Americas, Africa, and Asia.

The new form of warfare became so common that it acquired the title of "conventional" warfare. Fighting formations became larger, and almost exclusively male. It was necessary for all troops to have distinctive uniforms to distinguish them from the enemy. Martin van Creveld said that as regular forces grew stronger and more professional, they tended to specialize in external war until, finally, they were forbidden to do anything else.[34] The adoption of uniforms, meant to distinguish those who were allowed to fight in the name of the state from those who were not, was in place about 1660 and represented a crucial step. From 1715 on, more and more quasi-military tasks such as putting down riots and so on, were left to light forces, so that "to dragoon" emerged as a synonym for crowd-control and has remained so ever since. After about 1780, military specialization, backed by military power, reached the point where separate police forces were established. For the first time in modern history, the military were freed from day-to-day maintenance of law and order, administration, tax-collecting and other duties.

Armies and navies became more professional. Defense personnel were set apart from the rest of the community; they lived in separate buildings and were controlled by legal codes usually more extensive than those of the civilian legal system. While restrictions were placed on civilian access to weapons, warfare became the exclusive right of the government. The international humanitarian law of armed conflict, established at the Geneva and Hague Conventions, applied only to military personnel.

For the first time, there were professional soldiers who spent large chunks of time without fighting. Previous personnel had been recruited for specific campaigns and then demobilized as soon as the fighting stopped. Now personnel were in permanent employment, but fighting only consumed a part of their time.

The Decline of Conventional Warfare

During the first half of the twentieth century, the nature of conventional warfare changed again. It used to be about humans killing humans. But beginning in World War I, land warfare became far more mechanized: Warfare became a matter of machines killing machines.

While the last Allied cavalry charge was on November 8, 1917, when units of the Canadian army defeated a German cavalry regiment, few horses were used at all in World War II. In 1941, the United Kingdom had 100,000 vehicles in the Middle East. By the time of D-Day in June 1944, there was one vehicle for every 4.77 Allied soldiers. Between 1939 and 1945, the United Kingdom produced 130,000 aircraft, Germany 119,000 and the United States 303,000. Warfare had become an activity of quarter-masters general and production planners.[35] World War II, rather than the creation of the Welfare State, expanded the role of the government in the economy.

The "tail" became bigger than the "teeth." In order to keep one soldier at the front to bite the enemy, six persons needed to be drawn from such civilian occupations as catering, engineering, medicine, building, transportation, and law. Each arm of service became a society within a society.

World War II will remain the world's largest conventional war. Other wars have been longer, notably the Iran-Iraq war in 1980–1988. But none will be as extensive, intensive, and expensive.

The prime factor in the current decline of conventional warfare is the cost of the mechanization of warfare.[36] Governments cannot afford the same stock of equipment as they used to acquire. While humans, often available through conscription, have been comparatively cheap, machines are expensive both to purchase and to maintain. The machines are also much more destructive, and they travel further with more firepower than previous weapons. But this also means that machines can be destroyed at a faster rate, with less chance of ever being repaired.

All the major conventional wars since the early 1960s that have resulted in a clear victory have been won in about six weeks: most notably the two Middle East conflicts of 1967 and 1973, the Falklands/Malvinas in 1982 and the Gulf War of 1991. If one side cannot defeat the other in that time, the war will just drag on often inconclusively, as in the Iran–Iraq war, which ran for eight years. The crucial six-week-period is derived from the limitations of equipment and supply: Governments can no longer afford large reserves of equipment.

The Rise of Nuclear Warfare

Nuclear warfare was a direct outgrowth of conventional air warfare. Leaders in World War II wanted to avoid a repeat of World War I's trench warfare and so they looked for methods of moving firepower quickly over long distances.

Bomber aircraft were the favorite method throughout Europe. The technology of that period seems quaint by the standards of half a century later. One of the RAF's most famous raids was in May 1943 with the 617 Squadron's attack on some German dams. The British scientist Barnes Wallis devised a bomb that would bounce along the length of the lake behind the dam and then hit the structure itself. From an aircraft flying at 370km/h, the bomb had to be dropped from precisely 18 meters. But the bomb-aiming system itself was based on a coat-hanger so that when the two nails on the hand-held sight lined up with the towers on the dam, the bomb had to be dropped. The raid was largely successful in destroying the dams, and it was a good boost for British morale. However, only 11 of the 19 aircraft returned home.

The quest continued for much more powerful bombs and culminated in the creation of atomic bombs. As atomic weapons brought the war against Japan to an abrupt end, politicians reasoned that atomic weapons would be crucial in any future conflict. Later research shifted the emphasis from aircraft to nuclear missiles.

On a rate based on the number of potential deaths, nuclear missiles are cheaper than most other forms of killing. Their limitation arises, ironically, from their extensive capacity to kill. They are too destructive to use in the usual military campaigns. Nuclear weapons would destroy that which the attacker would like eventually to control.

Additionally for the first time in history, a powerful country cannot defend its people from an attack. Nuclear missiles cannot be shot down. Even if the proposed Strategic Defense Initiative ("Star Wars") had gone ahead and could have shot down some missiles, only about 2 percent of Soviet missiles were needed to destroy the United States' main cities. Much the same could be said about the National Missile Defense project now under consideration by the Bush Administration.

Both the 1987 agreement between the United States and U.S.S.R. on inter-mediate nuclear forces and their 1993 agreement on strategic nuclear weapons show that the countries realize the limitations of these weapons for political purposes. Even when the 1993 treaty comes fully into effect in the year 2003, the United States will still be vulnerable to nuclear attack because of the number of Russian strategic missiles still in existence. The United States was much safer from attack in 1945 than it will be in 2003.

Meanwhile, all societies will remain vulnerable to guerrilla groups using nuclear explosive devices. Nuclear weapons cannot be dis-invented. That knowledge is here to stay.

The Return of Extensive Guerrilla Warfare

Guerrilla warfare has grown rapidly since World War II. Almost every conflict underway today involves guerrillas in at least one party to the conflict. These are people fighting in small bands, often not in uniform, with weapons varying from very sophisticated ones, either donated by a great power or stolen from conventional forces, to old weapons and even home-made ones.

Guerrilla warfare turns conventional warfare's reasoning upside down. Essentially political, guerrilla warfare is about winning the hearts and minds of people. It is not so much about taking and holding a set piece of territory. Guerrillas do not need a large amount of firepower to do this because they are only carrying out sporadic raids. Too much firepower, as with the U.S. troops in Vietnam, can alienate the local population because there is a temptation to use the power wantonly. Indeed, the United States did not lose in Vietnam because of a shortage of firepower but partly because of the excessive use of it.[37] Guerrillas can lose battle after battle and yet still win the war because their warfare is a form of attrition, a wearing down of the conventional forces until exhaustion and frustration set in.

In contrast to most conventional leaders, General Gerald Templar in British Malaya in the 1950s succeeded partly because he recognized that economic and social reforms were necessary and that he was engaged in primarily a civilian activity.[38] Not surprisingly, he also was one of those who coined the phrase about winning hearts and minds. The United States failed to learn the lessons of Malaya for its Vietnam campaign, as the U.S.S.R. also failed to learn them during its Afghanistan campaign.

The mass media publicize guerrilla attacks. Although comparatively few people are killed in raids, the deaths attract a disproportionate amount of news coverage. Indeed in terms of the number of deaths involved, guerrilla warfare is by no means the huge problem that the mass media often suggest. For example, more people were killed on the roads of Northern Ireland each year than were killed in the warfare. But wars sell newspapers.

In 1985, the then British prime minister, Margaret Thatcher, called for the mass media to show greater restraint in reporting guerrilla activities:

We must try to find ways to starve the terrorist and the hijacker of the oxygen of publicity on which they depend. In our societies we do not believe in constraining the media, still less in censorship. But ought we not to ask the media to agree among themselves on a voluntary code of conduct, a code under which they would not say or show anything that could assist the terrorists' morale or their cause while the hijack lasted?[39]

Little has come from this suggestion.[40] While mass media continues to report extensively on this type of warfare, guerrilla groups seem ever more adept at using publicity to convey their point of view.

Modern life in large cities is one of anonymity. People living next door to each other often know little about each other. A guerrilla group could operate from a city district, and the neighbors would not know. This anonymity makes it difficult for the police to get information. Guerrillas can melt away in the crowd, like fish in a sea.

Therefore, guerrillas operate in a different way from conventional forces. An analogy with fighting lung cancer illustrates this; fighting lung cancer is futile if no attention is given to the primary cause of the disease—smoking. But conventional forces are trained for military action and not the analysis of why people go to war in the first place. Preferring what seem to be quick solutions, politicians like to use force rather than seek the underlying causes of conflict. For example, a more conciliatory approach to Tamil grievances some years ago could have reduced the subsequent Sri Lankan and Indian bloodshed.

This point is indirectly made in studies of military leadership. Lieutenant-General Phillip Davidson served with General Westmoreland in Vietnam and wrote a history of the war.[41] He argued that the main cause of defeat was Washington's failure to adopt a war policy. He believed that Congress should have declared war, thereby involving the United States in an all-out effort to win it. But I doubt if that would have been enough. After all, the North Vietnamese were not going to cooperate in fighting on the U.S. terms: The North Vietnamese avoided main force engagements. They had base areas protected by swamps, mountains, rivers, and dense vegetation. These bases housed supply areas, hospitals, and even small manufacturing plants. Enjoying the support of local people, the North Vietnamese could not have been forced by the United States to fight a conventional war. They could have gone on losing battle after battle and yet still won the war.

Edward Lansdale, by contrast, argued that the guerrillas (the Huks) in the post-1945 Philippines could only be defeated by a mixture of land resettlement, social welfare programs, elimination of government corruption, education— and military force.[42] When President Magsaysay was killed in an air crash in 1957, his successors and the United States simply reverted to the easier use of military force; the force helped explain the continuing conflict in the Philippines. Lansdale was posted to Vietnam in 1954 but had even less success in introducing his policies. The U.S. military preferred to use the conventional warfare techniques they knew best.

The U.S.S.R. did not learn from the U.S. experience in Vietnam either. Its operation in Afghanistan from 1979 to 1989, showed that it too did not understand the unique nature of guerrilla warfare. Much the same could be said about the Israelis in the Occupied Territories, the Burmese forces in Karen-controlled eastern Burma, and the Indian and Sri Lankan forces in Tamil-dominated parts of Sri Lanka.

A complicating factor is the availability of nuclear weapons to guerrilla groups. While there is now virtually no risk of a deliberate World War III, the risk that eventually guerrilla groups will get access to nuclear weapons is growing. The weapons need not be very sophisticated, and the delivery system could be the back of a truck or a civilian cargo ship moored in a port city.

The Decline of International War

Most wars underway today are not only guerrilla ones, but also not strictly international ones. Wars in which one country attacks another or groups of countries are now rare. The reason for the media's interest in the Falkland and Iraq/Kuwait wars is that these were the biggest conventional wars since the late 1970s, when the U.S.S.R. invaded Afghanistan and Iraq attacked Iran.

The modern trends in warfare are for groups to try to break away from an existing nation-state to create their own country, or for a group to try to overthrow its government and so form its own government. Guerrilla warfare is the preferred technique in both cases. A war may become internationalized by the intervention of other countries or through the deployment of an international force, such as a UN peacekeeping operation or a NATO operation.

This new era of warfare creates fresh problems. The military are not trained for guerrilla warfare. It is a much more complicated form than the conventional one, and it may not be clear just who is the enemy. For example during 1993, Mohammed Farrah Aidid, went from being just one of several Somali warlords to being the main enemy of the UN operations, with a $25,000 reward for his capture; he finally became one of the negotiators working on a long-term settlement to the country's conflict. A *Time* magazine report, around the time that Aidid was perceived as the main villain in Somalia, conveyed some of the highly charged atmosphere.[43] Gun battles had raged in the streets of Mogadishu almost daily since 23 Pakistani peacekeepers died in an ambush the previous month. Blaming Aidid, the U.S. led UN forces in an aggressive bid to flush him out, culminating in a particularly bloody daylight attack on a meeting of Aidid's top commanders. At the end of a 20-minute barrage of missiles and cannon fire from U.S. helicopter gun ships, dozens of bodies lay scattered around the demolished villa. When foreign journalists arrived to view the carnage, an enraged crowd turned on them with stones, guns, and machetes, killing four. Italy immediately threatened to withdraw its 2,400 troops unless the goals of the mission were reassessed. The Germans who had sent only 250 of a promised 1,700-strong contingent, grumbled that it was a mistake to have soldiers in Somalia at all.

These difficulties have made governments reluctant to supply forces to UN peacekeeping operations. *Time* magazine commented on the 1994 conflict in Rwanda to the effect that the tribal skirmishes recalled the wars of the Middle Ages when religion, politics, economics, and social conflicts all intertwined.[44] The hygienic, high-tech, buttons-and-bombs warfare that developed countries had spent the previous 40 years refining also was missing. The chosen weapons, like machetes, were often far more crude. There were no rules of engagement and no one reliable with whom to negotiate. The Hutu army chief of staff guaranteed safe passage to UN soldiers evacuating wounded Tutsi civilians. But soldiers along the road stopped the convoy, ordered the people out, and set upon them with machetes. They said they did not take orders from the army chief of staff. Without any discipline, warfare becomes an extension of crime by other means. The modern military model is the neighborhood gang—brothers and cousins roaming, rule-breaking, and terrorizing. UN peacekeeping forces, like all conventional forces, have had little training for this type of warfare.

Since the tragedies in Somalia and Rwanda in the early 1990s, there have been wars in Sierra Leone and Congo. Developed countries within the UN, led by the United States, have been most reluctant to get militarily involved in any further African conflict.

Post-Modern Warfare

To conclude, the world has moved into the era of post-modern warfare. The 1990–1991 Gulf War is an example of the new era. The person supposedly losing the war, President Saddam Hussein, remains in power. George Bush, Margaret Thatcher, and Mikhail Gorbachev, all of whom had beat him, have long since lost power. Saddam Hussein is now in conflict with the next Bush generation.

This is an era when our ideas of warfare are being turned upside down. First, it is no longer clear just when a war ends. As far as Saddam Hussein is concerned, the Gulf War is not over; after a setback in 1991, he continues to battle on. Much the same can be said about Argentina and the Falkland/Malvina Islands. Although Argentina lost the 1982 round, the country remains determined to get the islands. In former Yugoslavia, the conflicts throughout the 1990s are still not settled despite all the peace negotiations. The new Yugoslav leader, President Vojislav Kostunica, is less hostile to NATO than was President Slobodan Milosevic; however, he remains committed to maintaining Kosovo as part of his nation-state. In 1995, the United States deployed 5,000 personnel to Bosnia on the basis that they would be withdrawn in a year. At the end of 2002, the 5,000 troops were still there, along with an additional 6,000 patrolling nearby Kosovo.

Second, it is no longer clear just who wins a war. Although Germany and Japan lost World War II, their economies are stronger now than many of the countries which won it. With the introduction of the Euro based so much on German financial power and not even including the British pound, the United Kingdom is being eclipsed by the country it beat in two world wars. While the United States won the Cold War, the country has found little joy in that victory. The Cold War damaged the economies of both the United States and U.S.S.R. Having fought the Cold War to contain Soviet expansionism, the United States is now troubled that Moscow is too weak to govern and so is lending money to help in the country's recovery. The part of the country credited for holding Russia together is, ironically, the defense force. After half a century of worrying that Moscow was too strong, the United States now is worried that Moscow is too weak.

Third, there is the decline of national patriotism. On the one hand, there has been the creation of a global consumer culture, which transcends national tastes. This is based on such items as CNN, MTV, pop music, Coca-Cola and McDonald's fast food. On the other hand, there has been a growth of micro-nationalism, the politics of identity. Peace for Russia has not come about with the end of the Cold War. There are around the world probably as many conflicts underway today as at the height of the Cold War; but they are almost all internal wars, with groups wanting to break away from a central national government to form their own countries.

Fourth, in most developed countries military expenditure is not so much a matter of safeguarding the people as protecting corporate profits. John Pike of the Federation of American Scientists has claimed that the "current military spending levels are largely driven by corporate interests rather than national security."[45] Therefore, the end of the Cold War was in some respects irrelevant: The key issue is to find ways of maintaining high levels of military expenditure at a time when the taxpayers want a peace dividend. Dana Mead was CEO of Tenneco, one of the most troubled conglomerates in the United States when he took over in the early 1990s. Part of his story about how Tenneco was restructured back into high profitability is an account of how the company lobbied its government to ensure continued work within its shipbuilding program.[46]

Finally, it is dangerous being a civilian. A key component of conventional warfare was the clear distinction between professional soldiers and the civilians; the professionals protected the others and in return received a special status in society. Senior officers have a priority standing in orders of precedence at official government functions as a part of the reward for being willing to lay down their lives for protecting the rest of society. However from World War II onwards, the percentage of civilians being killed in warfare has increased. Traditionally, military personnel and buildings were to be the only targets. Nowadays, the targets could be anything—including office blocks and passenger aircraft. Civilian deaths may now be as high as 90 per cent of the total deaths in warfare. During the period of the Vietnam War, more U.S. ambassadors were killed worldwide than were generals killed in Vietnam.

To conclude, warfare used to have clear boundaries and distinctions: winners/ losers, beginnings/endings, military/civilians, and patriotic motivations. In post-modern warfare, we are all lost in the fog of battle.

INTERNATIONAL LAW AND THE BREAK-UP OF NATION-STATES

Secession, the desire of a group of people within an existing nation-state to form their nation-state, has been one of the main themes of this chapter. But there is no consistent international law or diplomatic practice on this subject. For example, the United States does not support the Basque separatists in Spain. However, the United States did assist the Kosovo Liberation Army in 1999 and did not discourage the Chechen guerrillas from fighting against the central Russian government until after September 11 when Russia was needed in the international alliance against terrorism.

The secession issue brings many basic principles into conflict. People have the right to self-determination so that they can decide their own futures. There also is the precept of nonintervention in the internal affairs of another country, which should stop a country from interfering in another country. Meanwhile, upholding the principle behind the international protection of human rights means that governments ought not to be standing by and passively accepting the violation of human rights in another country.

There are also many broader practical matters. How is a people to be defined and could a specified group change over time due to, for example, demographic factors? Are nationalism, ethnicity, and religion enough to hold a country together? The experience in the original Pakistan shows that Islam was not enough to hold together the two ends of the 1947 version of the country, and East Pakistan broke away in 1971 to form Bangladesh. Would the creation of a separate nation-state be enough to end a guerrilla struggle, or would dissident groups continue to fight on? The various Tamil groups seem to fight each other almost as much as they fight the national government. How are we to determine that a guerrilla group does in fact speak for the ethnic group it claims to represent? Has the international community created problems for itself through inadvertently providing incentives and mechanisms for a people to seek independence as a way of achieving direct international benefits of statehood? For example, having become a nation-state, a people can call for international assistance to defend their state, as happened in 1991 with the breakaway of Croatia and Slovenia from Yugoslavia.

The intention here is not to solve these problems. That is impossible because there is very little agreement on them among scholars.[47] I simply want to note that these problems will continue in the twenty-first century with governments and the UN remaining reluctant to deal with them within broad policy. Instead, these leading bodies will lurch along pragmatically from one instance to another. Dealing with the difficulties is a key matter for the Westphalian System, yet it is being avoided.

THE CAMPAIGN AGAINST TERRORISM

The September 11, 2001, tragedy has again revived debate over the need to combat international terrorism.[48] For those of us who have written about various concepts of terrorism over the decades, there is a sense of weariness. In my case, living with terrorism came via the development of the law of armed conflict from the late 1960s onwards; I attended the Geneva Diplomatic Conference on the Reaffirmation and Development of the International Law of Armed Conflicts in 1974–1977, where there were various discussions of the subject.[49] For the veterans of these discussions, there is a sense of here we go again with yet another fresh bout of enthusiasm and determination to oppose terrorism. Each flurry of activity may produce declarations and treaties, but none of these amount to very much by way of practical action. The problem is essentially political—not legal. Once the political dimensions have been resolved, progress can be made in developing effective international law.

No Agreed Upon Definition and Application

Terrorist or Freedom Fighter?

The basic problem with trying to create an international regime against terrorism is that there is no agreed upon definition of it for practical purposes.[50] The International Law Association (ILA) had this issue on its agenda for many years. At its 1984 Paris Conference, the ILA defined "acts of terrorism" as including but not being limited to "atrocities, wanton killing, hostage-taking, hi-jacking, extortion or torture, committed or threatened to be committed whether in peacetime or in wartime for political purposes."[51]

The practical problem, of course, is that one government's terrorist is another's freedom fighter.[52] Indeed, it is possible for a person to move from being a terrorist to a freedom fighter to even a head of government. For example, Nelson Mandela recalls in his memoirs how his liberation movement decided not to use terrorism but instead opted for what it termed sabotage; he defines neither phrase.[53] However, the South African government regarded him as a terrorist and throughout the 1960s to the late 1980s refused to negotiate with him.[54] Later, political circumstances changed. Released from prison, Mandela went on to become South Africa's president. Similarly, the Jewish Irgun group that fought against the British for the creation of an independent Israeli state in 1947 was considered terrorist—by the British. Yet Menachem Begin, leader of the Irgun group, later became a prime minister of Israel. Indeed, many of the first generation of leaders in the new countries created out of the former

British and French colonies had served time in prison or had been on the run for offences considered to be terrorist by their colonial masters. Thus, terrorism is a pejorative and politically colored phrase devoid of legal meaning.

Inconsistent State Practice

This lack of a generally accepted definition helps explain the inconsistent pattern of state practice as in the following four sets of examples.

First, the first major use of aerial hijacking was made by East Europeans fleeing communism in the early years of the Cold War. They stole aircraft to land in western Europe, usually West Germany. Viewed as heroes in western countries, these people were not returned to their communist rulers as demanded. Western countries only began to regard aerial hijacking as a crime when their own aircraft were being used.

The 1963 Convention on Offences and Certain Other Acts Committed on Board Aircraft (the Tokyo Convention) deals with the safety of aircraft and maintenance of order on board. However, the problem of unlawful seizure is considered only in Articles 11 and 13; there is no obligation for state parties to prosecute or extradite the alleged offender. Their obligations concern only the release and safe return of the crew, passengers, aircraft, and cargo.

Then in the late 1960s, the hijacking of aircraft for political motives, distinct from asylum-seeking, spread, particularly against western governments. The 1970 Convention for the Suppression of Unlawful Seizure of Aircraft (the Hague Convention) goes considerably further than the Tokyo Convention and deals explicitly with aerial hijacking. This was followed by the 1971 Convention for the Suppression of Unlawful Acts against the Safety of Civil Aviation (the Montreal Convention). The 1988 Protocol on the Suppression of Unlawful Acts at Airports Serving International Civil Aviation further adds to the definition of offence established at the Montreal Convention. Taken together, these treaties represent a very different attitude towards aerial hijacking from the cavalier approach of western countries in the early Cold Wars years.

Thus, some progress has been made in devising ways of clamping down on aerial hijacking. However, the September 11 tragedy showed that such hijacking is still possible, irrespective of the considerably increased range of treaties and airport security. This is a problem for all legal systems despite laws prohibiting hijacking in many countries. Similarly, all countries have laws against murder, but murder is still committed. All legal systems need to continue addressing the problem.

Second, the current round of conflict in Northern Ireland began in the late 1960s. British politicians and Northern Ireland Protestant groups complained about the way in which elements in the United States, such as nongovernmental fund-raising, assisted the IRA (Irish Republican Army). This issue arose at the 1985 annual conference of the American Society of International Law. Professor Rubin of The Fletcher School explained the situation.[55] He recalled that the British regarded the IRA as a criminal conspiracy. According to the IRA, however, they were an army of national liberation. For the United States, the problem of determining the IRA status arose only in an extradition context. In all the cases that had arisen thus far, the United States had refused British extradition requests on the grounds that as long as the offense would have been legitimate for a soldier in armed struggle, the political offence exception applied. Thus, U.S. courts had applied the political offence exception under their own law, which meant that the United States could grant asylum for honorable soldiers when they had opted out of struggle. Rubin also noted that nothing in international law required all states to use the same labels for a situation.

However, the United States in 1996, pursuant to the Immigration and Nationality Act as amended by the Antiterrorism and Effective Death Penalty Act of 1996, began designating certain organizations as FTOs, or Foreign Terrorist Organizations. This Act makes it illegal for persons either in the United States or in any country subject to U.S. jurisdiction to provide material support to FTOs, requires U.S. financial institutions to block assets held by FTOs, and enables the U.S. Government to deny visas to representatives of FTOs. The October 2001 list identified 28 FTOs (with the breakaway faction Real IRA listed, rather than the main branch of the IRA).[56] A further list was issued on December 5, 2001, with the number of FTOs increased to 39.[57] The statement foreshadowed that this was not the last version, and presumably other groups will be added in due course.

Third, Russia has its own inconsistencies. *The Economist* magazine reported in late September 2001 how a former KGB officer reminisced about playing football with "Carlos" (Ilyich Sanchez) a "terrorist" trained in the USSR, who operated against western interests and is now in a French prison.[58] The article also noted that in the 1990s Russia flirted with terrorism as a way of destabilizing bits of its former empire. Igor Giorgadze, an ex-KGB man wanted in connection with the attempted assassination in 1995 of Georgia's president, Edward Shevardnadze, escaped on a Russian military aircraft to Moscow. Although Russia has brushed off Georgian extradition requests and pleaded ignorant about his whereabouts, journalists have had no trouble finding him.

Finally, there is the role of rogue states. The term has been used by the United States to describe countries which, among other things, facilitate overseas terrorism against it. The 1998 list from the State Department included Cuba, Iran, Iraq, Libya, Syria, North Korea, and Sudan.[59] But there is little consistent state practice. Not all other countries agree with the list, and some countries move on and off the list. For example, most countries in the UN, except for Israel, do not agree that Cuba is a rogue state; each year the UN General Assembly adopts by a very large majority a nonbinding resolution calling on the United States to end its unilateral sanctions against Cuba.

Meanwhile, Libya is no longer being considered as such a rogue state. On December 21, 1988, a bomb exploded in the cargo hold of Pan Am Flight 103, killing all 259 passengers and crew as well as 11 residents from the Scottish town of Lockerbie, where the wreckage of the Boeing 747 crashed. Two Libyan agents were suspected by western intelligence agencies of planting the bomb. Throughout the 1990s, Libya refused to hand the suspects over for a trial in a western country. The subject of international sanctions, Libya was isolated from most of the rest of the world. Eventually, in 2000 the United Nations brokered an arrangement whereby the two suspects went on trial under Scottish law in a former NATO base in The Netherlands. In February 2001, one suspect was found guilty and the other released. The sanctions now have been lifted against Libya. Western companies are back trading with the oil-rich country. There remains, of course, the mystery of how one or two agents were able to mount such an operation and the extent to which members of the Libyan Government were also involved in the operation.

State Terrorism

A second problem is that the word "terrorism" is usually applied to only nonstate actors and so ignores the role of governments. Terrorism is what is done to a government—and not by it. Again, depending on the approach to terrorism, it could be argued that the worst perpetrators in the previous century have all been recognized leaders of government: Stalin, Hitler, Mao Zedong (Mao Tse-Tung), and Pol Pot. The 1984 ILA definition of "acts of terrorism" certainly applies to the activities of these leaders: through purges and other means, these leaders brutally killed many of their own people, almost all of whom were not armed opponents of any regime. In almost all cases, the victims were killed in appalling circumstances with no adequate trial. They were simply in the wrong place at the wrong time or had the incorrect economic, social, ethnic, or religious background.

Similarly, a number of regimes in the post–Second World War era used what may be called terrorism on their own people and were supported by the United States. Chile in the 1970s provides one example. One of the few, if not only, countries in Latin America with an established tradition of democracy, Chile elected President Salvador Allende in 1970 and instituted a program of socialist reforms. Under President Richard Nixon, the U.S. government retaliated with a destabilization program, and General Augusto Pinochet led a military takeover on September 11, 1973, to stop the reforms. President Allende was killed in the military coup. The military then cracked down on its opponents. In October 1998, Pinochet in retirement was arrested in the United Kingdom on a Spanish warrant for offences committed against Spanish citizens during his time in power. However, he evaded a trial and eventually returned to Chile. The most well-known U.S. citizen implicated in the Chilean tragedy is Henry Kissinger, who was the U.S. Secretary of State at the time. Some have claimed that he is vulnerable to a similar indictment as one of the chief architects of the destabilization program.[60]

The destruction of the Greenpeace vessel "Rainbow Warrior" is a good example of both state terrorism and inconsistent state practice.[61] The vessel was destroyed in New Zealand's Auckland Harbor on July 10, 1985 by members of the French secret service (DGSE: Direction Generale de Securite Exterieure). Forty kilos of explosive were used to sink the ship, thereby also killing one crew member. The ship had been campaigning against nuclear testing in the South Pacific. All but two of the French agents escaped back to France. The two who were caught on July 12 pleaded guilty on November 4, 1985 to the lesser charge of manslaughter, rather than murder, and were each sentenced to 10 years in a New Zealand prison. The New Zealand Government was subjected to considerable pressure by France for the agents to be released immediately. Eventually, the UN Secretary-General provided a mediation of the dispute in which the agents were transferred to serve in a French prison (from which they were released prematurely), with the payment of compensation by France. In July 1991, one of the agents even received a French decoration.

The destruction of the "Rainbow Warrior" was conducted by French agents. Not even the French Government denied that. But there remains a lack of clarity as to why France did it because the vessel had also been monitoring the impact of U.S. nuclear tests three decades earlier in Micronesia and who in Paris authorized the attack. Given the amount of resources involved, the attack must have involved more than just a few agents operating on their own initiative.

Meanwhile, the allies of France, also supposed to be allies of New Zealand, never described this attack as terrorist. New Zealanders were angered by the lack of support from their erstwhile allies, not least the United Kingdom where the "Rainbow Warrior" was formerly the "Sir William Hardy," a British fisheries research vessel. New Zealand, with David Lange as prime minister, was an outspoken critic of the nuclear arms race and had alienated itself from the United States and Australia, leading to the suspension of the Australia/New Zealand/United States (ANZUS) defense alliance.[62] Therefore, New Zealand received no assistance over the "Rainbow Warrior" tragedy; the other countries did not regard France as a rogue state.

To sum up so far, terrorism is far more a political term than a legal one; its use varies according to the political expediency of each government at the time. This helps explain the lack of real progress in international legal action against terrorism.

The First Attempt to Curb International Terrorism

Terrorism has often described assassinations. These have been a staple item of political life since at least Brutus stabbed Julius Caesar in 44 B.C. In the European Middle Ages, kings, queens, and heirs to the throne were often killed. In the late nineteenth century, victims of this form of terrorism included Tsar Alexander of Russia, President Carnot of France, President McKinley of the United States, the Empress of Austria, the King of Italy, and Archduke Franz

Ferdinand, the latter assassination providing the June 1914 trigger for the First World War.

The first international treaty on terrorism arose out of the assassination of King Alexander of Yugoslavia in October 1934. After Hitler had come to power in Germany in 1933, France, then a great power, was positioning itself vis-a-vis Hitler and Mussolini in Italy. The King had been invited to France by the French Foreign Minister Louis Bathou as part of the country's plan to improve its strategic situation in the Balkans. In Marseilles, a Macedonian revolutionary incited by a fanatical group of Croatians assassinated the King, and Barthou was struck at the same time.

Elizabeth Wiskemann, a journalist at the time of the murder and later Professor of International Relations at the University of Sussex, noted:

The murder at Marseilles was one of the most appalling events of the inter-war period and it was most injurious to France which had been unable to protect its royal visitor; Barthou's death was said to have been due only to delay in supplying medical care.[63]

She also noted that the British politician Lord Avon, previously Sir Anthony Eden who had served as the Foreign Secretary for part of the 1930s and 1940s said, "These were the first shots of the Second World War."[64] The murder was also caught on news film and so was well-publicized by the media standards of the day.

In 1934, the League of Nations Council, in pursuance of a proposal made by France and concerned by the King's assassination, took steps to prepare an international convention for the prevention and punishment of acts of political terrorism. The Council took the view that states had a duty to suppress so-called terrorist activity and comply with any request for help in putting down adventurers forgathering within their jurisdiction.

A treaty was adopted at Geneva in November 1937: the League of Nations Convention for the Prevention and Punishment of Terrorism. Under this treaty, the contracting states undertook to treat acts of terrorism as criminal offences; these acts would include conspiracy, incitement and participation in such acts, and in some cases could be granted extradition However with ratification only by India, the treaty never entered into force and therefore set the pattern for a subsequent flurries of activities. The pattern follows a tragedy extensively reported in the media, a demand from the public for something to be done, an agreement on an international text (declaration or treaty) condemning terrorism, and then little if any action to follow it up. The issue then lies dormant until there is another tragedy.

The United Nations and Terrorism

While, for political reasons, it has not been possible to obtain international agreement on a definition of terrorism, this has not prevented countries from cooperating extensively in adopting measures against specific acts. The United

Nations website (http://untreaty.un.org/English/tersumen.htm) has a list of 12 treaties adopted under its aegis. The list is probably longer than is commonly thought. Besides the four treaties mentioned above dealing with aerial hijacking and airport offences, there are also:

1973 Convention on the Prevention and Punishment of Crimes Against Internationally Protected Persons, Including Diplomatic Agents

This applies to the crimes of direct involvement or complicity in the murder, kidnapping or attack, whether actual, attempted or threatened on the person, official premises, private accommodation, or means of transport of diplomatic agents and other "internationally protected persons," such as heads of government.

1979 International Convention Against the Taking of Hostages

This applies to the offence of direct involvement or complicity in the seizure or detention of, and threat to kill, injure, or continue to detain a hostage, whether actual or attempted, in order to compel a state, an international intergovernmental organization, a person or a group of persons, to do or abstain from doing any act as an explicit or implicit condition for the release of the hostage. This entered into force in 1983.

1997 International Convention for the Suppression of Terrorist Bombings

This applies to the offense of the intentional and unlawful delivery, placement, discharge or detonation of an explosive or other lethal device, whether attempted or actual, in, into or against a place of public use, a state or government facility, a public transportation system or an infrastructure facility, with the intent to cause death or serious bodily injury, or extensive destruction likely to or actually resulting in major economic loss. This entered into force in May 2001.

1999 International Convention for the Suppression of the Financing of Terrorism

This applies to the offense of direct involvement or complicity in the intentional and unlawful provision or collection of funds, whether attempted or actual, with the intention or knowledge that any part of the funds may be used to carry out any of the offences described in the treaty's annex, or an act intended to cause death or serious bodily injury to any person not actively involved in armed conflict in order to intimidate a population, or to compel a government or an international organization to do or abstain from doing any act. This has not yet entered into force.

1980 Convention on the Physical Protection of Nuclear Materials

This deals with the protection of nuclear materials being used for peaceful purposes while in transport or storage. The treaty entered into force in 1989.

1988 Convention for the Suppression of Unlawful Acts Against the Safety of Maritime Navigation

This applies to the offenses of direct involvement or complicity in the intentional and unlawful threatened, attempted or actual endangerment of the safe navigation of a ship by the commission of any of the following acts: seizure of or exercise of control over a ship by any form of intimidation; violence against a person on board a ship; destruction of a ship or the causing of damage to a ship or to its cargo; placement on a ship of a device or substance which is likely to destroy or cause damage to that ship or its cargo; destruction of, serious damaging of, or interference with maritime navigational facilities; knowing communication of false information; injury or murder of any person in connection with any of the preceding acts.

1988 Protocol for the Suppression of Unlawful Acts Against the Safety of Fixed Platforms Located on the Continental Shelf

This deals with the offenses described in the Convention for the Suppression of Unlawful Acts against the Safety of Maritime Navigation when committed in relation to a "fixed platform," defined as an artificial island, installation or structure permanently attached to the sea-bed for the purpose of exploration or exploitation of resources or for other economic purposes.

1991 Convention on the Marking of Plastic Explosive for the Purpose of Detection

This requires each state party to prohibit and prevent the manufacture in its territory of unmarked plastic explosives. For example, Semtex, which was probably used in the Lockerbie bombing, is almost impossible to detect by odor and is translucent: hence its popularity in some circles. This entered into force in 1998.

So some progress in the UN devising treaties against terrorism has occurred. There are also regional intergovernmental treaties, such as those devised under the aegis of the Council of Europe such as the 1977 European Convention on the Suppression of Terrorism. The international work, including the Sixth (Legal) Committee of the UN General Assembly, continues with more treaties still being considered.[65]

However, going back to the concerns raised at the beginning of this section, I again want to point out the irony that so many members of the UN condemn terrorism unequivocally and yet cannot reach a universal agreement on what is being condemned. Although all governments have labeled the September 11 attacks as terrorism and most have supported the campaign against Osama bin Laden and his al-Qa'ida network to some extent, I suggest that this international consensus will erode as time goes by—it always has.

AN ALTERNATIVE GRAND STRATEGY

Indeed, the first conflict of the twenty-first century has been fought with techniques much like those of the previous centuries. It remains to be seen how successful the U.S. grand strategy will be against the al-Qa'ida network. I was opposed to that strategy on the grounds that anyone smart enough to plan the September 11 attacks would have also factored in a U.S. military retaliation. Indeed, an overreaction may have been part of the calculations. Terrorism is partly designed to provoke a harsh response by a government so that the resulting oppression theoretically will lead to a public backlash in favor of the terrorist organization's political aims. Although I am skeptical of the theory, that is stated by some as a justification for terrorism. Therefore, a standard military campaign, which is what the United States has been conducting, means fighting according to the terrorist agenda, drawn up by Osama bin Laden in the current situation. In accordance with this agenda, the United States could be led into an ambush of some sort. The military response could isolate the country rather than Osama bin Laden's network.

An alternative grand strategy could have been based on trying to build up the international legal order in order to deny the other side an opportunity to win martyrdom status in the many developing countries where U.S. economic and foreign policy is not liked. Here are four steps that could have been followed. First, the United States could have said that it would not attack Afghanistan because the Afghanis had already suffered so much from the Soviet invasion as well as subsequent civil war and drought. Second, the United States could have decided to provide extensive amounts of foreign aid, to win the hearts and minds of Afghanis as well as others in the Islamic world. This would have emphasized that the United States was not anti-Islamic and that it wanted to work with all people of goodwill irrespective of religion. Third, a very big reward, perhaps $500 million U.S. dollars, could have been offered to entice groups such as the Russian mafia (or even the Taliban) to hand over Osama bin Laden dead or alive.[66] Fourth, the United States could have sought to follow the Lockerbie solution by having an ad hoc international tribunal try Osama bin Laden, if he were captured alive.[67]

Any of these plans would have required a great deal of advocacy, not least because so many Americans seemed to just want Afghanistan destroyed. However, such is the leadership role of U.S. presidents—if they want to assume it. It would have required President Bush to ask if there were another way to behave and so encourage creative thinking.

In a broader sense, the lessons of September 11 suggest that the expansion of international law will lead to a better world. This is not to recommend simply the creation of still more treaties on terrorism. Instead, it is necessary to first recognize that terrorism may take place no matter what arrangements are made (just as murder is still committed within societies, even though it is prohibited and there are the police and prison services which do not exist at the international level). At the personal level, it is important to note that the object of terror is to terrorize. Therefore, people who cancel travel plans etc. are giving into terrorists. As Winston Churchill said at the height of the German bombing blitz on London on July 14, 1941: "You do your worst—and we will do our best."[68] People need to carry on regardless and to live by hope rather than by fear.

Also the potential for terrorism can be reduced by addressing the underlying causes of violence in the first place. This would mean, among other things, a greater sense of U.S. multilateral engagement with the world, rather than a withdrawal from multilateral involvement in global affairs. For example, President Clinton in 1999 was angered by the Congress's refusal to provide sufficient funds for U.S. foreign operations: "It is another sign of a new isolationism that would have America bury its head in the sand at the height of our power and prosperity." America's fiscal year 2000 foreign operations bill totaled $12,600 million, $199 million less than the president had requested. "It is about half the amount available in real terms to President Reagan in 1985 and it is 14 percent below the level that I requested," Clinton continued. He further warned: "If we under-fund our diplomacy, we will end up over-using our military."[69] That turned out to be a good prediction.

Finally, the grand strategy that I proposed would require the reinvolvement of the United States in creating a better international legal order. The country needs the international cooperation it has thrown away. The isolationism identified by President Clinton has increased. Indeed, not only has the United States decided not to become a party to the Rome Treaty for the International Criminal Court (ICC), but also Congress was debating a proposal to further reduce contributions to the UN to "undercut" the ICC initiative only three weeks prior to the September 11 tragedy.[70] In July 2001, the conservative British magazine The Economist, asked rhetorically if "George Bush has ever met a treaty he liked?" and went on to list a number of decisions by the president that blocked U.S. acceptance of international treaties.[71] Therefore, the United States should reaffirm its commitment to wanting to work with other countries through international organizations in order to develop the international legal order. Conferences of nongovernmental organizations, such as the International Law Association have also provided many ideas for projects that could enhance this order. The problem is not so much a shortage of legal ideas as a shortage of political will.

To conclude with the Westphalian System having so many difficulties within itself, it is now necessary to look at the new global actors. These powers are eroding the strength and dominance of nation-states.

NOTES

1. Alastair Horne, *Macmillan,* London: Macmillan, 1989, p. 190.

2. Text in: *The United Nations and Human Rights 1945–95,* New York: United Nations Department of Public Information, 1995, p. 205.

3. Keith Suter, *East Timor, West Papua/Irian and Indonesia,* London: Minority Rights Group, 1997.

4. Lansell Taudevin and Jefferson Lee (Editors), *East Timor: Making Amends?* Sydney: Oxford Press, 2000.

5. Elie Kedourie, "A New International Disorder" in Hedley Bull and Adam Watson (Editors), *The Expansion of International Society,* Oxford: Clarendon, 1985, pp. 353–354.

6. Karl Maier, *This House Has Fallen: Midnight in Nigeria,* New York: Public Affairs, 2000.

7. See: Thomas Pakenham, *The Scramble for Africa: The White Man's Conquest of the Dark Continent from 1876 to 1912,* London: Random House, 1991.

8. Milan Sahovic and William Bishop, "The Authority of the State: Its Range with Respect to Persons and Places" in Max Sorensen (Editor), *Manual of Public International Law,* London: Macmillan, 1968, p. 321.

9. See: Basil Davidson, *The Black Man's Burden: Africa and the Curse of the Nation-State,* London: James Currey, 1992; Basil Davidson, *The Search for Africa: A History in the Making,* London: James Currey, 1994.

10. Centre for Human Rights, *The Rights of Indigenous Peoples,* Geneva: United Nations, 1991, p. 5.

11. This is the 1966 First Optional Protocol to the 1966 UN International Covenant on Civil and Political Rights, under which governments may agree that persons within their jurisdiction may complain to the UN Human Rights Committee about alleged violations of their civil and political rights. Less than half of the UN member-nations have agreed to this process (the U.S. not being one of them).

12. See: Julian Burger, *The Gaia Atlas of First People,* London: Robertson McCarta, 1990.

13. Department of Public Information, *Indigenous People,* New York: United Nations. 1992, p. 1.

14. See: *American Indian Civil Rights Handbook,* Washington, D.C.: U.S. Commission on Civil Rights, 1980; *Indian Rights Human Rights,* Washington, D.C.: Indian Law Resource Center, 1988; A.M. Josephy, *Now That the Buffalo's Gone,* University of Oklahoma Press, 1986.

15. See: Robert Milliken, *No Conceivable Injury: The Story of Britain and Australia's Atomic Cover-Up,* Melbourne: Penguin, 1986.

16. See: Keith Suter, "British Atomic Tests in Australia" *Medicine and War* (London), Vol 10 No 3, pp. 195–206.

17. This also includes the country's property. For example in 1975, the Cambodian government fell to Pol Pot's forces, and its embassy in the Australian capital city Canberra became vacant. The Australian government did not recognize the new Cambodian government, but it did have the duty to look after the small piece of "Cambodia" in Canberra. The Australian government therefore arranged for commercial tenants to use the property, with the rent being used for the property's maintenance. Following the UN intervention and the election of a democratic government, the property was handed

over to the ambassador-designate in 1994, along with the residue of the rent that had been collected since 1975. See: *Insight* (Canberra), September 26, 1994, p. 2.

18. For a recent example of the old-fashioned approach to the study of diplomacy which, for instance, omits virtually any reference to economics, see: Henry Kissinger, *Diplomacy*, London: Simon & Schuster, 1994.

19. For example in 1792, Thomas Jefferson, while Secretary of State in George Washington's Cabinet, noted that nothing had been heard from the U.S. ambassador in Madrid for over two years; if another year went by with no word from him, Jefferson said that he would write him to see if everything was all right.

20. David Thomson, *Europe Since Napoleon*, London: Pelican, 1970, p. 501.

21. For a critique of modern diplomacy, see: Harold Nicolson, *Diplomacy*, Oxford: Oxford University Press, 1963, pp. 244–262.

22. See: Keith Suter, *The New Law Sea of the Sea*, Sydney: World Wide Fund for Nature, 1995.

23. Igor Janev, "Legal Aspects of the Use of a Provisional Name for Macedonia in the United Nations System," *American Journal of International Law*, January 1999, pp. 155–160.

24. Declaration of the UN Conference on the Human Environmentquoted in: Peter Stone *Did We Save the Earth at Stockholm? The People and Politics in the Conference on the Human Environment*, London: Earth Island, 1973, p. 148.

25. For example, one writer evidently based his criticism of the Stockholm Conference on mass media reports and thought the conference consisted almost exclusively of these rituals; he missed the more fundamental achievements. See: Angus Martin *The Last Generation: The End of Survival*, London: Fontana, 1975, pp. 100–101.

26. I suggest that three explanations for the mass media's interest in such rituals were: (i) the events were more straightforward for the ordinary reader than most of the substantive items on the agenda; (ii) the events were definite conference decisions, rather than agreements to defer items until the next conference session; and (iii) they normally occurred at the beginning of each session, when journalists were present for the opening speeches.

27. One achievement was the admission of the Palestine Liberation Organization with "observer status" into the UN on November 22 1974; see: "Status of the Palestine Liberation Organization at the United Nations," *American Journal of International Law*, January 1999, pp. 179–181.

28. The Sea Change Web site is: www.seachange.org

29. Hugh Sidey, "Motion Sickness" *Time*, January 20, 1992, p. 10.

30. John Kenneth Galbraith, *The Culture of Contentment*, Boston: Houghton Mifflin, 1992, pp. 112–113.

31. Valerie Pakenham, *The Noonday Sun: Edwardians in the Tropics*, London: Methuen, 1985, pp. 16 and 18.

32. Tom Stonier, *The Wealth of Information*, London: Thames Methuen, 1983, pp. 87–88.

33. Martin van Creveld, "High Technology and the Transformation of War: Part I," *Journal of the Royal United Services Institute*, October 1992, pp. 76–77.

34. Martin van Creveld, "High Technology and the Transformation of War: Part II," *Journal of the Royal United Services Institute*, December 1992, p. 61.

35. Alec Cairncross, *Planning in Wartime*, London: Macmillan, 1991.

36. See: Mary Kaldor, *The Baroque Arsenal*, London: Andre Deutsch, 1982.

37. In South Vietnam in 1974 during the war, I interviewed some of the villagers near the site of the My Lai massacre. They expressed little support for the Viet Cong/ National Liberation Front. But they pointed out to me that at least these forces were better disciplined and far less prone to gratuitous violence than the U.S. forces; the VC/ NLF had to be careful about their use of violence because they had far less ammunition.

38. For a study of a rare example of conventional troops defeating guerrillas, see: Noel Barber, *The War of the Running Dogs: Malaya 1948–60*, London: Collins, 1973.

39. "Thatcher Unfolds Strategy to Beat Hijack Terror" *The Times* (London), July 16, 1985, p. 1.

40. The suggestion was not unprecedented. The British media are careful in how they report suicides, for fear of others following suit. Movie stars and entertainers do have their deaths reported; they are as famous in death as in life. But the suicide of ordinary individuals may be easier for others to identify with, so reports on them are limited.

41. Phillip Davidson, *Vietnam at War: The History 1946–75*, London: Pan, 1989.

42. Cecil Currey, *Edward Lonsdale: The Unquiet American*, New York: Houghton Mifflin, 1989.

43. "Peacemaking War" *Time* July 26, 1993, p. 30.

44. "The Killing Fields of Rwanda" *Time*, May 16, 1994, p. 30.

45. John Pike, "Buying Votes with B-2," *The Bulletin of Atomic Scientists*, May 1996, p. 4.

46. Dana Mead, *High Standards, Hard Choices: A CEO's Journey of Courage, Risk and Change*, New York: John Wiley, 2000, pp. 139–182.

47. For example: Allen Buchanan, *Secession*, Boulder, CO.: Westview, 1991; H. Gros-Espiell *The Rights to Self-Determination: Implementation of United Nations Resolutions*, New York: United Nations, 1980; Ted Robert Gurr, *Minorities at Risk: A Global View of Ethnopolitical Conflicts*, Washington: United States Institute of Peace, 1993; Robert McKim and Jeff McMahan (Editors), *The Morality of Nationalism*, Oxford: Oxford University Press, 1997; Thomas Musgrave, *Self-Determination and National Minorities*, Oxford: Clarendon Press, 1997; Guntram Werther, *Self-Determination in Western Democracies: Aboriginal Politics in a Comparative Perspective*, Westport, CT: Greenwood, 1992; David Wippman (Editor), *International Law and Ethnic Conflict*, Ithaca: Cornell University Press, 1998.

48. The U.S. Government's Web site on September 11 and subsequent events is: http://usinfo.state.gov.topical/rights/law/warlaw.htm. The American Society of International Law (ASIL) has a free e-mail information service ("Insights"), with some articles dealing with the events surrounding September 11: http://www.asil.org/insights

49. Keith Suter, *An International Law of Guerrilla Warfare: A Study of the Politics of Law-Making*, University of Sydney, 1976, Volumes I and II (PhD dissertation); and Keith Suter, *An International Law of Guerrilla Warfare: The Global Politics of Law-making*, London: Pinter, 1984.

50. See: Keith Suter, "What Is Terrorism?," *British Army Review*, No. 55, December 1977, pp. 66–72.

51. *Report of the 61st Conference, Paris, 1984*, London: International Law Association, p. 320.

52. For a study of legal developments, particularly in the 1980s and 1990s, see: Alex Obote-Odora, "Defining International Terrorism" at http://www.murdoch.edu.au/elaw/issues/v6n1/obote-odora61nf.html

53. Nelson Mandela, *Long Walk to Freedom: The Autobiography of Nelson Mandela,* Boston: Little, Brown & Co., 1994, p. 246.

54. Ibid., p 458.

55. "Should the Laws of War Apply to Terrorists?" *Proceedings of the American Society of International Law,* Washington, D.C.: American Society of International Law, 1985, p. 125.

56. "Fact Sheet: State Department Identifies 28 Foreign Terrorist Groups," Washington, D.C.: State Department, October 5, 2001.

57. "U.S. Places 39 Groups on Terrorist Exclusion List," Washington D.C.: Statement Department Media Statement, December 6, 2001.

58. "Poacher Turned Gamekeeper," *The Economist,* September 22, 2001, p. 50.

59. Raymond Tanter, *Rogue Regimes: Terrorism and Proliferation,* London: Macmillan, 1998.

60. The "poor Henry" argument, as it is called, is one explanation for the U.S. refusal to support the Rome Treaty for an International Criminal Court (ICC). In fact, an eventual ICC could not deal retrospectively with the Chilean tragedy from the 1970s. But the argument has been widely (if wrongly) used in the US. See: Nicholas Guyatt *Another American Century? The United States and the World After 2000,* London: Zed, 2000, pp. 101–102. Also see: Christopher Hitchens, *The Trial of Henry Kissinger,* London: Macmillan, 2001.

61. See: Keith Suter, "French Nuclear Testing in the South Pacific," *The Contemporary Review* (London), September 1992, pp. 126–129.

62. See: Keith Suter, *Is There Life After ANZUS? New Directions for the Peace Movement,* Sydney: Pluto, 1987.

63. Elizabeth Wiskemann, *Europe of the Dictators 1919–1945,* London: Fontana, 1971, p. 106.

64. Ibid., p. 106.

65. "Measures to Eliminate International Terrorism: Report of the Working Group," UN General Assembly document A/C.6/56/L.9, October 29, 2001.

66. Keith Suter, "Our Taskforce," *The Age* (Melbourne), October 19, 2001.

67. Keith Suter, "Assault on Terror," *The Age,* September 25, 2001.

68. "A Tonic for Today," *Finest Hour* (magazine of the International Churchill Society), Autumn 2001, p. 6.

69. "Clinton on Veto of Foreign Operations Bill," Washington, D.C.: State Department Media Statement, October 18, 1999.

70. "U.S. Foes of World Court to Block Fees for UN," *The International Herald Tribune* (Paris), August 17, 2001.

71. "Stop the world, I want to get off," *The Economist,* July 28, 2001, p. 39.

4

The New Global Actors

INTRODUCTION

Nation-states are having to share their power with three groups of global actors: transnational corporations; international, or more accurately intergovernmental, organizations such as the United Nations; and nongovernmental organizations (NGOs). This chapter looks at the new global actors.

The process of globalization, which is causing so many problems for national governments, is also having an impact on the study of international relations. The late Susan Strange, of the University of London, commented in 1992 that the standard texts in international relations subscribed to the dominant realist school of thought; this thinking held that the central issue in international society was war among nation-states, and the prime task was the maintenance of order in the relations among those states.[1] This traditional view of international relations also held that the object of study was the behavior of states towards other states and whether the outcome of the various behaviors meant that the states were better or worse off, less or more powerful, or less or more secure. Although transnational corporations may be mentioned in passing, they were seen as adjuncts to or instruments of state policy. However, Strange argued that transnational corporations should now be put at center stage because their corporate strategies in choosing host countries as partners were already having a great and increasing influence on the development of the global political economy.

Globalization has crept up on much of the academic study of international relations. Like Professor Strange, I think that international lawyers, international political economists, and business writers have a better awareness of the new global order than of the traditional state-centric, international relations writers. Much the same could be said, in general terms, about the need for attention to intergovernmental organizations and NGOs. Not of course as influential as transnational corporations, they are often just as marginalized in the study of international relations.[2]

The good news, from this book's perspective, is that in the long view of history, cooperation is spreading. The Westphalian System is giving way to greater cooperation across the planet for the overall benefit of humankind.The bad news is that the pace of change is so slow, particularly where governments are directly concerned. Although the Westphalian System is ending, no specific replacement is being devised. Instead, there are instances of what I have previously described as disorder. Governments are not working with the new global actors to create a new order. Therefore, each of this chapter's sections ends with a comment on how the new actors are contributing to the global disorder.

Chapter 4 finishes with a case study of global crime. Crime can be global, but there is little that is global in police work. Indeed, nation-states with federal jurisdictions often have a problem with even obtaining a national focus on fighting crime. Although criminals can roam across boundaries within a nation-state, local police forces cannot and may even require some form of extradition to have an alleged criminal transferred from one jurisdiction to another. Therefore, a case study of global crime provides an illustration of the weakness of the Westphalian System in its inability to deal with new actors.

TRANSNATIONAL CORPORATIONS: GLOBAL BUSINESS

For the purposes of transnational corporations, the boundaries that separate one nation-state from another are no more real than the equator. They are merely convenient demarcations of ethnic, linguistic, and cultural entities. They do not define business requirements or consumer trends. The world outside the home country is an extension of the single global market.

A transnational corporation is a company that engages in foreign direct investment and owns, or controls, activities in more than one nation-state. These corporations are now the main global economic force: national economies have been replaced by a global one. Sprawling across national political boundaries, transnational corporations can change character to maximize profits. For example, if a government tries to protect its own industries by keeping out imports, such a corporation will try to buy local companies so that it can produce goods within that country.

Frederick Clairmonte and John Cavanagh, writers based in the United States, argued in the early 1980s that transnational corporations had by then evolved through three stages.[3] In the first stage, from 1895 to 1945, there was the emergence and consolidation of oligopolies, large corporations in small numbers that dominate a market, in key sectors in North America, Western Europe, and Japan. In the second stage, from 1946 to the mid-1960s, transnational corporations rose to their position of prominence. For example, they were responsible for roughly 80 percent, a rough figure according to Clairemonte and Cavanagh, of the trade conducted outside the Communist bloc. In some commodities, there was a high degree of what has been called vertical integration, a system of complete ownership in which, for example, a corporation might own its own tea plantations that sold tea to its own blenders who then sold the tea to retailers. This represented 100 percent ownership. In other commodities, however, corporations had to buy from independent producers, so that the percentage was lower. In the third stage, from the mid-1960s to the present, the corporations have consolidated their dominance. For example, there have been mergers across national boundaries. There has also been a rise in the significance of corporations not from the United States, but from Japan and Western Europe.

I think that there is now a fourth stage. The process of consolidation is continuing with the ending of the Cold War and the opening up of the former Soviet bloc to transnational corporations. China is also more willing to have corporations invest in it. For example, there is a new oil rush by the corporations into the countries that were largely off-limits during the Cold War. These countries include Kazakhstan, the Russian Arctic Circle, China's Tarim Basin, and the waters off Vietnam; they strive to develop their resources and earn hard currency. Former communist countries are also opening up to the capital, technology, and management skills which international oil firms offer.

Virtually the entire globe is now within reach of the corporations. Libya is now ending its international isolation because it is cooperating with the trial of the alleged criminals involved in the December 1988 Lockerbie Pan Am aircraft bombing. North Korea is on the verge of joining the global economy. Although the United States maintains trade sanctions against Cuba, almost all other countries, including U.S. allies, now ignore them. Only countries with appalling human rights records, such as Burma/Myanmar and Iran, are still subject to some trade restrictions. Overall, however, there are now far more opportunities for trade than there were at any time in the twentieth century.

The corporations are also helping to solve the problem identified in chapter 1 by Jean-Jacques Servan-Schreiber: how to transfer Western technology to developing countries.[4] The corporations are doing it. Dana Mead, former CEO of Tenneco, in his case study of how the corporation was returned to profitability, has two chapters on Tenneco's investment in Romania following the collapse of communism.[5] This was the largest investment of its kind by a U.S. corporation in Romania, and one of the largest anywhere in Eastern Europe. Admitting that the change has been a big challenge, Mead points out that younger Romanians are more able than older ones to acquire an entrepreneurial culture Creating such a culture cannot be done quickly because of the deep-seated changes which are required. Nor can it be done via a set of government foreign aid grants. The U.S. Marshall Plan of the late 1940s for the rebuilding of Western Europe worked well because Western Europe already had such a culture; a similar influx of money will not have the same good result in Eastern Europe or the developing countries in Africa. Instead, a new entrepreneurial culture has to be instilled, and this is best learnt on the job, under the instruction of the corporations.

Another development fostering globalization is that the corporations are staffed by a form of global civil service, rather than national personnel. Corporations have been far more successful than the United Nations in encouraging their staff to see themselves as global workers rather than ones with national loyalties. Business consultant Kenichi Ohmae (a great admirer of transnational corporations) has argued that the corporations have been able to create a commitment to a single, unified global mission which transcends nationalistic feelings by individual staff.[6] For example, a person does not think that he or she is working for a Japanese automaker trying to build and sell its products in the United States. Instead, such a person works for either Honda, Nissan, or Toyota. The customers are the people who love the products everywhere in the world. The mission is to provide them with exceptional value. Country of origin does not matter; location of headquarters does not matter. Not only the products for which the staff person is responsible, but also the company served have all become denationalized.

This is linked to the recognition that a national market is rarely large enough for a corporation. Michael Osbaldeston and Kevin Barham have said that because companies recognize that they cannot thrive on domestic markets alone, national loyalties are diminishing as companies coordinate business assets in multiple countries.[7] For example, the Swiss firm Nestle has only 4 percent of its employees based in Switzerland and generates only 2 percent of its sales there. The Swiss/Swedish company ASEA/Brown Boveri (ABB) has no more than 15 percent of its employees in any one country. Unilever employs 350,000 spread across 78 countries.

A report from the UN Conference on Trade and Development (UNCTAD) showed how corporations are increasingly organizing themselves into multitier networks including parent firms, foreign affiliates, firms linked through sub-contracting, licensing as well as similar contractual arrangements, and firms tied together through alliances.[8] Including all the major corporate functions such as research and development, procurement, manufacturing, marketing, finance, accounting, and human resource development, these networks exist in both developed and developing countries. Thus, these developments are fostering worldwide economic integration.

The UNCTAD Report also says that the telecommunications revolution means that workers can be employed in cheap labor areas to do data processing for an entire corporation. For example, Swissair (Switzerland) has created an affiliate in Bombay, India to handle revenue accounting functions for the corporation as a whole. A New York insurance corporation has located all the data processing in Ireland. This also takes advantage of the time zone differences because the New York office can offer an overnight service: While the paperwork is processed in Ireland, a check is ready to be collected the following day in New York time. A U.S. airline company has located its booking system in

Jamaica. British Telecom has relocated some of its administration, finance, personnel, and customer service operations to Australia; while the northern hemisphere sleep, Australian staff work on software development, fixing problems that occurred during the day in the European and United Kingdom network.

The Cathay Pacific airline has been relocated from Hong Kong to Sydney. The return to China of Hong Kong in 1997 meant that Cathay Pacific wanted a secure home base. Still in Hong Kong amid the fears about Chinese policy, the Hong Kong Jockey Club (HKJC) is governed by a committee that sits around a large conference table split between Hong Kong and the Queensland's Gold Coast in Australia. The committee works via video-conferencing. The HKJC is the horse-racing world's most ambitious user of information technology. The Gold Coast offers skilled computer personnel, a secure future, and pleasant working conditions.[9]

To conclude, transnational corporations are themselves becoming global entities.[10] Raymond Vernon, one of the pioneers of research into these corporations, noted in the early 1990s that the transnational corporation was widely regarded as a peculiarly U.S. form of business organization four decades earlier.[11] But by the early 1990s, every industrialized country provided a base for a considerable number of TNCs which collectively were becoming the dominant form of organization responsible for the international exchange of goods and services.

Global Impact

The impact of transnational corporations on the Westphalian System may be seen in three ways.

First, global business has changed the pattern of economic relationships. James Carrier of the University of Virginia described economic life before the industrial revolution in the eighteenth century, when most English people were peasant farmers living in villages.[12] Their village institutions were dominated by the values of localism and self-sufficiency. People could and did travel beyond the village in order to trade; they were not forestalled by poverty or lack of transport. However, compared to the later eighteenth century, there was relatively little trade, most of it among acquainted people who were defined and linked by a common local social structure. The local market, bringing together local producers and consumers, typifies this trade. Furthermore, most market towns were oriented towards local rather than specialist trade. That pattern of life has now gone. For an American to drive to the supermarket to buy food for the weekend is in itself an experience in global trade, though the consumer would probably be unaware of it. Very little of the trip would be defined by anything local: the consumer's wants, clothes, car, gasoline, as well as the supermarket design products all have global dimensions.

Second, the corporations not only do not need a host government to open up or guarantee foreign markets, but also may do better on their own. National identification can be a burden. If a product is identified with a particular country, as Coca-Cola is with the United States, a government may try to keep it out simply in order to express displeasure with U.S. foreign policy. It is notable that the few countries which do not permit Coke to be sold, including Iran and North Korea for the time being, are those that are antagonistic. While corporations can enter national economies under the guise of providing goods and services to the consumers, they generally can elude the complaints about colonialism that would haunt a foreign government enterprise.

Finally, national governments no longer have full national control over their economies. An example of this problem is the inability of governments to generate full employment. There has been a transfer of some jobs from developed to developing countries, where labor costs are low or where there is a shortage of specialist workers. For example, more than 30 companies, including Motorola, IBM, Texas Instruments, Hewlett Packard, and Citicorp, have set up software programming offices in Bangalore, India.

Many of the jobs lost in developed countries will never return. Jobs in the manufacturing industry are going the way of agricultural jobs; few people work on the land but those that do are now more productive than ever before. Much the same can be said for people working in factories in developed countries. While only some of the jobs will remain, workers will be more productive than ever before, thanks to assistance from machines.

Transnational corporations are encouraging the intertwining of national economies. Moving across national boundaries and forging links among countries, the intertwining corporations and woven together economies limit the scope of government action. For example, U.S. corporations want to increase their trade in China. Therefore, the Clinton Administration, which had promised to take a firm stand in favor of human rights protection in China, was under pressure not to alienate the Chinese leadership by American comments, such as over the Chinese occupation of Tibet. Appropriate action by the national government was avoided for fear of damaging trade links.

Paradoxically, as a developing country becomes more economically developed, its people (particularly in the middle class) want a greater say in how the country is governed. However, the government generally has less influence in economic matters because the country is increasingly locked into the global economy.

GLOBAL PRODUCTS

Although there are periodic "Buy American," "Buy British," or "Buy Australian" campaigns urging consumers to buy local products and help employment in their own nation-states, transnational corporations have undermined the potential success of such campaigns.

First, many consumers themselves are obviously uninfluenced by such campaigns. Denationalized, consumers are global customers. Wanting the best and cheapest products, they are unconcerned about the origins of the goods. The exception to this trend are so-called conspicuous consumers, people who ostentatiously buy expensive products expressly to show that they have a great deal of money. Not interested in mixing with the common herd, these consumers are not attracted to the cheapest items—only the most expensive and least common.

Second, it is increasingly difficult to tell the nationality of a product. What is the nationality of a Reebok sneaker that has an African name, is made by an American company in South Korea, and displays the British Union Jack as a label? This is "the era not only of multinational enterprises, but of multinational goods."[13] This was the conclusion of two North American lawyers trying to make sense of a long-running trade dispute between the United States and Canada. Honda led the way among Japanese automobile manufacturers in setting up "transplants" in the United States; by the 1990s, Honda's Accord had become a best-selling car in the nation. When Honda also shipped parts to be assembled in Canada, the U.S. and Canadian customs services had to determine, for the purposes of duties, the nationality of a Japanese car made in Canada with an American engine.

To conclude on a light-hearted note, *Business Week* magazine in 1999 carried a story about French fries.[14] The distinctive fried potato is a Belgian invention sold in a "friterie." (Belgium has been growing potatoes since 1583 soon after the Spanish brought the potato back from the indigenous people in Peru.) But World War I American soldiers mistook the French title for a French invention and so called them French fries when they copied the process back home. The magazine reported that the company B. Frites plans to franchise 300 to 500 U.S. stores within five years to introduce Belgian fast-food into the American fast-food market.

GLOBAL CONSUMERS

Consumerism is the leading edge of the globalized economy. The Washington-based Worldwatch Institute has reported that, particularly in the United States, shopping seems to have become a primary cultural activity.[15] Spending six hours a week doing various types of shopping, Americans on average go to shopping centers once a week, more often than they go to church or synagogue. Some 93 percent of American teenage girls surveyed in 1987 deemed shopping their favorite pastime. Similarly, British management consultant Francis Kinsman found that British teenagers placed greater value on cash than on either love or friendship.[16] Their short-term goals are mostly practical and materialistic. While money is the doorway to modern life, work is a means of providing status rather than fulfillment. They also are determined to become adults as quickly as possible. The fear of unemployment has shaped their lives with a sense of conformity very different from their elders, who recall their own teenage years in the 1960s as exploratory and rebellious.

Consumerism is a global process. For example, many Indians are now active participants in the global economy. Mahatma Gandhi had hoped that his country would be economically self-sufficient. Thus, he stopped wearing foreign shirts and wore a "khaddar," made with home-spun cotton as a political trademark. This set an example for others, and it became the symbol of India's campaign for freedom. Beginning in the early 1990s, however, foreign shirts have increased in popularity and are being made in India under license from transnational corporations. In addition, satellite television reaches about 600[17] million Indian people, out of a total of about 1 billion; it appeals particularly to the emerging middle-class, which is growing at about 20 million per year. Unlike China, India has imposed few restrictions on what advertising is broadcast, so the demand for consumer goods is fueled. The problem is, of course, that expectations are rising faster than the capacity of any Indian government to satisfy them. That the Indian standard of living could ever reach U.S. levels is hard to believe. But politicians are obliged to keep assuring voters that living standards are going to get better. If they do not give that promise, other candidates will certainly do so and get elected. For the emerging middle class, the standard of living may rise; but many people will not enter that class. Additionally, there will be environmental limits to India's growth, as with the economic growth of all countries. Thus, there will be great strains imposed on the Indian nation-state.

Meanwhile, the impact of this form of globalization has even been felt among the apparently isolated tribes of Papua New Guinea. Michael O'Hanlon of the British Museum has found that the Wahgi people in the Highlands have added motifs to their traditional fighting shields drawn from advertising and rugby league football.[18]

To conclude, a global middle-class has been created. This class often has more in common with members of the middle-class in other countries than it has with its own working class/peasants. For example, a corporation based in the United States will be more concerned with selling to the emerging middle-class in India and other parts of Asia than to Americans who cannot afford to buy its products. Thus, Coke is the global soft drink, Macs the global fast-food, and CNN the global television. These are the commodities of a new, global middle-class. Globalization goes better with Coke.

TRADE, WAR, ORDER AND DISORDER

Order

Although probably as many conflicts exist today as at the height of the Cold War the wars are increasingly internal rather than international, as noted in the previous chapter. Economic factors play an important role in both international and internal conflicts. This section ends with how the corporations add to both global order and disorder.

The decline of international conflict has been credited partly to the growth of free trade and democracy. Governments are now committed to free trade and free politics. Capitalism creates a thriving middle-class. War is bad for their interests. Middle-class people are more globally oriented: Spinning webs of affiliation around the world, they create nongovernmental organizations such as Amnesty International and Greenpeace, as well as transnational corporations. These people prefer a world where they can travel freely, making money and satisfying their curiosity. Middle-classes are less tolerant of prolonged wars. Although Mrs. Thatcher could unite the British in 1982 for the short, sharp Falklands campaign of six weeks, President Johnson could not unite the United States for the six years of his Vietnam campaign.

Besides, little is now to be gained by one nation-state invading another. Invasions used to be about the conquest of new territory and resources or the imposition of a religion among new converts. In the new era of information technology, much of a country's wealth is in the heads of its people or in cyberspace. What would a country gain, for example, from invading Japan? It has few natural resources. By the same token, Iraq's August 1990 invasion of Kuwait was a bad investment because so much of Kuwait's financial reserves were held offshore.

Of course, old rivalries will remain, and there are traditional border disputes. When a country has problems at home, focusing attention on an external threat, as Greece has done with Turkey and India with Pakistan, is always tempting. However, there are few international wars underway at present. Governments are finding that they have more to gain from peace than from war. Even the Indians and Pakistanis, with all their posturing with nuclear weapons, seem reluctant to have another war.

Disorder

However, the corporations are adding to global disorder because of their inadvertent contribution to the growth of internal conflict. First, there is a growing gap between rich and poor, especially in the developing countries. For example, there is concern about so-called Islamic fundamentalism: Islamic groups espousing violence recruit young, unemployed, alienated men, who fear that they have lost out in the race for wealth.

Third World governments have defense forces not so much to defend their countries from external attack as to defend themselves from their own citizens. Owing to a lack of democracy, dissent is prohibited so that people often feel that they have no choice but to use violence. The Third World has eight times more soldiers than doctors.

Thanks to the mass media, for the first time in history, people now know they are poor. In all previous eras, people were poor but did not know it; they lived in small villages, with the rich people in castles or country houses. Life was settled, and few poor people could journey out of the village and gain any basis of comparison for life style. Now people in Third World villages can see on television (because of *Dallas* and *Sylvania Waters*) how well Texans and Australians live. While Texans and Australians may not take these programs seriously, other people tend to believe what they see on television.

Second, there is the volatility arising out of the way in which about $1.8 trillion in U.S. dollars is traded each day in foreign exchange. There is a growing concern about financial instability because about 90 percent of it is speculative.

There has been the partial collapse of the 1944 Bretton Woods System and growing foreign currency speculation. In 1944, at Bretton Woods in New Hampshire, Allied governmental financial delegates met to create the post-war international financial system. This system entailed a bold vision to ensure the world avoided another Great Depression. The Bretton Woods System fixed currencies to the U.S. dollar, which itself was pegged as $35 dollars per ounce of gold. Working very well for the first two or so decades, the system provided for the greatest period of economic expansion in world history.

But the United States debased its currency in the 1960s, printing extra money to fight the Vietnam war among other things; so the system of fixed exchange rates started to collapse in the early 1970s. Thus, in financial terms, the world has moved from the strict order of the Bretton Woods System to the disorder of floating exchange rates, excessive currency speculation, and the flight of "hot money" (which Asian governments held responsible for the 1997 Asian financial crisis). With exception of the European Union's Euro, a fixed national currency over the long-term has hardly been attempted.

The development of electronic communications has meant that money can be transferred at the speed of light. Young screen jockeys working on foreign currency speculation transfer millions of U.S. dollars and other currencies around the globe in seconds. London is the world's most important city for this speculation; in 1998, foreign exchange trading was 118 times greater than the total British gross domestic product (GDP).

Transnational corporations have become the major players in the global economy, with greater combined assets than those of the national reserve banks of each country. More money is traded each day than is held in all the treasuries of the national reserves banks.

All these developments have been reflected in greater currency instability. For example, on "Black Wednesday" September 16, 1992, the Bank of England tried to defend the pound from speculators but the United Kingdom was driven out of the European Exchange Rate Mechanism by the speculators. Other crises have occurred over the 1994 Mexican peso and the Asian newly industrialized countries in 1997. Therefore, the world is moving into a period of even greater financial volatility and instability.

Finally, environmentalists are concerned about what the global consumer culture will do the global environment. According to that perspective, the twentieth century was the century of economics, with the emphasis on economic growth. In contrast, the twenty-first century will be of the environment, not because humans will suddenly become environmentalists but because related problems will force themselves upon humankind to such an extent that people will have no choice but to give more attention to the environment.[19]

INTERGOVERNMENTAL ORGANIZATIONS: THEIR EVOLUTION[20]

National governments have found it necessary to create international, or more accurately intergovernmental, organizations to facilitate cooperation across national frontiers. While most popular attention has been focused on political and military cooperation such as UN peacekeeping operations, the real breakthroughs have been in economic and social cooperation.

The process has been underway for almost two centuries. Rivers and diseases, for example, do not conform neatly to political boundaries. The British international lawyer Sir James Fawcett pointed out that in 1815, the first permanent administrative body was set up by governments—the Commission for the Navigation of the Rhine.[21] The European Commission for the Danube was established in 1856. This cooperation increased in the second half of the nineteenth century as technological progress, trade, and commerce developed further. The International Telegraphic Union, now a UN specialized agency, was established in 1865 with a permanent bureau and some participation by private telegraph companies. In 1874, there followed the Universal Postal Union, also now a UN specialized agency with a permanent bureau, participation by postal administrations regardless of their political status, and a system of financial contributions.

These pioneering intergovernmental organizations had three important advantages over the holding of ad hoc diplomatic conferences, such as the 1815 Congress of Vienna. First, these public international bodies transcended the diplomatic conference in their permanence because they had an enduring common purpose, unlike the transitory objectives of diplomatic conferences. Second, these organizations had a constant membership of nation-states, unlike the varying participation according to subject matter in the diplomatic conference. Third, they had a permanent structure, consisting of a bureau and perhaps a directing council.

THE LEAGUE OF NATIONS[22]

World War I came as a great shock to everyone. No one expected such a large or lengthy conflict. There was widespread agreement that this should be, in the phrase of British writer H.G. Wells: "The War that will end War."[23]

But how was this to be brought about? Much of the debate derived from disagreement over who or what caused the war. U.S. President Woodrow Wilson, several nongovernmental groups, and individuals, such as HG Wells, said the fault was due to the system of competing nation-states. The Westphalian

System encouraged rivalry. Since the system itself was at fault, there should be a new international system. On the other hand, most politicians believed that the system was basically sound, though destabilized by the unification of Germany in 1870. This unification had disrupted the 1815 Concept of Europe's balance of power; so Germany ought both to be punished for its past deeds in the war and be prevented from trying to repeat them.

This basic disagreement was never resolved. The punitive peace settlement inflicted upon Germany helped Adolf Hitler into power in 1933 on the wave of German resentment. Ironically, the so-called appeasement policy of the United Kingdom and France was initiated by people who believed that Germany had been too harshly treated and soothed by some concessions.

Meanwhile, the League began operations in 1920.[24] It was designed principally as the place where two or more governments would bring their international disputes. The League had no automatic right to intervene; governments had to agree to bring their disputes to it. Most governments did not.

President Wilson could not get Congressional approval for U.S. membership in it. Indeed, the United States not only rejected League membership, but also had a mood of isolationism, which entailed a restrictive immigration policy and the imposition of high tariff barriers.

Meanwhile, the United Kingdom and France, the League's two most important members, were wary of it. They were not accustomed to working through international organizations. For example, Sir Austen Chamberlain, whose half-brother Neville went on to champion appeasement of Germany, won the Nobel Peace Prize for his work on Franco-German reconciliation culminating in the 1925 Locarno Treaty. But even he had a limited vision of what the League could achieve. Lord Robert Cecil, a great supporter of the League, recalled Chamberlain's views of the League: "He thought of it as just one cog in the diplomatic machine, to be used or not at the discretion of the Cabinet. I regarded it as the essential international organ for the maintenance of peace."[25] Thus, the United Kingdom's most distinguished Foreign Secretary of the 1920s and 1930s regarded the League as being useful merely as a strong moral force.

The League, then, had a troubled career. It was able to make some progress in world health, care of refugees, the suppression of slavery and drug trade, the protection of minority populations, and improvements in employment conditions in factories as well as elsewhere. The League also settled, particularly in the 1920s, some international disputes. For example, Yugoslavian forces suddenly invaded Albania in late 1922 and looted the villages on their way to the capital, Tirana. The League Council called on Yugoslavia to withdraw, and the Yugoslavian currency lost value on the international money market. The forces withdrew after two days, and Yugoslavia apologized to the League Council for the invasion.[26]

Once militarism built up in Japan, Italy, and Germany, however, the League was powerless to stop the dictators because the member-nations were reluctant, if not downright opposed, to introduce coercive measures. Consequently, the League ceased to have much political relevance by the early 1930s.

THE UNITED NATIONS[27]

The League's most significant impact was the way in which it convinced governments to persevere with creating international organizations; while the UN retained the League's basic structure, it has, of course, flourished in ways that the League was unable to, especially in economic and social co-operation.

The UN contains six principal organs: General Assembly, Security Council, International Court of Justice (ICJ), Trusteeship Council, the Secretariat, and the Economic and Social Council (ECOSOC).

The General Assembly is the world's main political forum. It meets for about the last four months of each year, with all UN member-nations (now 191) present. It adopts resolutions which indicate how the world's governments think on particular issues. General Assembly resolutions are not binding, except in relation to domestic UN affairs.

The UN is the global debating chamber—but not the global parliament because it does not pass laws. Governments are not obliged to follow any resolution. Indeed, governments may even vote for a resolution and then ignore it. In such a way, most developed countries have refused to increase their level of foreign aid to developing countries to the level endorsed in General Assembly resolutions.

The Security Council is designed to meet day or night to handle threats to international peace and security. Its core consists of the Permanent Five (P5), which were the Allied leaders in World War II: the United States, Russia, United Kingdom, France, and China. The other 10 countries serve two-year terms and are elected via the UN caucus system to maintain a representative balance of the world. All UN member-nations agree to be bound by Security Council resolutions, the only part of the UN system with such power; all member-nations "shall hold immediately available" (UN Charter, Article 45) defense forces to be deployed as required by the Security Council. A Military Staff Committee was created, drawn from the representatives of the Chiefs of Staff of the five permanent members, to coordinate the military operations.

Because of the Cold War, this elaborate system was never used. Instead, an ad hoc system of peacekeeping evolved for intervention in disputes in which the two super powers agreed not to intervene if that lack of action was mutual. Instead of the five permanent members controlling the UN's military work, peacekeeping almost always avoided any involvement of the P5. The bulk of the peacekeeping operations has also been financed by non-P5 countries. The ending of the Cold War has seen a great increase in the UN's peacekeeping work. Although the UN is now mounting more peacekeeping operations than at any other time in its history, most of the operations have been controversial. Each one has been haunted by a lack of political will and resources.

The International Court of Justice (ICJ) is the world's main legal body.[28] Its roots go back to the end of the nineteenth century when it was hoped that wars could be avoided by encouraging governments to use an international court to settle their disputes. The ICJ has been able to settle some disputes so that what could have become international conflicts were avoided.

However, the ICJ is not a court in the sense understood by the general public. Individuals who are alleged to have committed offences are obliged to attend a court hearing. If they refuse to attend, that in itself is an offence. Government attendance at the ICJ is not compulsory.[29] Only about a third of the UN's membership (62 out of 191 states) accept its jurisdiction. The United States does not accept ICJ jurisdiction. Because of the Westphalian system's principle of national sovereignty, no government can be obliged to accept any international obligation. Thus, a government can rightfully have nothing to do with the ICJ and refuse to attend its hearings when another state complains about that government.

Another difference between the domestic and international legal systems arises from the structure of the courts themselves.[30] In the domestic legal system, the lower courts deal with the facts of what actually happened while the higher (appellate) courts deal with matters of law interpretation. In contrast, international legal bodies, principally the ICJ, have to be both a court of trial and of last resort. Although there are pioneering examples of international dispute settlement over the centuries, almost all of the work of these bodies has been done only in the twentieth century. Therefore, the international structure is still rather unsophisticated. Compared with the centuries over which the English and U.S. legal systems have evolved, time for the ICJ has been short.

The ICJ is hampered on procedural matters by various factors. Judges are often appointed with an appellate court; they often have an academic or government background with an interest in treaty creation, which is useful for appellate work. But they may have limited experience in the work of lower courts in sifting through the evidence. Only governments may take cases to the ICJ. Because of an assumption that governments provide evidence honestly, the ICJ task is to weigh the legal arguments of both sides. That the evidence may be accidentally or deliberately false is still a risk, however. Since ICJ judges are drawn from all over the world, there may also be cultural differences in how the evidence is interpreted. Various national legal systems also are involved as the English system, forming the basis of the U.S. one, is not necessarily the standard form for all national legal systems. The world is a long way from a uniform legal system.

The Trusteeship Council is rooted in President Wilson's admonition after World War I that the colonies of losers should not be absorbed into the colonies of the winners. Instead, the colonies would become "mandated" territories, with a view to their being put on the road to independence. Japan, which was an Allied country in World War I, lost its colonies after World II. Both the mandated territories and the Japanese colonies, after World War I, what were named trust territories.

A total of 11 territories were administered by the seven member-states on the UN Council. The Trusteeship Council has worked itself out of a job as the Axis colonies have been given independence. The last territory to go was Palau in November 1994. The Council has now been suspended. It cannot be formally wound up because that would require an amendment to the UN Charter, and member-states presently are unwilling to entertain any major amendments to the UN Charter.

The Secretariat, headed by the Secretary-General, supplies the personnel for the main UN bodies. While UN staff promise not to take instructions from their national governments, there is a temptation to maintain close links. The U.S.S.R. and former Eastern European bloc staff provided the worst examples of how UN staff were influenced by their governments.[31] This type of influence has improved with the ending of the Cold War. The lower levels of the staff work hard, and promotion is on merit. However, some of the senior positions unfortunately are used by governments as dumping grounds for retired politicians, active politicians more conveniently placed outside of their own countries, or members of royal households. This kind of expedience or favoritism has eroded the principle that the UN Secretariat should be an international civil service recruited on merit.

The Economic and Social Council (ECOSOC) initiates reports and makes recommendations to the General Assembly, UN member-nations, and specialized agencies on economic, social, and cultural matters. Until the recent expansion of the UN peacekeeping work, at least 80 percent of UN money was directed into the areas under ECOSOC: the International Telecommunications Union (ITU), the Universal Postal Union (UPU), Food and Agricultural Organization (FAO), and the World Health Organization (WHO).

Minute, the sums of money involved in these areas are often highly effective. For example, the World Health Organization (WHO) coordinated the international campaign to eradicate smallpox. Canadian medical practitioner Dorothy Goresky pointed out that the United States alone, saved $130 million a year by no longer having to vaccinate its population against smallpox.[32] What was saved each year amounted to more than the U.S. total annual contribution to all of WHO.

This type of work is characterized by the functional co-operation described earlier.[33] In other words, specialists get together out of the political spotlight and devise methods of cooperation on particular functions. For example, the national telephone systems has been standardized so that people can telephone around the world. This work was not hampered by Cold War political bitterness. Instead, all governments recognized that it would be in their interests to have a global telephone system and left the experts alone to create one through the ITU.

THE UN AND THE NEW GLOBAL ORDER

The UN is a much more ambitious organization than the League of Nations. Whereas the League only hesitatingly paid attention to economic and social cooperation, the UN has made great progress in this area. The UN is helping to erode the Westphalian System. This is not as obvious and dramatic as the activities of transnational corporations. But the process is underway.

First, the mere fact that the UN exists is in itself proof that governments acknowledge, albeit reluctantly, that they do need to work together on an increasing range of issues, such as health and protecting the environment. A comparison between the range of issues being discussed at the 1950 and the more wide-ranging 2000 annual sessions of the General Assembly exemplifies this cooperation. Rosalyn Higgins, then of the University of London and now a Judge at the ICJ, pointed out in 1963 that many countries in 1960 argued that even to discuss their internal affairs was a form of intervention prohibited by the UN Charter.[34] Four decades on, few countries would try to make that claim. While discussing internal affairs may not seem dramatic today, the present system of world affairs, as argued by this book, has to be seen in the context of the long sweep of history. The actuality is that until a few decades ago, even discussing the internal affairs of another country was regarded as an unfriendly action, which contradicted international law and the Westphalian System. For example, as recently as the 1930s, governments refused requests from Western NGOs to complain about Hitler's treatment of the Jews because it was seen by the governments as an internal German matter.

Second, the UN Charter is ambivalent towards the Westphalian System. According to Article 2(1), "[t]he Organization is based on the principle of the sovereign equality of all its Members." This is the standard Westphalian principle.

However, Article 2(7) hints of erosion in that system in two ways:

Nothing contained in the present Charter shall authorize the United Nations to intervene in matters which are *essentially* [emphasis added] within the domestic jurisdiction of any state or shall require the Members to submit such matters to settlement under the present Charter; but this principle shall not prejudice the application of enforcement measures under Chapter VII.

The word "essentially" undermines the absolute prohibition of the UN against intervention in domestic affairs; the League of Nations Covenant had been much more strict in this regard. Chapter IX (Articles 55–60) of the UN Charter deals with international economic and social cooperation and so foresees a role for the UN in such domestic matters as economic development, health, and human rights. Indeed, in June 1943, H.V. Evatt (Australian Minister for External Affairs and Attorney General and one of the key authors of the 1945 UN Charter) predicted that:

[I]t may become necessary for governments to accept obligations of [an] international character affecting matters which, in the past, have normally been regarded as matters of domestic concern only, and to accept responsibility for standards of living and for economic development in countries beyond their own borders.[35]

Additionally as Article 2(7) itself acknowledges, some conflicts, which may have domestic origins, can be become a threat to international peace and security; thus, these conflicts potentially can come within the scope of the Security Council. With the ending of the Cold War and the increase in secessionist movements, there is likely to be far more work for the UN Security Council as nation-states fragment and their disputes spill over into adjoining states, as in the former Yugoslavia. Whether the UN is equipped to cope with the new era of guerrilla warfare and fragmenting nation-states is, of course, another matter.[36]

THE UN AND GLOBAL DISORDER

Despite the optimistic analysis immediately above, it is now necessary to look at how there are some forms of disorder. The insistence upon national interest results in some of the disharmony.

National Interests

Governments use the UN not, despite their claims, out of any sense of idealistic high-mindedness but because the UN is a vehicle for national foreign policy. For example, no country is going to sign any international agreement that it perceives will be to its disadvantage. It will not forego its own national interest in the higher interests of the greater good.

This is contrary to what often happens in domestic politics. For example, a state within a federation will agree to something even though it will lose out because it wants to maintain harmony within the federation, and it expects that in a fraternal feeling it will later derive benefits at the temporary expense of other states on some other matter. There is a sense of give and take, and a belief that temporary losses should be sustained because the federation is generally worth belonging to. This worldview is missing when governments operate at the global level.

Lack of a Central Vision

The UN lacks a central transforming vision. Instead, the UN is a decentralized organization, with its various components acting independently of each other. The General Assembly, Security Council, and Secretary-General may attract the daily media coverage. However, at least 80 percent of the UN's work is conducted through specialized agencies with their own governing boards, such as the UN Educational, Scientific, and Cultural Organization (UNESCO), World Health Organization (WHO), and the Food and Agricultural Organization (FAO). The governing boards are linked back to different government departments at the national level.

Each agency has its own membership. Thus, each country may choose which specialized agency to join. The United States and United Kingdom, for example, both resigned from UNESCO in the early 1980s. (Both have rejoined after an abscence of almost two decades.) In Switzerland, the voters themselves remain bitter about their experience in the League of Nations and until 2002 voted in all referenda against joining the UN General Assembly.[37] Prior to the 2002 vote, the Swiss government had joined the specialized agencies. Given the importance of functional co-operation, Switzerland would lose out from not being in these agencies.

Each agency has its own method of operating and its own objectives. This means that some agencies overlap in the field, with resulting confusion. In 1992, the UN took over much of the running of a member-nation Somalia. The obvious way to have done this would have been for the Secretary-General to appoint some form of commissioner or administrator to not only govern all UN activities including peace-keeping, relief, and reconstruction as the Allies did in Germany and Japan immediately after World War II, but also to requisition money and personnel from member-nations to be deployed for this task. However, the political reality is that such a centralized approach was impossible. Governments now lack the political will to implement such an approach.

Lack of Money[38]

The UN seems to be in a perpetual financial crisis. The total amount of money that goes to the UN, with the exception of the loan money which passes through the World Bank, is about $8 million in U.S. dollars per year. This is well less than the amount of money the world spends on defense forces each week. But governments are very slow to make their contributions. At any one time, many countries are in debt to the UN. The current debtor is the United States at about $1.5 billion.

In December 2000, the UN General Assembly agreed to reduce the U.S. percentage of the UN budget from 25 percent to 22 percent. This would allow the U.S. Congressional critics of the UN, such as Jesse Helms and Joseph Biden, to permit the flow of American contributions, which they had blocked for sometime, to go the UN. Perhaps as a sign of the times and corporate power overshadowing the ability of governments to meet their own international commitments, media magnate Ted Turner, formerly of CNN, offered to help the Clinton Administration with the cash shortfall. Turner, who in 1997 provided the UN with the largest donation in its history of $1 billion American dollars for humanitarian purposes, offered to donate $34 million to assist in paying off the U.S. debt. The UN, however, does not allow individuals to pay a government's debts. With the revision of the funding formula, which means that some other countries will now have to pay more, the U.S. contributions deadlock has now been broken. But on September 25, 2001, Congress suddenly agreed to the payment of $582 million in back dues. Voting finished in a few minutes, the Senate agreed 99 to 0. The United States now has need of the UN owing to September 11.

By the standards of government expenditure, the UN runs on minute sums of money. The UN's central budget is less than that of the Council of the City of New York. One and a half days of the cost of "Desert Storm," the operation which finally liberated Kuwait, would have paid for all UN peacekeeping world-wide for one year. The total cost of operation "Desert Storm" probably cost the same as all the peacekeeping operations the UN has ever conducted since they began in 1948 until 1991.

In short, if governments regard something as particularly important, they will find the money for it. On this reckoning, the UN is obviously a low priority item.

Peacekeeping

"Peacekeeping" is not referred to in the UN Charter. It has been an ad hoc measure which the UN devised to cope with the Cold War's freezing of the procedure which is laid down in the Charter.

Generals always prepare to fight the last war; diplomats design methods to avoid having to fight the last war. The ghost of Hitler (who had died only two months before the 1945 San Francisco conference which finalized the UN Char-ter) underpins the original vision for the Security Council. If enough countries had worked together in the League of Nations, according to that vision, Hitler would have been deterred from his aggressive foreign policy. For example, Winston Churchill wrote to Lord Robert Cecil that World War II should be called the "Unnecessary War" because it "could easily have been prevented if the League of Nations had been used with courage and loyalty by the associated nations."[39] Consequently, the UN, was given—on paper, anyway—immense power to learn from history.

The UN Security Council was probably flawed from the outset. Based on an incorrect interpretation of governmental behavior, it assumes that all countries are willing to fight any other country. But all governments, in line with their perception of national interest, have a policy of selective indignation: There are some incidents they feel strongly about and others that they overlook. Thus, the United States and its allies assisted Kuwait in 1990 but had done little to help East Timor when it was invaded by Indonesia in 1975.

Whether the UN Security Council could ever have recovered from that de-sign flaw will never be known because the Cold War froze that system so that it was never used as designed. The ending of the Cold War has had four impacts on the UN peacekeeping work. First, there has been an increase in operations: The UN since 1988 has created as many operations as it did in the years 1948 to 1987. Second, the UN has gone even deeper into debt over these operations. Governments vote for them but are slow to pay for them. Third, the United States has exploited the demise of the U.S.S.R. and Russia's vulnerability to foreign aid bribery by manipulating the Security Council to its own ends. Operations "Desert Shield" and "Desert Storm" were not UN operations. They were conducted by a coalition led by the United States.[40] Finally, the UN Charter's elaborate system has still not been used as it was designed. The UN Security Council continues to lurch from one crisis to the next.

The peacekeeping operations since the end of the Cold War generate five basic questions which the UN Security Council has not resolved. First, how is the UN to select in which disputes it should get involved? The ending of the Cold War has not seen an outbreak of peace. On the contrary, many tribal and ethnic disputes frozen by the Cold War have now been revived—not least in the former U.S.S.R. itself. What system of priority-setting is the UN to develop to help select crises?

Second, when does the UN leave a situation? By what criteria does the UN decide that its work is over? As in Cambodia in the late 1980s, Somalia in the early 1990s, and Yugoslavia in the late 1990s, the UN has taken on a more ambitious task than keeping warring factions apart, in itself a difficult job. The UN is now in the business of state-building.

Third, will governments continue to agree to supply forces for these operations? This book has pointed out that, under the UN Charter's elaborate system, all member-nations have to supply forces. But that system has never been used, and the Secretary-General instead can only ask if governments are willing to supply forces. For example, in late 1999, Australia supplied its own force to East Timor because there was no certainty that the UN Secretary-General could mount one early enough.

Fourth, there is the issue of how the UN's work on peacekeeping should be coordinated with its work on protecting the environment and promoting economic growth. Poverty is related to environmental decay, and both are in turn related to armed conflicts. As the quality of local land declines, people move into adjoining areas and onto the land of other people. These environmental refugees unintentionally contribute to local conflicts by occupying the land of others. When that new land is damaged, people again move on and create even more conflict. Poverty and environmental decay played a part in Somalia's conflict.

Finally, how far the UN can intervene in domestic affairs to resolve a problem affecting a region is a problem. Somalia's internal problems spilled over into neighboring countries, by creating wartime refugees and environmental refugees. That prompted the UN into action. Additionally, global television galvanizes viewers into action. No longer having patience with the niceties of the

Westphalian principle of sovereign independence of nation-states, viewers see people suffering and want something done quickly to help them.

REFORMING THE UN

Given that the UN has so many problems, what are the prospects for reforming the organization? There is no shortage of ideas for reforming it—only a lack of political will to do so.

Options for reforming the UN may be divided into "micro-reform" proposals, not requiring an amendment to the UN Charter, and "macro-reforms," requiring an amendment to the UN Charter.[41] I have coined the distinction between these two reforms because amending the UN Charter is very difficult. There has been no substantial amendment to the Charter since it was written in 1945. Having to be adopted by a vote of two-thirds of the General Assembly, these amendments have to be ratified in accordance with their respective constitutional processes. The Permanent 5 (P5), the United States, Russia, China, France and the United Kingdom, can each veto any proposed amendment. Since 1945, the only changes have been to the number of member-nations on UN bodies; these changes have arisen because of the increase in the UN's overall membership. For example, the UN Security Council's membership was increased in 1965 from 11 to 15.

On the other hand, all "micro-reform" proposals could be introduced immediately. My following suggestions are not in any order of priority.

Governments should pay their UN dues on time. It is hardly a novel idea to suggest that governments pay subscriptions on time. Individuals who belong to clubs or associations know that their continued membership depends partly on their paying subscriptions. But UN member-states are slow to pay and show no remorse for their lateness.

More women should be appointed to senior positions. The senior level of the UN has traditionally had none or only a few women. This parallels the lack of women as heads of national delegations. However, just as some countries are now making more of an effort to ensure equal opportunity at the head of delegation level, so the UN's own employment practices could reflect that same determination. Although the UN Secretary-General has little leverage over countries, such as in demanding prompt payment of their dues, the Secretary-General does have much greater scope for action in employing women in the Secretariat's senior level.

The International Court of Justice (ICJ) is the world's main legal body. However, attendance at it is not compulsory; only about a third of the UN's membership accepts its jurisdiction. I propose that all states should accept its jurisdiction, thereby allowing much greater use of international arbitration rather than war.

The Secretary-General could be appointed for only one, seven-year term. The present arrangement is for the person to have five-year terms, with the understanding that only two terms will be served. There is a temptation to use the end of the first term as an election campaign to get reappointed. One term in office would remove that need and perhaps make the office-holder a little more independent.

The UN Secretariat could be a truly international civil service. UN staff promise not to take instructions from their national governments, but there is a temptation to maintain close links with their governments. Similarly, national governments ought not to use the UN as a dumping ground to reward retired politicians or relatives of the ruling households who need a job. All recruitment should be on merit.

In summary, putting the micro-reform proposals into effect would make the UN a very different body from the one it is today. Effecting these proposals also could happen overnight.

Based on amending the UN Charter, macro-reform proposals would be much more difficult to achieve. The post-Cold War era does not mean that amendments to the UN Charter will be any easier to achieve. For example, Japan and Germany would like to become members of the Security Council and are trying to give the impression that their inclusion would represent only a minor change to the UN Charter. However, the change would be major. There are valid reasons for these memberships, not least because of the countries' economic power. The P5 are no longer necessarily the world's main countries as they were in 1945; the United Kingdom and France are the most obvious members to be dropped. Germany and Japan, ironically the two big losers of World War II, are the obvious candidates to join the Security Council. It was said of the United Kingdom in the early 1960s that it had lost an empire but not yet found a new role. It can be said of Germany that it has regained its unity, but it has yet to find a new role. Being on the Security Council would give a clear sense of direction to Germany, as the country clearly hopes. Japan has given the UN similar signals. Japan is increasing its financial contributions to UN operations. It is now giving more foreign aid, for example, than does the United States in an element of taxation without permanent representation.

However, making this change would encourage other countries from different regions to request similar status on the Security Council. Which other countries should be considered for equal treatment? In Asia, should it be India, Pakistan, or Indonesia? In Latin America, Brazil, Mexico, and perhaps Argentina would be contenders. Among African countries, reference is made most often to Nigeria, but other countries may have strong claims, including the democratic and multiracial South Africa.

Meanwhile, the United Kingdom and France would resist any move to be dispensed with in favor of Germany and Japan. For example, the United Kingdom could approach Pakistan, drawing its attention to the fact that India would like to get on the Security Council. Pakistan would prefer the status quo to having India on the Security Council. The United Kingdom could do the same with Argentina vis-a-vis Brazil. The net effect would be countries preferring to stick with the known devils rather than taking on the unknown devils. All this politicking would assure that the United Kingdom remains on the Security Council.

Therefore, the chances of achieving macro-reforms are not necessarily very good. This means that as the UN gets older, it will have some fundamental faults that will become even more apparent as the years roll by.

In terms of some other macro-reform suggestions, an alternative approach to reforming the Security Council would be to break the nexus between the P5 and the veto power. Although the P5 would remain permanently on the Security Council, the veto power would be abolished entirely. The P5 would not have to worry about an election every two years, and the cost of retaining their permanent membership would be the surrender of the veto. The chances of major Security Council reform are slim if only because the P5 states could use their veto power to block reform.

The General Assembly is the world's main political forum and is composed of governmental delegations. The main debate on reforming the General Assembly has been generated by NGOs, especially the Campaign for a More Democratic United Nations (CAMDUN) and the International Network for a UN Second Assembly (INFUSA), to ensure that the General Assembly hears more from the people.[42] The UK Medical Association for the Prevention of War (now part of UK MEDACT) first proposed in 1982 that Article 22 of the UN Charter, which empowers the General Assembly to establish such subsidiary organs as it sees fit, be amended to create a subsidiary body for the General Assembly. The new body would have an advisory status and would be a forum for NGOs. Alternatively, the forum could be for individual representatives elected from each UN member-state, based on the size of national population.

Another NGO urging UN reform is the New York-based Center for War/Peace Studies, headed by Richard Hudson who has pioneered the Binding Triad proposal. The General Assembly each year adopts hundreds of nonbinding resolutions. Hudson has proposed a shift in power so that the General Assembly could adopt binding resolutions, thereby absorbing some of the Security Council's power. This would require a change from the present one state/one vote system to a system reflecting global population and economic realities. For a resolution to be binding, it would need to get two-thirds of the votes in three tiers of voting: the members present, a continuation of the present system; the world's most populated states, favoring the Third World and reflecting the majority of the world's people; and the world's richest states, favoring the developed countries and reflecting today's economic reality. While far fewer resolutions would be adopted under this system, any resolution that did make it would obviously reflect today's global realities.

The Trusteeship Council has worked itself out of a job. The Trusteeship Council structure could be retained, with its focus changed to either the environment or to the approximately 300 million Indigenous Peoples.

The Economic and Social Council (ECOSOC) has never been able to serve effectively as a world policy forum for economic, social, and related questions. ECOSOC is an organizational accumulation of institutional bodies which do not comply with political rationality and organizational efficiency. Over the years, the ECOSOC machinery has become extremely complicated. About 40 bodies are reporting directly to it. Since many of these bodies have their own subsidiaries, the total number of experts and intergovernmental committees in the economic and social field is close to 200. The main idea for reforming ECOSOC is to give it more power over the specialized agencies and the other bodies nominally within its jurisdiction so as to ensure better coordination and less duplication.

To conclude, there are many nongovernmental ideas in circulation for reforming the UN. However, due to a lack of political will and vision, the UN just drifts along from one crisis to the next.

OTHER INTERGOVERNMENTAL ORGANIZATIONS

The European Union is the world's best example of how an intergovernmental organization is eroding the Westphalian System.[43] Starting in Western Europe, the Westphalian System is being transformed in the same place. The EU is a unique intergovernmental organization. It is more than the confederal UN, where the authority resides largely at nation-state level, and yet less than a federal nation-state, such as the United States.

The EU began from a French proposal in 1950 to pool the coal and steel industries of France and the then West Germany into an organization open to all European democracies. The proposal had great symbolic significance: France and Germany had been at the center of the two World Wars; coal and steel are the basic industries for conventional warfare, the sinews of war. The European Coal and Steel Community was formed in 1951 with a membership of Belgium, France, West Germany, Luxembourg, Italy, and The Netherlands. After the success of this arrangement encouraged the six countries to apply the same approach to other parts of the economy, the European Economic Community (EEC) was created in 1957.

The EEC's membership and range of activities has continued to increase. With the end of the Cold War, negotiations are also underway to include some Eastern European countries. In 1993, with the entering into force of the Maastricht treaty, the EEC became known as the EU.

However, the EU has considerable problems. First, there is the problem of creating a sense of unity at the grass roots. Although old hatreds, such as between France and Germany, are certainly dying, no new pan-European nationalism is emerging.

Second, there is a debate over how the EU should evolve. On the one hand, there is a move for a deeper union, which would mean that the current member-nations would pool more functions and cooperate far more, which might lead to the creation of a single EU foreign policy. On the other hand, there is a move for the current membership to become wider so as to include some of Eastern Europe. While neither dilemma has been resolved, some member-nations (notably the UK) even have doubts about the possibilities of a deeper or a wider union.

Third, creating democracy and accountability within the EU is problematic. The real power resides with the European Commission at Brussels, rather than with the European Parliament; so citizens feel isolated from the decision-making. This alienation has given rise to a new fragmentation within the EU: a return to local, subnational concerns and the rise of local loyalties, like Scottish and Welsh nationalism.[44]

The standard reply to this concentration of power is called "subsidiarity"; the term means making all governmental decision at the lowest possible level. The theory is that the decisions should be made by the people who are going to have to live with the consequences. Subsidiarity is fine in theory, but it has a long way to go before being implemented. One argument against it is that local people do not have the big picture and that they will make decisions which benefit themselves but disadvantage the larger society in which they live. Additionally, subsidiarity offends the neat thinking of bureaucracies, which focus on the uniform creation and implementation of rules. Subsidiarity would permit too many local variations.

Finally, there is the problem of transnational corporations. They act as though national boundaries are no more significant than the equator. One example of their work is currency speculation. National currency restrictions, part of the Bretton Woods System, used to slow down the flow of capital, allowing central banks to control the value of their currency. Western governments, including those in the EU, have scrapped currency regulations. As noted earlier, $1.8 trillion in U.S. dollars can now flow through foreign exchanges in a day, looking for currencies to bid up or down. The EU created a European exchange rate mechanism to standardize the value of EU currencies. The corporations (some of which, ironically, are based in the EU) created a run on the United Kingdom pound in September 1992. The Bank of England tried to behave as it had done in the past to protect the pound's value. Although the Bank and West European central banks bought the United Kingdom pound to try to drive up its value, they did not have enough cash to compete against the corporations, which now have bigger reserves. Thus, the Bank of England surrendered after one day's trading, out of which some corporations made large profits. The EU has now created the Euro currency, which does not include the UK pound. It has had an unhappy initial period on the foreign exchange market.

In conclusion, the reason why books on regional intergovernmental organizations usually quote the EU example is that it is the only effective example to quote. The western European experience is well ahead of anything else being implemented in any other part of the world. For example on January 1, 2002, the largest currency reform in world history took place, with the introduction of the Euro as the common currency for most EU members. It is important, then, not to generalize too much from the EU case study for the rest of the world. World federalist activist Ernest Wistrich wrote in 1994 that a world federation would not come about immediately would likely emerge through the creation of regional federations and the consequent growing interdependence among them. Therefore, the European model could serve as a model for other regions.[45] The fact is that the European model has not yet been copied anywhere else around the world.

NONGOVERNMENTAL ORGANIZATIONS[46]

Introduction

A nongovernmental organization (NGO) is any organization outside the government, such as the public service and the defense forces, and business. The phrase nongovernmental is in itself Westphalian: Organizations are either "governmental" or they are not. This book uses the phrase simply because it is the standardone, as in UN circles. But a new, more positive (and less Westphalian) term is required. For example, the Worldwatch Institute has suggested that instead of naming such organizations in terms of what they are not, it may be more appropriate to call them what they are—civil society organizations (CSOs).[47]

The Numbers of NGOs

It is impossible to calculate the number of NGOs; they keep springing up in response to some need. There is no doubt, however, that NGOs are increasing both in number and in membership. Some examples will illustrate this claim.

The then UN Secretary-General, speaking at the 1994 annual UN/NGO Conference in New York, commented on the emergence of many new NGOs on every continent.[48] In France, for example, 54,000 new associations had been established since 1987. In Italy, 40 percent of the associations had been set up within the previous 15 years. This phenomenon was also occurring in developing countries. Within a short space of time, 10,000 NGOs had been established in Bangladesh, 21,000 in the Philippines, and 27,000 in Chile. In Eastern Europe since the fall of communism, NGOs had been playing an increasingly important role in people's lives.

Michael O'Neill, of the University of San Francisco, has examined the NGO situation in the United States.[49] The NGO sector, perhaps one of the biggest success stories in U.S. history, employs more civilians than the federal government, with a budget that exceeds all but seven countries in the world. Eighty million American adults and teenagers contributed the equivalent of $150 billion of volunteer work effort within nongovernmental organizations in 1987.

Time magazine reported in 1999 that the amount of money alone that Americans donated to charity in 1998 was $174.52 billion ($17 billion more than in 1997).[50]

O'Neill divides the nonprofit arena into nine sub-sectors including religion, private education and research, health care, arts and culture, social sciences, advocacy and legal services, international assistance, foundations and corporate funders, and mutual benefit organizations. The United States has 1,243,000 NGOs spread across these nine categories. While the United States is obviously the world leader, similar studies in other countries would produce a similar pattern.

Most of this book is focused on a narrow slice of the NGO spectrum: the politically oriented public advocacy ones working for social change in such areas as foreign aid, human rights, and the environment. Among the most high-profile organizations, these NGOs are easily, and wrongly, perceived as the major ones. But it is worth noting that they represent only a small slice of the full range of NGOs.

NGOs and the Decline of National Party Politics

Most NGOs were created in the twentieth century. Indeed, many were created since World War II. They are to be found in all aspects of life. Indeed, local and national political activities are increasingly about the competing pressures from NGOs. A parallel development to the decline in the significance of national governments, is the diminishing importance of political parties. Activists prefer to join single issue groups (NGOs). For example, there are probably as many members of the U.S. environment movement as there are members of all the U.S. political parties combined.[51] In other words, people are still active in political change. It is simply that they no longer see political parties as the best vehicle for that change.

People are disenchanted that when their political party does get into power, it is often unable to introduce the policies they would like. As this book is arguing, this disappointment is sometimes due to the fact that national governments are increasingly no longer masters of their own destiny.

Additionally, party politics polarize each issue. Opposition parties are virtually automatically obliged to oppose government policies in order to maintain their credibility as an being opposed. The mass media—always on the watch for clash and conflict—go to the opposition precisely to get a critical opinion of the government. By contrast, NGOs can bring people together across party lines to work for a greater goal.

Characteristics of NGOs

An Expanding Role

NGOs have moved a long way from their image in the nineteenth century of mainly dealing with people in crisis. For example, people who were made homeless or destitute went to these organizations, usually Christian-based, for assistance. NGOs were the forerunners of the welfare state created in many developed countries in the twentieth century.

But governments in the twentieth century accepted that they must carry out much of the crisis intervention work. Owing to the twentieth-century changes in taxation, governments now have far greater resources to do this work. NGOs now share crisis intervention work with governments, thereby permitting them to take on other complementary roles, such as research and advocacy.

In the field of foreign aid, for example, NGOs developed to deal with an immediate crisis, such as a famine, like the Oxford Committee for Famine Relief (OXFAM) formed in 1942.[52] An extension to the work was long-term development. This may be illustrated by the difference between supplying food in a famine and helping people plant their own crops. The next extension was questioning why people were poor when others in the same society were rich. This questioning brought NGOs into the debate over the best way for a country to develop. Another extension was to bring the development issue back home via education about it, whereby people in developed countries were challenged to reflect on what contribution they may be making, albeit unintentionally, to the plight of the Third World.

Thus, the work of NGOs is now more sophisticated than, say, a century ago. For example, NGOs are now involved in multi-track diplomacy. In single-track diplomacy, national governments deal directly with another; the limitations involve governments finding it domestically inconvenient to be seen dealing directly with each other, or perhaps of being devoid of ideas about settling a dispute. In addition, Douglas Johnston and Cynthia Sampson have explained the role of a so-called second track diplomacy by private citizens and NGOs; an example was the Moral Re-Armament that helped to bring about Franco-German reconciliation after World War II.[53]

Much the same could be said about the increasing role that NGOs play in international litigation. Dinah Shelton of the Santa Clara University School of Law has done a study of the participation of NGOs, primarily as amici curiae, in the proceedings of four permanent international courts: the International Court of Justice, the European Court of Justice, the European Court of Human Rights, and the Inter-American Court of Human Rights.[54] It is evidence of globalization that three of these four institutions did not exist at all before 1945. Further evidence lies in the way that NGOs are permitted to play their role.

People Helping People

NGOs mobilize the community. They enable individuals to take an active role in working for a better society. NGOs are a vehicle whereby people can volunteer their services. People will volunteer their time, money, and gifts-in-kind to NGOs—but they will not volunteer to do the same for official government bodies. Playing a very important role in NGOs, volunteers either provide supplementary services to the staff or, in some small areas, actually make up the staff.

Despite the volunteers, NGOs are now more professional, having lost the lady bountiful image of the nineteenth century. The staff are paid, not necessarily very well, and are often well qualified. NGOs now provide career structures for people who wish to help their fellow human beings. Some tertiary educational institutions have taken the concern for a professional image a step further by creating courses for managing NGOs. For example, I teach at the University of New South Wales' Department of Social Work in a master's course which is aimed at equipping people for service in NGOs.

NGOs can themselves be very important to the volunteers. They provide these men and women with opportunities to take active roles in community welfare. Further, NGOs help the self-image of those volunteers who through unemployment or retirement from the paid work force may feel marginalized and even unwanted. Thus, NGOs provide therefore a vehicle out of the self-absorption and self-obsession which characterize so much of contemporary life.

THE WARNING VOICE

Not trying to foretell the future, NGOs warn people that if they persist in their current actions, dire consequences will come about.

In 1993, for example, the United Kingdom and Australia reached agreement on the British payment for cleaning up the Maralinga (South Australia) site at which the some British atomic weapons had been tested in the 1960s.[55] The tests were conducted amid great secrecy, and only in recent years has the truth about the health hazards fully emerged. The peace movement opposed the tests from the outset, and its stand has been vindicated. Like all governments, the Australian one never likes to admit that it has given in to pressure from the peace movement.[56] But the peace movement was the power to oppose the tests, to be skeptical about governmental assurances concerning the health consequences, and to campaign in the 1980s to get the Maralinga site cleaned up. It was peace movement pressure, among other things, that led to the Australian Government creating the 1985 Royal Commission into British tests in Australia. The Commission's report was the basis of Australian demands for greater British help in cleaning up the test sites. Even though the 1993 outcome was not fully to the peace movement's liking, the whole episode for four decades has vindicated the stand of this movement.

NGOs are also good at research. This is important because universities in many countries are going through various financial crises, and there is not so much scope for research to be conducted. NGOs are now recruiting people with high academic qualifications, who previously may have been employed in universities when appropriate jobs were available. This means that NGOs also produce some important research. Additionally, much of the university research that is conducted and written up is too detached from the general public. Academics talk too often to each other and too little to the general public. Conducting their own research, NGOs can popularize esoteric university research. They also are good at using the mass media to publicize their findings.

The Leading Edge

NGOs show that a good way to bring about change is to establish a model of how things should be. In other words, providing warnings is not enough: It is also necessary to provide an alternative. Thus, NGOs are often on the leading edge of change. Through their advocacy work, they provide innovations, fresh thinking, and new visions. They—rather than governments—often set the pace.

An example of this is the London-based Intermediate Technology Development Group, founded by Dr. E.F. Schumacher. ITDG has popularized Schumacher's ideas characterized by "Small is Beautiful."[57] ITDG is not advocating some romanticized return to nature. It wants a change in economic policies It wants the economic policies to be based on technology with four principles: Workplaces should be located where people live, avoiding the need for migration into the overcrowded cities; workplaces should be cheap to organize, avoiding borrowing a great deal of capital to get started; the manufacturing systems should be uncomplicated, avoiding the demand for high skills; and the production should be based on local materials for local use, avoiding high transportation costs. Many NGO projects in the Third World are now based on these principles, though they might not explicitly acknowledge Schumacher and the ITDG.

CONTINUITY

NGOs survive the fads and fashions of governments; they outlive the terms of elected governments. They provide a continuity of care and a continued focus on social justice issues—when governments might prefer to ignore those issues.

One example is the consumer boycott against the makers of infant-formula powdered milk.[58] The argument over infant-formula in the Third World rested on three points. Use of it detracts from breast milk, which provides initial near-perfect nutrition, protects against disease, and is virtually costless. Lactating mothers are less likely to conceive than mothers who are not breast-feeding. Second, because powdered milk is often mixed with unclean water in villages and served in unclean bottles, its unnecessary use can lead to malnutrition, disease, and even death. Finally, powdered milk, which is often supplied free in hospital, has to be paid for when mother and child return home; then it becomes a financial burden for the family, especially when the alternative is free. Of course, there are some circumstances in which infant-formula is justified. Consequently, the critics have not campaigned against formula in principle, but against the aggressive marketing techniques of the companies, as in offering inducements to hospital employees to recommend infant-formula.

In the late 1970s, groups began to call for boycotts of other products made by the infant-formula companies, such as Nestles. The boycott was coordinated by the Infant Formula Action Coalition (INFACT) in the United States. Two major supporters were the National Council of Churches and the NCC-sponsored Interfaith Center on Corporate Responsibility, which acts for Protestant denominations and Catholic orders in trying to persuade corporations in which they invest to adopt voluntarily more socially responsible business practices. Other churches such as the United Church of Canada and the Anglican Church of Canada, took up the campaign.

The World Health Organization (WHO) responded to the campaign by drawing up a voluntary set of marketing guidelines. The International Code states, among other things, that there should not be free samples, promotion of products in health facilities, or gifts to health workers. An International Baby Food Action Network (IBFAN) was established to stop the unethical promotion of bottle-feeding products. It has also been encouraging governments to adopt binding legislation to assist the observance of the voluntary code.

The infant-formula campaign has become the classic case study of the effectiveness of consumer boycotts. It has greatly influenced international organizations, changed the practices of transnational corporations, and has been a good medium by which to inform people in developed nations about economic and social development. Although the campaign has still not achieved all that was hoped for it, it showed that the boycott technique could be effective. It was an example of thinking globally and acting locally: The individual or family had a specific task to do which would contribute to a better world. Every time people buy a product, they vote in favor of that product and yet seldom think of the ethical consequences of casting that vote. The campaign called upon people to think about the social responsibility of their consumer patterns.

A key factor in this campaign was the NGO continuity. Annelies Allain of IBFAN pointed out that influencing intergovernmental organizations was hard and often boring work.[59] It was also something that could not be done off-the-cuff. Exerting influence required continuous public support, local organizing, lobbying at home, and building expertise on a specific issue. To focus on single issues and set ambitious but achievable goals seemed the right recipe for success. Staying power to follow through on favorable intergovernmental decisions was necessary to ensure continued commitment by the organization and by individual governments. Few governments will act without public pressure.

A second case study concerns one of the world's oldest human rights organizations: the British Anti-Slavery Society, the origins of which go back to 1787, and which is now known as Anti-Slavery International. Slavery, when the Belgian government was forced in 1908 by international nongovernmental pressure to curtail it in the Congo Free State which was 75 times the size of Belgium and had had a population decline of 50 per cent since colonization began in 1885, did not end.[60]

Anti-Slavery International, for instance, has been monitoring the use of debt bondage to collect "white gold," or sugar cane, in Haiti and the Dominican Republic.[61] For about 500 years, the histories of sugar and slavery have been interwoven. The island now shared by Haiti and the Dominican Republic was Columbus' first port of call in his quest to discover a new route to the East. The settlers who followed him found wealth in the planting of "white gold" and in exploiting the native population. Many workers in the sugar cane fields went to the plantations voluntarily, pushed by the terrible poverty of their own country. But many more were compelled to work cutting sugar cane in the Dominican Republic when there were not enough workers for the harvest. The Dominican authorities resorted to extreme measures to ensure that the supply of labor was adequate to harvest the cane.

Anne-Marie Sharman used a photograph of a sugar cane worker in slavery-like conditions for an annual review of Anti-Slavery International.[62] She said that it was a sad reflection on the standards of the late twentieth century that Anti-Slavery International, more than 150 years after slavery was abolished in the sugar plantations of the West Indies, was still finding such pictures. However, there was some good news. Information now flowed more rapidly and in much greater volume despite being still difficult to find and sometimes dangerous to collect. But once this was done, detailed facts could be disseminated in ways and at speeds undreamt of by the abolitionists in the nineteenth century. With the international community mobilized, notably through press, radio, and television, and with abuses put in the public domain, it becomes possible to hope that change is on the way.

A third case study of continuity is the environment movement's Greenpeace, which has a trade mark that is now almost as famous as Coca-Cola's. Greenpeace started in Canada in 1971.[63] The environment debate was then dominated by conservationists, who were concerned about trying to preserve parts of Canadian wild-life. Greenpeace argued that this was too simplistic and that there was more involved. Because the entire global ecosystem was under threat, there had to a more sophisticated approach to saving the earth. This coincided with the preparations for the 1972 UN Conference on the Human Environment, where the UN was also taking a broader view of the environmental crisis.

Greenpeace has grown in strength. It has a larger budget than the UN Environment Program, which was created a year later by the UN Conference. It is one of the world's most famous environmental NGOs. What was dismissed as a trendy NGO, with a flair for publicity, such as against French nuclear testing in the South Pacific, is now recognized as a major factor in shaping the environment debate. Incidentally, most national departments of the environment were created around the time of the 1972 UN Conference, in order for governments to be represented by ministers of the environment. Therefore,

Greenpeace is older than many national ministries for the environment and the UN Environment Program.[64]

People work in NGOs to make a difference. They are not there simply to make money, which is unlikely, given the salary scales. Volunteers donate their time and skills similarly to make a difference. There is, then, a degree of commitment here which may be lacking in politicians and public servants who are simply doing their job. Politicians and public servants may be fine individuals, with a dedication to the task then occupying their time. But they are unlikely to be focused on that task for long; they will be transferred or promoted elsewhere, and new staff will arrive. NGOs keep on keeping on.

NGOs and the Westphalian System

The Westphalian Facade

Nation-states, according to the concept of the Westphalian System, are the masters of their own destinies. Thus, governments rarely admit that they have given in to NGO pressure: To do so would be a public admission that governments are not really masters of destiny. Such an admission would also encourage other NGOs to be equally active in the expectation of changing government policy.

It is also very difficult to follow a governmental decision-making process to find out how any decision was made and what influenced whom. For example, Amnesty International, whose members write letters to governments asking for the release of political prisoners, is careful not to claim that its adopted prisoners are released due to Amnesty pressure. Amnesty International cannot establish a clear chain of causation between its campaign and the release of the political prisoner.

Similarly, an NGO may advocate a policy change and a government may later change its policy—but it is usually very difficult (if not impossible) to say precisely that one caused the other. For example, there was an NGO campaign throughout the 1980s against mining in Antarctica. This coincided with an upsurge in concern generally about the environment in the later 1980s. Suddenly and unexpectedly, the Australian and French governments completely changed their policies to also oppose mining. This killed the attempt to create a treaty to regulate mining in Antarctica.[65] While the NGOs were triumphant, it is not so easy to form a chain of causation linking the NGO campaign with the governmental back down.

Therefore, the refusal of governments to acknowledge the role of NGOs in changing particular policies is also part of the Westphalian logic. This chapter's brief case studies have provided examples of when, coincidentally, governments have changed their policies around the time of NGO campaigns, and even those of transnational corporations as in the case of the infant-formula campaign.[66]

The NGO Impact

NGOs cut across the Westphalian System in five main ways. First, they can provide an alternative focal point for loyalty, such as the peace movements in many countries which opposed the arms race in the 1980s. Citizens do not always think that their own governments know best. Indeed, some NGOs provide an alternative foreign policy transcending national boundaries; the NGOs working together in the 1980s in many countries to defeat the proposed treaty to regulate mining in Antarctica offered these different foreign policies. Since national governments may not necessarily represent the views of their citizens on all issues, NGOs are very important.

Second, NGOs show that governments have no monopoly over information and ideas. For example, NGOs undertake public education work, such as alerting people to the dangers of pollution and generating new ideas for coping with problems. NGOs develop close ties with politicians and, even more importantly, public servants to work on new treaties and so on.

Third, NGOs are adept at using the mass media for their campaigns. They sometimes challenge governments and corporations to do better.

Fourth, NGOs provide an alternative route for people who wish to work for a better world. Political parties are not the sole route for working for that objective. Indeed, given the widespread disenchantment with politicians, NGOs are important avenues for peaceful social change.

Finally, the importance of NGOs is being recognized in the intergovernmental organizations which grant various forms of consultative status to NGOs to enable them to take part in the work of the organizations. Also, national governmental delegations to UN conferences now sometimes contain NGO personnel as "observers" and expert advisers.

The Limitations of NGOs

To conclude this section, the future is not necessarily bright for NGOs. It is a pessimistic sign about the Westphalian logic at work that some governments at the UN are now feeling uncomfortable with the extent of NGO involvement. The discomfort has led to moves to reduce that involvement. At the 1999 Stanley Foundation conference on the UN and NGOs, Richard Stanley, the Foundation's President, surveyed some of those concerns.[67] First, that NGO numbers at UN meetings are growing causes some administrative and security concerns. Second, NGOs are not necessarily representative in the sense of having externally defined geographic or community constituency. Additionally, developed countries, with a total population now forming a small minority of the total world population, are disproportionately represented in the NGO community. Third, NGOs are seen as part of the process of globalization; in so far as governments are trying to block that process, they are resisting the growing influence of NGOs.

A theme of this book is the way in which the nonstate actors have grown in a haphazard way. This is to be expected because that is how most institutions, including the Westphalian System itself, do evolve. However, the disordered growth encourages people and other institutions, after a few years or decades, to suddenly decide that the growth of NGOs, or any other particular trend, is not to their liking. There is now a reaction against globalization in general and the nonstate actors in particular.

Thus, the backlash against NGOs was to be expected. Not only happening at the UN, the reaction is also occurring in the field where, for example, humanitarian NGOs are having to reassess their methods of operating due to their now being the targets of guerrilla groups. For example, to what extent should relief convoys now have armed guards? It is a sign of the times that World Vision International, one of the world's largest development NGOs, should have a director of corporate security to address the U.S. Defense Intelligence Agency at the Pentagon in Washington D.C. on NGO security.[68]

In this post-Westphalian world, NGOs can help us think through the issue of representing people and being represented. The rise of liberal democracy through the Westphalian system, as noted in chapter 2, is based on politicians representing their constituents in a congress or parliament. However, any person, in theory, can form an NGO and begin a world wide campaign. Who does such a person actually represent?

It may well be that in the post-Westphalian world, NGOs rise and fall based on consumer demand: Fulfilling a need, they will continue; not meeting a need, they will fail. For example, Jody Williams, coordinator of the United States-based International Committee to Ban Landmines and co-winner of the 1997 Nobel Peace Prize, ran the campaign largely from a Vermont farmhouse and through the Internet. Her success was due to the way in which she touched a nerve in the global body politic: Other people, and eventually governments, also agreed that landmines ought to be banned and so were willing to join her campaign. By the same token, other NGOs may slip into decline because they are no longer so much in tune with public feelings; groups opposed to alcohol, like the Woman's Christian Temperance Union, might fall into this category.

This ad hoc rise and fall of NGOs is obviously less satisfactory than the Westphalian System of geographically defined areas, electoral rolls, and free elections. But the post-Westphalian world will be more flexible and less bureaucratic than the era to which we have become accustomed.

THE GLOBAL DIMENSION OF CRIME

Introduction

The September 11 tragedy has been a reminder of the global dimension of crime. Modern technology in the banking, communications, transportation, and electronic sectors have provided criminals with new tools enabling them to steal millions of dollars and to launder their huge, illicit profits across borders and continents. During the 1980s, the profitability of the drug trade led to a situation in which the "narco-dollar" began to assume the economic significance of the "petro-dollar" in the 1970s. The capital generated during the 1980s by illegal drug trafficking alone was in the order of $3,000 billion to 5,000 billion U.S. dollars. Indeed, it is possible that drug trafficking has become the world's second most lucrative manufacturing business, worth $400 billion per year in U.S. dollars[69] after the arms trade.[70]

There are three main trends in the globalization of crime. First, the computer and communications technology have developed. Electronic funds transfer systems can move billions of dollars around the globe in seconds. Faxes and cellular telephones can be encrypted, making it all but impossible to trace calls from them. Drug-cartel aircraft flying north to the United States have internal interceptors to plot radar and avoid monitoring.

Second, there has been the collapse of communism. In the former Soviet Union and in Eastern Europe, the rebirth of the profit motive has combined with weak governments to form an entrepreneurial criminal culture. While the Chinese communist government has called growing rich good, it has been unable to control the crime unleashed.

Third, there is the declining significance of borders. As late as the 1960s, the Japanese were not allowed to travel abroad for pleasure. As recently as the 1980s, exit visas for those living in the Soviet Union, Eastern Europe, and China were a rarity. Now Czech prostitutes work the Italian Riviera, and Chinese immigrants to North America are trans-shipped through Central America. In Western Europe, people, goods, money, and arms move around in a virtually borderless world.

This section will look, in particular, at cases of the global drug trade. The following paragraphs also will discuss the lack of control over global banking, especially the issue of money-laundering, and people smuggling.

The Drug Trade

The global dimensions of the drug trade may be seen in eight ways. The most obvious dimension is that peasants grow coca bushes, which produce cocaine, and opium poppies, which produce heroin, to meet foreign demand for them.[71] Attempts to get peasants to grow alternative crops, such as potatoes in Bolivia, have usually failed because these are not as profitable as drugs. If there were no overseas demand, the peasants would be obliged to cultivate other crops.

Second, the United States, the world's largest importer of drugs, and other developed countries have difficulty in discouraging countries from supplying the market, which is indifferent to U.S. interests or those of other countries. The American population is so fond of drugs that marijuana is now their second largest cash crop (after corn); therefore, peasants from the supplying countries can argue that if U.S. citizens are so determined to have drugs, they should not be denied. If a group of peasants were to give up growing drugs, this also would only reduce the supply, forcing the price up and encouraging others to get into the trade. Additionally, there is the irony that drugs kill fewer Americans, along with Australians, Britons and others, than tobacco and alcohol; yet these latter substances not only remain legal, but also are a source of lucrative taxation for governments. Peasants cannot understand why their products should attract odium while others do not. Rensselaer White wrote that the solution does lies not in the Andean jungles but in the United States: the six million people who now consume cocaine must be persuaded to change their habits.[72]

Third, given the extent of foreign trade, it is difficult for customs officials to locate drug shipments. For example, drugs are often shipped in foodstuffs, such as yams, hollowed-out coconuts and canned oranges. U.S. customs officials can only check about 3 percent of the nine million shipping containers that enter ports annually. Meanwhile, Colombia (the world's fourth largest opium producer after Burma, Laos, and Afghanistan) has found a new market in Europe. Much of the traffic is going through Eastern Europe, arriving via large-container cargo shipments and moving into the West by truck or rail. The hottest new market for cocaine is Russia, a country in which the drug has become a status symbol of the newly rich.[73]

Fourth, foreign responses to drug growing and trafficking may clash with other priorities. Burma (Myanmar), which is the world's largest opium producer providing 60 percent of the heroin on the U.S. market, provides a good example of this conflict. The ruling regime, still generally known as the State Law and Order Council (SLORC) does not control the drug-producing areas. Although the U.S. Drug Enforcement Administration (DEA) has worked with SLORC to oppose the drug barons such as Khun Sa, the SLORC-DEA cooperation has been opposed by the State Department. SLORC nullified a general election won by opposition leader Aung San Suu Kyi and killed thousands of protesters. The United States and most other western countries have minimal contact with SLORC. Thus, the DEA claims that this concern with human rights is eroding the campaign against the drug barons.

In Afghanistan, where the strict Islamic Taliban regime opposed the growing of opium poppy, a conflict of interest also has arisen. Afghanistan has been for some years one of the world's major producers of the poppy. The U.S. government, while never recognizing the Taliban regime, did welcome its strong stand against poppy production—which was a change from the policy of earlier regimes. (Ironically, the Taliban regime hosted Osama bin Laden and provided a base for his activities.) The U.S. attitude toward the Talban regime obviously changed after September 11.

Fifth, U.S. drug enforcement policy does not always recognize two basic principles of the Westphalian System: the sovereignty and self-determination of other countries. These two principles theoretically mean that a country cannot without permission invade the territory of another to capture a fugitive. To address this problem, countries have bilateral extradition treaties with each other which govern the handing over of such fugitives. However, to observe such treaties takes time and warns the fugitives that they are being pursued; to just go into a country and smuggle out the pursued is easier. The United States has done this several times in recent years with alleged drug traffickers, such as General Noreiga who was grabbed with much publicity and full-scale invasion of Panama in 1989.

A less dramatic grabbing, that of Humberto Alvarez-Machain, resulted in a case before the U.S. Supreme Court in 1992.[74] Enrique Camarena-Salazar, Special Agent of the U.S. DEA, was abducted, tortured and murdered by drug dealers in Mexico in 1985. The DEA went to great lengths to bring the murderers to justice. It resorted to kidnapping, from Mexico, some of those believed to be responsible for Camarena's death to then appear in U.S. courts. Mexico officially protested the kidnappings. On April 2, 1990, Humberto Alvarez-Machain, a medical practitioner and a Mexican citizen, was abducted from his office in Guadalajara, Mexico, by several armed men and flown by private aircraft to the United States where he was arrested by the DEA. Accused of using his medical skills to keep Camarena alive during the interrogation, Alvarez complained to the U.S. Supreme Court that his abduction violated the 1978 U.S.–Mexican Extradition Treaty. The Court decided that the U.S. courts could try a Mexican national, even though his presence was the result of abduction rather than extradition pursuant to the 1978 treaty.[75] A country with the resources of the United States apparently can run its own kidnapping operations, rather than wait for extradition proceedings to take their course.[76]

Sixth, there is the irony that poor countries sell drugs to developed countries in order to earn money for repaying the banks in those developed countries. Susan George, of the Amsterdam-based Transnational Institute, has spent over three decades monitoring the economic crisis in the developing countries, especially the consequences of those countries owing money to foreign banks.[77] She looked at six ways in which the actions of indebted countries to earn money to repay the debt bounce back to harm people in the developed countries. One of the six ways is the drug trade, especially in Bolivia, Colombia, and Peru, whose foreign currency-earning activities create problems for the U.S. law enforcement system.

Seventh, Alvin Toffler included the leaders of drug cartels as members of the "global gladiators."[78] Governments find it increasingly difficult to deal with these new actors on the world stage. Governments are too bureaucratic; their response times are too slow. Linked into so many foreign relationships requiring consultation with allies and catering to so many domestic political interest groups, governments cannot react quickly to initiatives by drug lords, religious fanatics, and guerrillas. By contrast, many of the "global gladiators," guerrillas and drug cartels in particular, are nongovernmental and nonbureaucratic. While a single charismatic leader often makes the decisions, identifying the leader and knowing whom the government can make a deal with is sometimes unclear. If a deal is possible, how is one to know if the people making it can actually deliver? Can they really return hostages, stem the flow of drugs, prevent bomb attacks on embassies, or cut down on piracy?

Finally, ironically, there are allegations that U.S. intelligence agencies profit from some aspects of the drug trade. Peter Dale Scott and Jonathan Marshall have examined the CIA's role in drug and weapons sales in Central and Latin America.[79] They argue that trafficking flourishes under the protection of intelligence agencies because these agencies find the traffickers' political influence and arms networks useful. When drug barons are removed, their place is simply taken by a new set of people; so little is to be gained by "wars on drugs."

Money Laundering

The biggest bank fraud in world financial history was centered on the Bank of Credit and Commerce International (BCCI), in which about $9.5 billion in U.S. dollars was lost or stolen. The British newspaper *The Guardian* commented at the time that the first lesson of the BCCI collapse was that an international mechanism to police the highly mobile funds—legal and illegal—which can be shifted around the world via computers without adequate control, needed to be created.[80] Governments in the 1980s opted for international financial deregulation, but not for the international surveillance which should go with it. (As has been noted above with the UN, governments are often slow to work together). BCCI was based in the secret tax havens of Luxembourg and the Cayman Islands. Owned by Arab money and run by Pakistanis, it was not only rudderless but stateless as well, with no central bank standing behind it. Although the Bank of England did well to marshal a global clampdown at short notice, the question of why a bank which had been indicted for laundering drug money and which secretly bought control of two American banks was allowed to get away with it for so long was not answered.

BCCI was formed in 1972 by Agha Hasan Abedi, born at Lucknow, India. A major backer was the very wealthy Sheikh Zayed of Abu Dhabi, President of the United Arab Emirates (UAE). Opening its first branch in 1973 in London, BCCI was incorporated in Luxembourg, with a holding company in the Cayman Islands. It particularly attracted overseas Asians as clients and claimed to be the Third World's banker (especially for those actually living in the First World). It also sponsored activities such as the Third World Foundation, the magazine *South*, and the journal *Third World Quarterly*, which published articles from respected writers. Before closing, BCCI had operated in 73 countries—and in all the major financial centers; it was one of the world's fastest growing banks.

However, BCCI had three major defects. First, it always had a shaky financial foundation: Most of its equity capital was fake. Equity capital is the foundation of a company. When any company is established, investors contribute money and receive shares of stock in return. If the company becomes profitable, some of the profits may be retained by the company to strengthen the capital base. If the firm loses money, the equity serves as a kind of shock absorber. If a bank loses money, the equity capital gives it time to reorganize itself. BCCI reassured people that its equity capital came from some of the world's richest men, the oil-rich sheikhs in the UAE and elsewhere in the Persian Gulf. While some of the initial money had come from these men, some of the rest had been lent by BCCI to those men, who in turn supplied it to BCCI as equity capital.

Second, BCCI operated on the basis of the world's largest Ponzi racket: BCCI senior staff looted the deposits in their reckless lending and trading, necessarily using current deposits as the operational capital of the bank. As long as people continued to make fresh deposits, there was a flow of money to cover the losses.

Third, as reported by financial writers Peter Truell and Larry Gurwin, BCCI had some shady customers.[81] BCCI was a banker for Abu Nidal, the Palestinian guerrilla leader. It was a financial intermediatory between the United States and Iran (the "Irangate" arms scandal). It also lent money to both sides during the Iran-Iraq war to buy weapons. Looking after the money of rulers who wished to keep their funds (often stolen from their citizens) offshore, BCCI provided superannuating schemes in the event of such rulers being overthrown. BCCI was also the bank of drug traffickers; Burma's Khun Sa, for example controlled 80 percent of the region's drug trade and had at least $300 million in U.S. dollars deposited with BCCI in mid-1991.[82]

The question then arises as to why BCCI got away with so much for so long. Partly it was because, as Truell and Gurwin explained, BCCI had friends in high places, such as the CIA. BCCI generated tremendous goodwill at the CIA by assisting in a series of sensitive covert operations. BCCI's relationship with U.S. intelligence was so close that questions have been raised about whether the CIA was one of the original sponsors of BCCI—and even one of the beneficiaries of its larceny.[83] It also attracted respectable figures of high profile, such as former British Prime Minister Jim Callaghan, former President Jimmy Carter and former Secretary of State Henry Kissinger. Although none of these people was involved in any of BCCI's illegal activities, they gave a veneer of respectability to the organization. BCCI also was ruthless in using libel laws to punish any newspaper or magazine trying to expose it; for example, it contributed to the demise of the *New Statesman* magazine in the United Kingdom through litigation.

However, the primary reason for the BCCI getting away with so much was that is operated globally. There is, as *The Guardian* newspaper pointed out, no global system for regulating banking or, for that matter, checking on auditing arrangements. National banking authorities may have had information about potentially criminal activities, but they had no way of focusing their concerns.

Ironically, demise of BCCI happened through the decision of Manhattan District Attorney Robert Morgenthau to investigate alleged BCCI crimes in New York (an interesting example of thinking globally and acting locally). It was the threat of their tolerance of inappropriate banking behavior being exposed in a New York court that suddenly forced national authorities to act on the information which they had accumulated over the years but had done nothing about. The shutdown came swiftly. On July 5, 1991, national authorities, such as the Bank of England, closed down BCCI operations throughout much of the West, the Caymans, and Hong Kong, then British crown colonies, The shutdown revealed another problem for banking authorities: Almost all of the BCCI small customers were honest people having no connection with the criminal activities but having their assets frozen and perhaps dissipated for good. By allowing the scam to go on for so long, national banking authorities had made the eventual shutdown all the more painful for small customers.[84] BCCI owed money to 800,000 depositors with 1.2 million accounts in over 70 countries. Some progress has been made in securing some repayment to the account holders.[85]

BCCI founder Agha Hasan Abedi was sought on criminal charges in the United States and United Arab Emirates. He fled to Pakistan that refused to extradite him. He died there a free person in 1995.

People-Smuggling

People-smuggling is a global crime worth $7 billion per year in U.S. dollars and involving four million people each year.[86] The International Organization for Migration estimates that there are at least 50 criminal gangs involved in smuggling people. It is ironic that ministers for immigration do not know who runs each network, but a poor rural peasant in can find out and use the scheme to travel overseas via Central America to Los Angeles or New Jersey.[87]

The smuggling of people has five features worth noting in a study of globalization. First, it shows the weakness of national governments in fighting crime. Crime is global, but police forces are only national. There is not only no international police force, but also only limited cooperation between national forces in combating people smuggling.

Second, this level of people-smuggling could only take place because there is a high degree of corruption in national and local police forces as well as immigration services. Fifty-eight Chinese nationals from Fujian province in June 2000 perished in a air-tight refrigeration section of a truck amid a cargo of tomatoes on route to England's port city of Dover. They had been traveling for four months. They had passed through more countries and immigration control posts than the ordinary foreign tourist from a developed country would do on an annual vacation. Traveling from Fujian province to Bejing, they had passed through Moscow, the Czech Republic, and the Netherlands before reaching England. Although the Chinese nationals had crossed half of the world and passed many officials, the operation was only detected when it went wrong finally in Dover. They almost succeeded in their quest for freedom.

Third, people-smuggling is not done by the quickest or most direct routes. Instead, the routes zigzag via the countries with the weakest defenses. The smugglers use routes where officials can be bribed or where the immigration posts lack the modern technology to detect forged documents, such as fake passports.

Fourth, people-smuggling is lucrative and low-risk; criminals easily can make money and get away with it. The few people who do get caught are the people being smuggled or the people transporting them. Sometimes called "snakeheads," the main organizers usually are not apprehended.

Finally, the process is just an additional form of smuggling for all the other items that already get illegally transported across borders, such as drugs and pornographic videos. Since smuggling links were already in place and doing well, people could simply become another form of cargo. The most tragic problem with this cargo of course, is that people die. The Chinese at Dover died because of a lack of air. People trying to get into Australia die at sea or land in deserted places on the northern coast where they die from thirst and hunger. Most of their bodies are never found. In hot climates, a body rots away in only a few hours. People landing in crocodile-infested waters get eaten. Therefore, many aspects of people-smuggling are horrific, yet some states may only half-heartedly discourage the practice.

Desperate, knowing that international cooperation will do little to stop them, and not always discouraged by their own countries, illegal migrants continue to take the risk. China is one state that may not dissuade its people from such migration. The extent to which Chinese authorities publish foreign material discouraging people from trying to leave China illegally is questionable. The Chinese authorities tell citizens that their state is a good place to live. Publishing foreign governmental material that warns of the punishments to illegal migrants would be a tacit admission that Chinese are trying to escape from a life that is not so good. Additionally, the success of people-smuggling may show that some Chinese authorities are corrupt and also involved in the criminal activities. With a population of 1.2 billion people, China also might not mind having a few of its citizens going to live overseas.

CONCLUSION

To conclude, criminals have been among the main beneficiaries of the globalization process. "Law and order" is often a popular issue at election times and political parties make promises about being "tough on crime" if elected. But their adherence to Westphalian logic blinds them to the need to work together to combat crime globally. Although they may want to tackle crime, they are unwilling to leave the Westphalian System's comfort zone and really work together. Interestingly, given the public concern about crime, this would be one area where such global co-operation would enjoy wide public support.

But politicians are still not willing to embark upon the level of global functional cooperation required to combat global crime.

It is interesting to note that the first international criminal treaty ever created by the UN was not done until December 2000: The treaty is the Convention Against Transnational Organized Crime. The agreement provides a legal framework for concerted action, including some possible domestic legislation, that would criminalize various activities: belonging to a criminal group, laundering money, and corrupting various processes. It also involves corporate liability, investigative techniques, witness and victim protection, law enforcement cooperation, and exchange of information, as well as technical assistance and training. The United States was one of the signatories. As with most UN treaties, the one against organized crime will take some years to come into effect. This is a welcome, if belated and modest, move.

If governments are not willing to have more functional cooperation on crime, it is not surprising that they have such a poor record on so many other matters. Thus, the globalization process rolls along by default, as will be seen in the next chapter.

NOTES

1. Susan Strange, "States, Firms and Diplomacy" *International Affairs*, January 1992, p. 11.

2. For a case study of the role of NGOs in the development of international humanitarian law, see: Keith Suter, *An International Law of Guerrilla Warfare: The Global Politics of Law-Making*, London: Pinter, 1984.

3. Frederick Clairmonte and John Cavanagh, *"Transnational Corporations and Global Markets: Changing Power Relations,"* Sydney: Transnational Corporations Research Project, University of Sydney, 1984, pp. 3–9.

4. Jean-Jacques Servan-Schreiber, *The World Challenge*, London: Collins, 1981, p. 250.

5. Dana Mead, *High Standards, Hard Choices: A CEO's Journey of Courage, Risk and Change*, New York: John Wiley, 2000, pp. 83–135.

6. Kenichi Ohmae, *The Borderless World*, London: Collins, 1990, p. 94.

7. Michael Osbaldeston and Kevin Barham, "Using Management Development for Competitive Advantage" *Long Range Planning*, December 1992, p. 19.

8. United Nations Conference on Trade and Development, *World Investment Report: Transnational Corporations and Integrated International Production*, New York: United Nations, 1993.

9. Peter Young, "Why the Royal HK Jockey Club Rode South," *MIS Magazine*, September 1992, pp. 26–31.

10. It has even been argued that not only are corporations often too big for government control, but also are even beyond the effective control of their own shareholders; managers run corporations for their own benefit. See: John Kenneth Galbraith, *The Culture of Contentment*, Boston: Houghton Mifflin, 1992, pp. 51–64.

11. Raymond Vernon, "Transnational Corporations: Where Are They Coming From, Where Are They Headed?" *Transnational Corporations*, August 1992, p. 7.

12. James Carrier, "Alienating Objects: The Emergence of Alienation in Retail Trade" *Man: The Journal of the Royal Anthropological Institute*, June 1994, p. 363.

13. Frederic Cantin and Andreas Lowenfeld, "Rules of Origin, the Canada-US Free Trade Agreement and the Honda Case" *American Journal of International Law*, July 1993, pp. 375–390.

14. "French Fries? Non! Frites? Oui!" *Business Week*, May 31 1999, pp. 4A2–4A8.

15. Alan Durning, "Asking How Much is Enough" in Lester Brown et al. (Editors) *State of the World 1991*, New York: Norton, 1991, p. 163.

16. Francis Kinsman, *Millennium: Towards Tomorrow's Society*, London: WH Allen, 1990, 135.

17. Louise Williams, *India's Consuming Passions*, The Sydney Morning Herald, June 4 1994, p 7.

18. Michael O'Hanlon, "Modernity and the 'Graphicalization' of Meaning: New Guinea Highland Shield Design in Historical Perspective," *Journal of the Royal Anthropological Institute*, September 1995, pp. 470–492.

19. See: Ernst von Weizacker et al., *Factor 4: Doubling Wealth—Halving Resource Use: The New Report to the Club of Rome*, London: Earthscan, 1997.

20. For an introduction, see: Clive Archer, *International Organizations*, London: George Allen & Unwin, 1983; Inis Claude, *Swords into Plowshares: The Problems and Progress of International Organization*, London: University of London Press, 1964.

21. J.E.S Fawcett, *The Law of Nations*, London: Penguin, 1971, pp. 176–177.

22. For an introduction, see: Elmer Bendiner, *A Time for Angels: The Tragicomic History of the League of Nations*, London: Weidenfeld & Nicolson, 1975.

23. H.G. Wells as quoted in: Ray Monk, *Bertrand Russell: The Spirit of Solitude*, London: Jonathan Cape, 1996, p. 370.

24. For an evocative photographic study of the League—with its delegations of elegant white male diplomats—in an era when it was a great deal easier to get access to VIPs than in the present security-conscious time, see the photographs of Erich Salomon (the man who inspired the phrase "candid camera"). Erich Salomon, *Portrait of an Age*, London: Macmillan, 1967.

25. Robert Cecil, *All the Way*, London: Macmillan, 1949, p. 190.

26. James Avery Joyce, *Broken Star—The Story of the League of Nations 1919–39*, Swansea: Christopher Davies, 1978, pp. 118–119.

27. For an introduction, see: *Basic Facts About the United Nations*, New York: United Nations Department of Public Information, 1992; M.R. Bustelo and P. Alston (Editors) *Whose New World Order? What Role for the United Nations?* Sydney: Federation Press, 1991; Adam Roberts and Benedict Kingsbury (Editors), *United Nations, Divided World*, Oxford: Clarendon, 1993; Keith Suter, *Reshaping the Global Agenda: The United Nations at Forty*, Sydney: United Nations Association, 1986.

28. See: Shabtai Rosenne, *The World Court: What it is and How it Works*, Dordrecht, The Netherlands: Kluwer, 1994.

29. See: Stanimir Alexandrov, *Reservations in Unilateral Declarations Accepting the Compulsory Jurisdiction of the International Court of Justice*, Dordrecht: Kluwer Academic Publishers, 1995; Renata Szafarz, *The Compulsory Jurisdiction of the International Court of Justice*, Dordrecht: Kluwer, 1993.

30. See: Richard Lillich (Editor), *Fact-Finding Before International Tribunals*, New York: Transnational Publishers, 1992.

31. See: Arkady Shevchenko, *Breaking with Moscow*, New York: Ballantine, 1985.

32. Dorothy Goresky, "Lanterns for Peace" in Thomas Perry (Editor), *Peacemaking in the 1990s: A Guide for Canadians*, West Vancouver: Gordon Soules, 1991, p. 61.

33. See: David Mitrany, *The Functional Theory of Politics*, London: Martin Robertson, 1975.

34. Rosalyn Higgins, *The Development of International Law Through the Political Organs of the United Nations*, Oxford: Oxford University Press, 1963, pp. 69–70.

35. H.V. Evatt as quoted in: Peter Crockett, *Evatt: A Life*, Melbourne: Oxford University Press, 1993, p. 212

36. See: Keith Suter, "The United Nations in 1992: Moving Out into Uncharted Waters," Graeme Gill et al. (Editors), *Beyond the Headlines: Politics—Australia and the World*, Sydney: Department of Government, University of Sydney, 1993, pp. 247–263.

37. The Swiss people were very great supporters of the League, which was based in their city of Geneva. But their enthusiasm was not matched by the political will of governments in other countries; so they feel let down by how those governments treated the League.

38. A good overview of this problem is: *Financing an Effective United Nations: A Report of the Independent Advisory Group on UN Financing*, New York: Ford Foundation, February 1993.

39. Quoted in supra note 25, p. 224.

40. See: Keith Suter, "The United Nations and the Gulf Conflict" in St. John Kettle and Stephanie Dowrick (Editors), *After the Gulf War: For Peace in the Middle East*, Sydney: Pluto, 1991, pp. 56–66.

41. Keith Suter, "Reforming the United Nations" in Ramesh Thakur (Editor), *Past Imperfect, Future Uncertain: The United Nations at Fifty*, London: Macmillan, 1998, pp. 189–204.

42. See: Frank Barnaby (Editor), *Building a More Democratic United Nations*, London: Frank Cass, 1991.

43. For an introduction, see: Clive Archer, *Organizing Europe: The Institutions of Integration*, London: Edward Arnold, 1994; Arthur Cockfield, *The European Union: Creating the European Market*, London: John Wiley, 1994; Andrew Evans, *A Textbook on European Union Law*, Oxford: Hart, 1998; Charles Grant, *Inside the House That Jacques Built*, London: Nicholas Brealey, 1994; Peter Stirk and David Weigall (Editors), *The Origins and Development of European Integration: A Reader and Commentary*, London: Pinter, 1999.

44. Lord Slynn of the British House of Lords has surveyed the extensive legal changes underway, such as the British Parliament having to ensure that its laws conform to those of the EU, the growth of Europe's mechanisms for protecting human rights, and devolution of power from Westminster to regional assemblies. See: The Lord Slynn of Hadley, "The United Kingdom is Changing: A Constitutional Look Around," *Australian International Law Journal*, 2000, pp. 215–233.

45. Ernest Wistrich, "Building and Extending the European Federal Union," *World Federalist Magazine*, # 2, 1994, p. 8.

46. For an introduction, see: Elise Boulding, *Building a Global Civic Culture: Education for an Interdependent World*, New York: Columbia University Teachers' College Press, 1988; Michael Edwards (Editor), *Beyond the Magic Bullet: NGO Performance and Accountability in the Post-Cold War World*, New York: Kumarian Press, 1996; Thomas Rochon, *Mobilizing for Peace: The Anti-Nuclear Movements in Western Europe,*

London: Adamantine, 1988; Peter Willetts (Editor), *Pressure Groups in the Global System*, London: Frances Pinter, 1982.

47. "The Decline of Nations and the Future of the UN," *World Watch* (Washington, D.C.), March/April 1996, p. 2.

48. "Statement by the Secretary-General on the Occasion of the Forty-Seventh Conference of Non-Governmental Organizations," New York: United Nations Press Release SG/SM/94/142, September 20, 1994, p. 2.

49. Michael O'Neill, *The Third America: The Emergence of the Non-Profit Sector in the United States*, San Francisco: Jossey-Bass, 1990.

50. "Numbers," *Time*, June 7, 1999, p. 22.

51. In New Zealand, the NGO dealing with the protection of birds alone has more members than all the political parties combined.

52. Maggie Black, *A Cause for Our Times: OXFAM, the first 50 years*, Oxford: Oxford University Press, 1992.

53. Douglas Johnston and Cynthia Sampson, *Religion: The Missing Dimension of Statecraft*, Oxford: Oxford University Press, 1994.

54. Dinah Shelton, "The Participation of Non-Governmental Organizations in International Judicial Proceedings," *American Journal of International Law*, October 1994, pp. 611–642.

55. See: Keith Suter, "British Atomic Tests in Australia" *Medicine and War*, July 1994, pp. 195–206.

56. A 1993 example of how the Australian Government is loathe to admit the existence of the peace movement is in a book by the Australian foreign minister: Gareth Evans, *Co-operating for Peace: The Global Agenda for the 1990s and Beyond*, Sydney: Allen and Unwin, 1993. An excellent book, it nevertheless ignores the work of the peace movement in all the issues discussed, including the fact that the peace movement had spent decades encouraging the Australian Government to pay attention to these issues in the first place!

57. E.F. Schumacher, *Small is Beautiful: Economics as if People Mattered*, New York: Harper & Row, 1975.

58. See: Andrew Chetley, *The Politics of Baby Foods: Successful Challenges to an International Marketing Strategy*, London: Frances Pinter, 1986.

59. Annelies Allain, "Influencing Inter-Governmental Organizations" in *Development Education: The State of the Art*, Geneva: United Nations Non-Governmental Liaison Service, 1986, pp. 143–144.

60. See: Adam Hochschild, *King Leopold's Ghost*, London: Macmillan, 1999.

61. Jonathan Blagbrough, "The Price of Sugar," *Anti-Slavery Reporter*, London: Anti-Slavery International, 1992, p. 28.

62. Anne-Marie Sharman, "Facts and Faxes: Campaigning on a World Stage," *Anti-Slavery Reporter*, London: Anti-Slavery International, 1992, p. 5.

63. See: David McTaggart and Robert Hunter, *Greenpeace III: Journey into the Bombs*, London: Collins, 1978.

64. Also see: Thomas Princen et al., *Environmental NGOs in World Politics*, London: Routledge, 1994.

65. See: Keith Suter, *Antarctica: Private Property or Public Heritage?* London: Zed, 1991.

66. Also see: Jim Falk, *Global Fission*, Melbourne: Oxford University Press, 1982; Thomas Rochon, *Mobilizing for Peace: The Anti-Nuclear Movements in Western Eu-

rope, London: Adamantine, 1988; David Scott, *"Don't Mourn for Me—Organize": The Social and Political Uses of Voluntary Organizations,* Sydney: Allen & Unwin, 1981; Cora Vellekoop-Baldock, *Volunteers in Welfare,* Sydney: Allen & Unwin, 1990; Paul Wehr, Heidi Burgess and Guy Burgess (Editors), *Justice Without Violence,* Boulder, CO: Lynne Rienner, 1994.

67. Richard Stanley, "Opening Remarks," *The United Nations and Civil Society: The Role of NGOs,* Muscatine, IA: The Stanley Foundation, 1999, pp. 9–10.

68. Charles Rogers, "The Changing Shape of Security for NGO Field Workers," *Together,* January/March 1998, pp. 9–11.

69. By contrast, the annual budget of the UN International Drug Control Program is about $70 million in total; see: Roger Clark, "Stocktaking after Two Sessions of the Commission on Crime Prevention and Criminal Justice," *Criminal Law Forum* Vol 4, No 3 (1993), p. 486.

70. "Drug Business Rakes in $520 billion" *The Australian,* December 17, 1994, p. 12.

71. See: Ben Whitaker, *The Global Connection: The Crisis of Drug Addiction,* London: Jonathon Cape, 1987.

72. Rensselaer Lee, *The White Labyrinth: Cocaine and Political Power,* New Brunswick, N.J.: Transaction, 1989, p. 3.

73. See: Francisco Thoumi, *Political Economy and Illegal Drugs in Colombia,* Boulder, CO: Lynne Rienner, 1994.

74. Jacques Semmelman, *"United States v. Alvarez-Machain. 112 S Ct. 2188,"* *American Journal of International Law,* October 1992, pp. 811–820. Also see: Malvina Halberstam, "In Defense of the Supreme Court Decision in *Alvarez-Machain,"* *American Journal of International Law,* October 1992, pp. 736–746.

75. Thus, Alvarez-Machain went on trial, but he was acquitted through a lack of evidence. In 1993, he then unsuccessfully brought a civil suit against the U.S. Government for the alleged kidnapping, assault and battery, false imprisonment, negligent and intentional infliction of emotional distress, as well as cruel, inhuman, and degrading treatment. See: "US Abduction of Mexican National as Violation of International Law," *American Journal of International Law,* October 1999, pp. 892–894.

76. Much the same could be said about unilateral U.S. police action; see: Ethan Nadelmann, *Cops Across Borders: The Internationalization of US Criminal Law Enforcement,* University Park PA.: Penn State Press, 1993.

77. Susan George, *The Debt Boomerang: How Third World Debt Harms Us All,* Sydney: Pluto, 1992.

78. Alvin Toffler, *Powershift,* New York: Bantam, 1990, p. 461.

79. Peter Dale Scott and Jonathan Marshall, *Cocaine Politics: Drugs, Armies and the CIA in Central America,* Berkeley: University of California Press, 1991. Also see: Jonathan Kwitney, *The Crimes of Patriots: A True Tale of Dope, Dirty Money and the CIA,* New York: Norton, 1987.

80. "The Bank That Got Away" *The Guardian* (London), July 8 1991, p. 5.

81. Peter Truell and Larry Gurwin, *BCCI: The Inside Story of the World's Most Corrupt Financial Empire,* London: Bloomsbury, 1992, p. 101.

82. Ibid, p. 210.

83. Ibid, p. xviii.

84. A sympathetic account of how these people have been badly treated is: Nick Kochan and Bob Whittington, *Bankrupt: The BCCI Fraud,* London: Gollancz, 1991, pp. 167–202.

85. "BCCI: Silver Lining," *The Economist* (London), June 27 1998, pp. 82–83.

86. These are 1996 figures from the International Organization for Migration; see: *People Smuggling Factsheet*, Canberra: Department of Immigration and Multicultural Affairs, 2000.

87. *Time* magazine did a detailed study of the trip of a Fujian peasant to New Jersey; see: "Coming to America," *Time*, May 1 2000, pp. 46–49.

5

The Characteristics of Globalization

INTRODUCTION

The Westphalian System is similar to the view that gave the world Newtonian physics and the industrial revolution. That worldview is based on categorization, strict divisions, and neat arrangements whether these are of scientific theories, machines, or national boundaries.

But the earth's biosphere is inter-related, fluid and messy. It is a world of complex systems, with everything connected to everything else. Canadian scientists Ranjit Kumar and Barbara Murck pointed out that in order to understand the world, humans divide it up into concepts, pieces, categories, and disciplines.[1] But the world itself is a single whole. There are no clear dividing lines between chemistry and physics, between land and sea, between Iran and Iraq, between human beings and nature—except lines made in the human mind. Even when people do recognize the world's complex interconnections, they are often surprised by these interdependencies as well as causes and effects very far apart in place or time. A drought in Canada affects wheat prices in Ghana. Pesticides applied to agricultural fields may show up in ground water 10 years later, causing cancer 30 years after that. Many of these connections are traceable and knowable, if people look for them. However, if humans are not used to crossing conceptual categories and seeing interrelationships, they will not manage things very well and will sometimes be unpleasantly surprised.

This chapter argues that the world is becoming functionally more homogenous but politically more heterogeneous. In other words, factors such as technology, finance, and communications are overriding nation-state borders, while people within those borders are ceasing to have the national uniformity required by the Westphalian System. The previous chapter argued that there are signs of both global order and disorder. While signs of both also run throughout this chapter, the notion of disorder has predominance.

This chapter examines the five main characteristics of globalization that are sweeping over the Westphalian System: (i) the way that many problems are global in nature, (ii) fragmentation and reconfiguration of the world's political and economic systems, (iii) the erosion of the distinction between domestic and foreign policies, (iv) the importance of new technology, and (v) the reaction against globalization.

GLOBAL PROBLEMS

Transnational plagues, diseases, pollution, shortages of resources, and crime are not new problems. But in recent decades they have acquired a greater global character.

Thus, this survey of the characteristics of globalization begins with the most obvious characteristic: the expansion of global problems. The survey looks at four such examples: plagues, diseases, pollution, and the shortages of resources. It concludes with a note about the UN's lack of progress in protecting the environment.

Plagues and Diseases

Rats have killed far more people throughout history than warfare.[2] Bubonic plague is caused by the bacteria *Yersinia pestis,* which is carried by rats and the fleas which live on rats. When an infected flea bites a human, it can transmit the disease. Pneumonic plague occurs when the disease spreads to the lungs and can be passed from human to human through the air by coughing or heavy breathing.

Similarly, while natural disasters attract considerable media coverage, far more people are killed by disease. In 1999, while natural disasters killed some 80,000 people, 13 million people died from infectious diseases.[3]

HIV/AIDS

The HIV/AIDS epidemic is the most well known current crisis in infectious diseases. From a globalization perspective, there are nine points worth noting. First, there is the extent to which the disease has spread in just over two decades. The December 2000 figures from the Joint United Nations Program on HIV/AIDS (UNAIDS, website: http://www.unaids.org) show the following. There have been 21.8 million deaths from AIDS since the beginning of the epidemic in the late 1970s, 4.3 million of them children. Africa is the most affected region, with an estimated 25.3 million adults and children living with the virus. The global total of people living with AIDS is about 36.1 million.

Second, while the media devote so much attention to natural disasters and wars in Africa, the real problem is AIDS. More people died of AIDS in 2000 alone than in all the wars ever fought on the African continent. As was argued in chapter 1, the media do not always provide an accurate view of what is happening in the world. The colorful and dramatic events overshadow the more important matters.

Third, transnational corporations have been criticized for the high prices of their medicines to combat the disease. Most people in developing countries cannot afford them. Owing to intellectual property restrictions, developing countries cannot copy the medicines to make cheaper versions available. Additionally, the HIV virus has mutated; sub-type B, which is predominant in Western countries, receives 90 percent of the research attention. Yet up to 95 percent of people infected are in the Third World, where other viruses are involved.

Fourth, the HIV/AIDS epidemic is intensifying poverty. The disease is leading to a shortage of skilled labor because of the loss of educated people dying in the prime of their lives: Years of progress and investment are being reversed. It is not possible to predict what the long-term consequences will be for a country's economic development. It is clear that many African countries are in trouble. But there is far less information on, say, India, which is developing rapidly and could become a major economic power in the twenty-first century. If HIV/AIDS becomes a major health problem in India, as is currently being suggested by the infection rates, the state may not become a major power.

Fifth, HIV/AIDS is a major threat to national security. While countries think of national security in terms of military threats and the need to protect borders from attack, HIV/AIDS has slipped into countries across those borders. HIV/AIDS is overwhelming health systems, creating millions of orphans, and decimating health workers and teachers faster than they can be replaced. Military forces are irrelevant to combat this invasion. Further, military expenditure diverts funds away from health services in developing countries.

Sixth, the new era is being recognized by the UN. In January 2000, the UN Security Council devoted a meeting specifically to discussing HIV/AIDS in Africa. Sixty percent of the Security Council's agenda is devoted to military conflicts in Africa. This was the first time that the Security Council had discussed a health issue.

Seventh, despite all the western governmental rhetoric, action does not match words. For example, Rachel Sacks of Body Positive Inc. wrote in 1999 about how little money the United States gives to AIDS control and care programs overseas.[4] The budget of the U.S. International Aid Agency is about $900 million, which is a smaller proportion of its national budget than any other country's national budget in the West. In 1998, only 12 percent ($121 million in U.S. dollars) was allocated to HIV/AIDS programs. By contrast according to the UN HIV/AIDS figures, the sum of money spent annually across the United States on coping with the medical consequences of obesity was $52 billion.

Eighth, there is a limit to what any government itself can do to combat HIV/AIDS within its borders. HIV/AIDS provides a formidable challenge partly because of the difficulty of changing societal, cultural, and gender norms as well as creating open dialogue about sex, empowerment of women, and the recognition of the role of men in responding to the pandemic. No government decree or planning document can do this. It requires a broad-based national effort involving NGOs such as religious groups, women's groups, and trade unions. They all have far greater contact with local people.

Finally, for people critical of globalization, the rise of HIV/AIDS can be seen as a vindication of their views. Some critics of globalization see it as a modernizing, destabilizing force which encourages people to stray from the strict paths laid down by traditions and religions. They see people becoming too focused on consumerism, the low moral tone of Hollywood movies, and good times. Now people in general are paying the consequences.

By contrast, people in a state of denial may unintentionally contribute to the spread of HIV/AIDS by not recognizing its reality, one spreading in their countries. Chris Beyrer, an American epidemiologist, investigated the different infection rates in southeast Asian countries and noted the way that some governments were more willing than others to acknowledge that there was a problem.[5]

Other Infectious Diseases

The study of infectious diseases has gone through a major change. *Time* magazine reported that a generation ago, no one had ever heard of Lyme or Legionnaire's disease, much less AIDS.[6] In the 1970s, medical researchers were even boasting that humanity's victory against infectious disease was just a matter of time. The polio virus had been tamed by the Salk and Sabin vaccines; the smallpox virus was virtually gone; the parasite that causes malaria was in retreat; once deadly illnesses, including diphtheria, pertussis, and tetanus, seemed like quaint reminders of a former era. The first widespread use of antibiotics in the years following World War II had transformed the most terrifying diseases known to humanity into mere inconveniences; if caught in time, even tuberculosis, syphilis, pneumonia, bacterial meningitis and even bubonic plague could be cured with pills or injections. Medical students in the 1960s were discouraged from going into infectious diseases because it was a declining specialty. They were encouraged to go into lifestyle diseases, such as cancer and heart disease.

There are two issues here. One is the explanation as to why there is now an upsurge in infectious diseases in particular countries. The second is why a disease in one country now becomes a threat to other countries. The two issues overlap, but this is book is principally concerned with the latter issue.

The main explanation for the latter issue is, of course, the globalization of the planet. The late Jonathan Mann, formerly of WHO and then at Harvard before being killed in an airline crash, explained that international tourist arrivals increased nearly 17-fold since 1950 and 1.2 billion air passengers took scheduled flights in 1990, of which about one-fourth crossed national borders.[7] The travel and tourist industry is now one the largest in the world, employing over 6 percent of the global work force and generating about $2 trillion in U.S.

dollar sales. Increases in the speed and extent of human movements have been paralleled by the expansion of international commerce, rapid transfers of capital unconstrained by national boundaries, and the increasing transnationalization of labor market competition.

Along with increased transportation, tuberculosis is returning. It has been around for about 8,000 years but was reduced after World War II because of medical progress. Medical authorities lowered their guard against it, thinking that it was on the way out. While research funds were cut back, public health programs focused on other issues. But, as *Newsweek* magazine reported in 1993, it was unwise to drop the guard.[8] *Mycobacterium tuberculosis* got on the modern transportation systems, searching for new breeding grounds. It found them in the ghettoes of the Western world, where tuberculosis had been neglected. It also found them among the beneficiaries of advanced health care in rich countries, where cancer chemotherapy and organ transplants can depress natural immunities. It found them in Eastern Europe, where people are now so overwhelmed by economic challenges that they delay check-ups and medical consultations. It found them all over the Third World, where poverty and social unrest often outrank health care in the priorities of politicians. And it found them among the weakened immune systems of HIV-infected people. About 1.7 billion people—one-third of the world's population—carry the tubercle bacillus. The overwhelming majority of carriers, about 90 percent, never develop the disease. But enough people do fall ill to concern WHO, which estimates there are eight million new cases of tuberculosis each year worldwide and three million deaths.

More people in developed countries also are now dying from malaria, which is principally a Third World disease. WHO has an annual research budget of only $6 million U.S. dollars for malaria. Transnational drug corporations estimate that a new drug would cost about $100 million to research, test, and register. But since no Third World country could afford to buy it, the development is not profitable. Consequently, First World tourists are still using Chloroquine and Malopim on their exotic travels and risking encounters with mosquitoes which are now resistant to those drugs. Although malaria is one of the world's major diseases, it gets overshadowed by medical conditions, such as heart attacks, which are far more prevalent in First World countries.

Meanwhile, other diseases may be dislodged from their comparatively isolated natural habitats and transported by modern systems into other parts of the world.[9] The standard examples are AIDS as well as the Marburg and Ebola viruses in Africa. Viruses are named after the place where they are first discovered. Marburg is in northern Germany; in 1967, seven workers in a factory that produced vaccines using kidney cells from African green monkeys from Uganda died from an unknown and rabies-like illness, which dissolved the bodies of its victims.

Richard Preston traveled through central Africa as a boy.[10] Years later as a scientific writer, he was back searching for the source of the Ebola virus, which horrifyingly kills within hours with contagious blood pouring out of every orifice. The Kinshasa Highway in central Africa used to be a dirt track, but it is now a modern highway, one of whose main travelers has been HIV/AIDS. HIV/AIDS used this highway (which runs across central Africa from the Congo's Pointe-Noire to Tanzania's Mombasa, via Lake Victoria, Mount Elgon, and Kitum Cave) to spread from the rain forest in about 1979 into an outbreak. If the virus had been noticed earlier, it might have been named the "Kinshasa Disease" to note the fact that it passed along the Kinshasa Highway during its emergence from the African forest. The paving of the Kinshasa Highway affected people on all continents and turned out to be one of the most important events of the twentieth century. Already costing millions of lives, HIV/AIDS will likely cause an ultimate number of human casualties exceeding the deaths in World War II.

As humans delve deeper into rainforests, they are encountering more exotic diseases. The emergence of HIV/AIDS, Ebola, Marburg and other rainforest agents appears to be a natural consequence of the ruin of the tropical biosphere. The emerging viruses are surfacing from ecologically damaged parts of the earth. While the HIV virus is slow-acting, Ebola is not. African victims have perished within a few days, thereby limiting its range of dispersion. But today a virus from the rainforest lives within a twenty-four hour aircraft flight from every city on earth. All of the earth's cities are connected by a web of airline routes. The web is a network. Once a virus hits the network, it can shoot anywhere in a day—wherever aircraft fly.

In October 1989, a strain of Ebola started killing 500 monkeys held at Hazleton Research Products, Reston, Virginia. Swift action by the U.S. Army Medical Research Institute of Infectious Diseases prevented the virus getting to humans. The monkeys had been imported from the Philippines. Although how these monkeys became ill with an African disease is not clear, it has been alleged that wealthy Philippine business people illegally import African animals for their own rainforest hunting expeditions.

Diseases, whether global or just confined to a small locality, emphasize the individual's interdependence with neighbors (be they across the street or across the planet). Diseases move from one person to another. Each person has a vested interest in the health of neighbors. Thus, ironically, it is in the interest of rich people that they pay for the health costs of people who cannot, for example, afford injections. To avoid doing so produces a false economy.

POLLUTION

Pollution has always crossed national boundaries.[11] Nowadays, however, there is far more pollution, and the impact on other countries is far worse. Here are the four most well known examples of this problem: climate, the hole in the ozone layer, acid rain, and marine pollution.

Climate change is currently the most controversial issue in the global environmental debate. There are various positions. There is a difference of opinion over whether or not there is a change actually underway; some doubt it. Among the people who do accept that there is a change, some think that the global temperature is heating up while a few think that the temperature will suddenly drop, causing a new ice age. For those who accept that there is any change underway, there is also a difference between those who think it is due to a change within nature, the sun is getting hotter, and those who think that human activities, such as industrialization, are to blame.

Earth already has its own greenhouse effect. The ground is kept warm because the air traps heat, as if under a pane of glass like in garden greenhouses. Thus, certain gases in the atmosphere, water vapor and carbon dioxide, are more transparent to solar radiation than to thermal radiation. In other words, these gases permit the sun's heat to fall onto the earth but then prevent the heat from bouncing back into space. The heat is thus trapped on the planet. The greenhouse effect contributes to the miracle of life on our earth. If it did not exist, then the planet would be too cold to sustain life.

Thus, the problem does not involve the greenhouse effect per se but the pollution added to it by humankind. There is a great deal of scientific consensus about there being some form of human-made greenhouse effect. The differences arise in assessing the size of the human-made impact and what will be the implications of this impact.

One impact is that there could be a rise in sea levels. This change would come about partly because of the melting of the polar ice caps, especially the ice in Antarctica. This continent, over half the size of continental United States, has over 90 percent of the earth's supply of ice. As warming water expands, the sea levels rise. These developments could cause coastal flooding. A second impact could be on agricultural cultivation. Since tropical environments would increase, their traditional diseases would be spread even more.

Among the challenges arising out of the speculation over climate change, that scientific evidence is still so unclear is one of the main ones. If evidence in favor of some form of greenhouse effect becomes more precise, another problem will be added, stopping the pollution going into the atmosphere. As Sir John Browne, CEO of British Petroleum (BP) said in May 1997, "[We] must now focus on what can and what should be done, not because we can be certain climate change is happening, but because the possibility can't be ignored."[12]

In addition as already pointed out, governments are not geared up to thinking in the long-term. Attention is focused on the time to either the next election or palace coup. Economic problems always seem more immediate and acute than environmental ones.

Lastly, progress in international law on reducing atmospheric pollutants is only being made very slowly. The June 1992 United Nations Framework Convention on Climate Change (UNFCCC) was signed at the UN Conference on

Environment and Development (UNCED). It is designed to stabilize greenhouse gas concentrations in the atmosphere at a level that would prevent dangerous human-made interference with the climate system. A "framework" treaty, it sets the basic obligation, with the more specific commitments to be adopted via later treaties, orprotocols. Including the United States, 181 countries have ratified it.

The Conference of the Parties (COP), the international body under the UNFCCC containing the countries that have ratified the UNFCCC, normally meets annually. COP 3 met in Kyoto, Japan, in 1997 and adopted the Kyoto Protocol setting legally binding obligations on those countries which ratify it to reduce their greenhouse gas emissions.[13] This was the first time that developed countries accepted in principle being bound to specific targets and timetables on greenhouse gas emissions. The protocol requires industrialized countries to cut greenhouse gas emissions by a total of 5.2 percent of 1990 levels between 2008 and 2012. Countries are now considering the ratification of it.

Meanwhile, COP 6 met in November 2000 in The Hague to devise schemes to put the Kyoto Protocol into operation, on the assumption that it eventually enters into force. The conference broke down without any agreement. There were 182 governments, and 323 intergovernmental organizations as well as NGOs, all amounting to a total of about 7,000 participants. The United States and some of its allies refused to provide funds and the transfer of technology to other countries for them to develop production processes that would emit fewer greenhouse gases. Developing countries meanwhile were critical of carbon sequestration proposals by developed countries; schemes to encourage the planting of trees in order to gain "carbon credits" to offset the emission of greenhouse gases were frowned upon by less powerful countries. It is not clear how the Kyoto process will continue. Although the Bush Administration said in early 2001 that it would not ratify the Kyoto Protocol, Japan and the European Union may carry on regardless.

Climate change is an example of the Westphalian System's flair for creating disorder. On the one hand, there are a global environmental problems so that the threats to the environment are now much greater than ever before. On the other hand, governments remain locked into the system of national sovereignty, which means that they cannot be forced to accept any international agreement. Even though governments make statements acknowledging the dangers to the environment, they are often unwilling to make the real changes necessary to protect the environment. Governments cannot be forced to accept any international obligations. National sovereignty means that each government governs its own territory.

These challenges are also seen in the context of the holes in the ozone layer. A separate problem from the greenhouse effect, the disintegration of this layer of atmosphere shares a common root with unnatural temperature increases: pollution. The ozone layer limits the amount of solar ultraviolet radiation reaching the earth. Such radiation can cause skin cancer and cataracts, depress the human immune system, and reduce crop, animal and fish yields. Excessive exposure to the sun has always been a danger; the holes in the ozone layer will add to that risk. Chloroflourocarbons and halons have been released into the atmosphere by the use of refrigerators, air conditioning systems, hamburger cartons, paint, hair sprays, and fire extinguishers. These gases rise into the stratosphere where they destroy the ozone molecules. The holes in the ozone layers have been appearing over the polar ice caps. There is speculation that the holes will get larger and so affect the much more populated areas of northern Europe, southern Latin America, South Africa, and Australia.

Acid rain, more accurately "acid air," comes from the emission of sulfur and nitrogen oxides by coal-fired power stations, heavy industry factories, and motor vehicles. Undergoing changes in the atmosphere, the chemicals fall as sulphuric and nitric acid in rain, mist, and snow. The acid rain not only kills forests and their wild life, but also erodes ancient buildings, such as cathedrals, and modern concrete ones. The problem crosses national boundaries because the pollution is carried by the prevailing winds.

Finally, there is the problem of marine pollution.[14] The sea was, for thousands of years, traditionally viewed as: inexhaustible (no matter how many fish or whales were taken from the sea, there were always more left); limitless (a person could sail for years without necessarily retracing their route), and indestructible (the sea could always absorb the garbage of humankind).

That view is changing. The sea, of course, is not inexhaustible. Some whales have been hunted to extinction, and others have almost disappeared. Nevertheless, for economic gain, Japan now wishes to end the global moratorium on whaling and resume the hunting, which turned it into a major whaling country. Commercial fishing indeed has reached a plateau: there are two many hunters chasing too few fish. If the total world fishing fleet were cut in half, the same amount of fish would be caught.

Second, our view of the sea as being limitless is also changing. The sea covers 70 percent of the globe's surface but, compared with the diameter of the planet, the sea is shallow. If the planet were reduced to the size of an egg, the total amount of water would be the size of a tear drop.

Finally, there is a fundamental unity in the composition of the seas: pollution that goes into the sea tends to stay there. There is little other place for it to go. There is some mass media attention to maritime disasters involving oil spills from tankers running aground. These are dramatic and eye-catching. But they are not necessarily the worst examples of marine pollution.

A problem involving pollution by transporting marine life arises with ballast water. For example, Japanese bulk cargo ships, which carry woodchips from Tasmania to Japan, have to fill up with ballast water in Japanese sea lanes to maintain their balance for the voyage to Tasmania. The ballast water contains *Asterias amurensis*, the northern Pacific starfish. This was first seen in Tasmanian waters in 1986 but was not identified until 1987. The Australian magazine *The Bulletin* reported in 1993 that the starfish feeds on mussels, oysters, scallops, and abalone but also preys on farmed shellfish, fish caught in nets, crabs, and even its own kind.[15] Each year millions of eggs hatch, releasing larvae that float with the currents before settling. The larvae have a high survival rate, and scientists believe that *Asterias* poses a threat to most of southern Australia and New Zealand.

The pollution conveyed by ballast water is global. The United States and Canada, for example, are having to deal with infestations of the introduced European Zebra mussel. The mussel now occurs in such numbers that it is rapidly out-competing native species, and clogging inlet pipes for ships and power plants.[16] Infected ballast water from some Asian and Latin American ports carries diseases such as cholera from one continent to another. The ballast water problem threatens the health of people using the water, as for swimming, in other countries. It also threatens the development of fish-farming, or aquaculture—itself a response to over-fishing—in the coastal areas. As the bulk cargo ships travel faster, the risk of the organisms surviving long enough on board to be a problem in distant waters increases.

Additionally, it is worth noting that 90 percent of the pollution in the sea comes from the land, such as garbage and agricultural fertilizers. Thus, a person who lives well inland may still be contributing to the sea's destruction.

To conclude, pollution does not recognize national boundaries. Transnational pollution levels were small until recent decades, and governments attempted to solve national pollution problems by national means. But now pollution has gone global.

RESOURCES

Resources are not evenly distributed around the world. Resources do not recognize nation-state boundaries. Since the availability of resources and the demand for them are often mismatched, foreign trade is needed.

Water is an example of a resource the shortage of which has the capacity to create conflict. The International Institute for Applied Systems Analysis in Vienna complained that water was neglected by the 1992 UN Conference on Environment and Development (UNCED).[17] It recommended that far more attention be given to this subjectand that the basic unit of analysis not be the nation-state but the river basin. Water systems in many cities in developed countries are nearing the end of their useful lives.

Developing countries face even greater water problems, especially from population growth. Over 90 percent of the babies born today are born in developing countries. Several Third World cities already have populations in the tens of millions. It is estimated that the provision of reasonable water supply and sanitation in these cities, even with their present populations, would cost 300–400 billion in U.S. dollars. Future water shortages are almost inevitable. Modest economic growth would probably worsen scarcities: higher incomes usually mean higher rates of water use. Efforts to study these problems are hampered by a lack of data, especially at the river basin level. The possibility of changes in climate, which could affect water supply, demand, and quality, only further increase the uncertainty.

Dealing with these problems will require new approaches. Questions of water quality and quantity can no longer be addressed separately. Efforts much be made to break institutional barriers and to integrate policies for land use and water management. Therefore, it is important to address problems at the scale of river basins, the natural hydrological unity, rather than at the nation-state level.

The next major conflict in the Middle East is as likely to be over water as over oil.[18] Israel, for example, has a serious water problem. The water comes from three main sources: the Sea of Galilee and two aquifers (underground supplies). One aquifer runs down the coast of Israel, and the second begins in the territory of the West Bank, now under Palestinian control, before flowing underground into Israel itself. The Palestinians, with their high population growth rate, are even more short of water. A possible solution would involve one or two water pipes that would transfer water from eastern Turkey's rivers across to the Middle East and provide for all the countries of the region. Unfortunately, international politics, for the moment anyway, would rule out such a solution.

Another hydrological flashpoint is the Mekong River, one of the world's longest rivers, which begins on the Tibetan plateau and wends its way through southeast Asia into southern Vietnam and then into the South China Sea. The UN Development Program (UNDP) has been encouraging Thailand, Vietnam, Cambodia, and Laos to work together on how it is to be used. All four countries are anxious to use the river for hydroelectric purposes to fuel their economic revolutions. The work will be a major project for construction companies, bankers, and water engineers. But hydroelectric uses threaten the fishing and agricultural uses of the river. The Mekong's watersheds receive hardly any rain in the early months of the year, allowing salt water from the South China Sea to penetrate 500km inland, as far as the middle of Cambodia. But monsoon rains in May transform the Mekong. The water-flow into the Vietnam delta increases 30-fold and certain stretches of the river can rise by as much as a six-story building. The annual reversal of the flow of water back into Cambodia's economic heart, the Tonle Sap lake, fuels one of the world's most productive fresh-water fish industries. Ninety percent of the fish spawned in the Mekong river basin spawn not in the river but in submerged forests and fields. Among the many complex arguments against the rapid development of dams is that the dams might hold back silt and so decrease downstream fertility. Dams also risk increasing incursions of salt water and worsen flooding.

To conclude, the Westphalian System does not provide a good way of handling resources. Indeed, the very mixed interests between resources and national requirements may exacerbate tensions among countries and so help lead to armed conflict.[19]

THE WESTPHALIAN SYSTEM AND THE ENVIRONMENT

One of the UN's most important conferences in the 1990s was the 1992 Rio Conference on the Environment and Development (UNCED). This was held among speculation over both a hole in the ozone layer over Antarctica and a greenhouse effect. These were separate matters, but the media ran them together and got people worried about the environment. Environment NGOs reported increased memberships.

UNCED was one of the largest gatherings of heads of state/heads of government in world history. Including over 100 heads of state/government, 178 countries were represented. This was an indication of just how much attention was now focused on environment and development matters (especially by the global mass media and NGOs). There were also 1,420 accredited NGOs with a total of 15,000 personnel.

A number of important documents, including the UN Framework Convention on Climate Change, were adopted. However, not much else of substance came from all this effort. First, very little money was pledged at Rio—about $3 billion U.S. dollars. This amount equaled about three days' expenditure on the arms race. The UNCED Secretariat had estimated that $125 billion in U.S. dollars ought to be spent on the issues raised at the conference. The UN Environment Program itself operates on the minute budget of about $40 million U.S. dollars, less than the total international budget of Greenpeace. Governments remained reluctant to commit funds to international cooperation.

Governments from developed countries were under pressure to reaffirm their commitment to foreign aid. The UN General Assembly has had a target figure of 0.7 percent of gross national product (GNP) as foreign aid, which was originally set over three decades ago. Eventually the Western governments did reaffirm it at Rio, and a few said they would try to achieve it by the year 2000. But, a decade later, almost all of them have failed to do so. Indeed, there is a trend in reducing foreign aid, with some countries, including the United States, now giving the lowest amount gauged by the GNP since records began four decades ago. According to the UNICEF 2002 Report, only Denmark, the Netherlands, Sweden, Norway, and Luxembourg out of the 22 western countries have met their obligations; the average amount of aid is 0.22 percent; and the United States is at the bottom of the list with 0.10 percent.[20]

Second, UNCED did not deal with the problem of population growth which was seen as too divisive. Some Third World countries were sensitive to allegations that the world's environment problem were due to their population explosions, rather than the lifestyles of developed countries. Also the Bush Administration was influenced by pro-life, conservative, Christian NGOs into opposing any UN action on birth control. (1992 was a presidential election year, and Bush was anxious not to alienate conservative Christian NGOs.) The Holy See and Iran were among the delegations working together to prevent the item from being on the conference agenda.

Finally, the only explicit institutional change was the recommendation for a UN Commission on Sustainable Development. UNCED was not used as an opportunity, for example, to recommend the creation of a world authority for protecting the environment, to introduce an international environmental tax, or to act on any suggestions on UN reform then being circulated by NGOs. In other words, UNCED skirted around the structural challenges presented by the global protection of the environment.

The 1993, the UN General Assembly agreed to create the Commission on Sustainable Development. The Commission meets annually for two weeks with delegations from governments. NGOs have an observer status, watching the proceedings but not voting. While the commission monitors progress in environmental protection, it has no binding decision-making powers. It makes recommendations that governments are at liberty to ignore. By 2002, UNCED had achieved little.

FRAGMENTATION AND RECONFIGURATION

The Westphalian System gave the world a sense of order and predicability. Just how uniform was that system? In chapter 2, this book argued that the system from the outset contained four major ambiguities. Nonetheless, the mythic quality of the Westphalian System was substantial: It governed the outlook of people and governments for centuries. It still does hold tremendous sway over people, government, and the mass media. But the state of the today's world cannot be easily explained by the Westphalian System.

This section looks at three lots of instances in which the apparently neat nation-state system is being fragmented and reconfigured. The instances include the end of the traditional Third World, the rise of what is know as localization, and the changed role for governments.

THE END OF THE THIRD WORLD

The Third World, as a political term, arose during the Cold War as a way of identifying countries that did not want to be aligned with either the United States and its allies (the First World) or the U.S.S.R. and its allies (the Second World). Even at the height of the Cold War, the term was very elastic since some member countries tilted towards the United States, as Indonesia did after the Suharto coup in 1965, and some tilted towards the U.S.S.R., as did India and Cuba.

In economic terms which included UN standards, the Third World was called the G-77 (Group of 77), being 77 countries that were developing and not part of the other two worlds. The First World was grouped together within the Paris-based Organization for Economic Co-operation and Development (OECD), which had a membership of 24 countries. Membership of OECD carried with it the obligation to give foreign aid to the G-77.

In both political and economic terms, the Third World is in decline. Politically, it is difficult to have a "Third" world if the "Second" world has joined or is trying to join the "First" one. The Cold War is over, and some of the former Warsaw Treaty Organization countries have joined NATO. Additionally, the Third World has lost an important rallying point: All member-states were opposed to *apartheid* in South Africa. The ending, in 1994, of the white minority racist regime and the election of President Nelson Mandela meant that South Africa was itself able to join the NonAligned Movement.

Meanwhile, the economic basis of the G-77 is fragmenting. In 1994, Mexico was the first country to move from the G-77 to the OECD. Mexico's new status was not just due to its economic growth but also to the (US-Canadian-Mexican) North American Free Trade Agreement among the United States, Canada, and Mexico; this trade agreement made distinguishing between the U.S. and Mexican economies difficult. As the economic distinction between Mexico and the OECD largest economy, that of the United States, is fading rapidly, forecasters can easily count Mexico in.

Meanwhile, the former Second World is also fragmenting. The U.S.S.R. boycotted the UN's financial agencies, the World Bank and International Monetary Fund, and obliged its East European allies to do the same. The agencies were seen as tools of Western capitalism. However, the 15 constituent parts of the former Soviet Union, now known officially as "countries in transition," as well as the Eastern European countries, have all now joined the financial agencies, and receive loans from them.

The First World will also change. It has become a victim of its own success. The new members will bring fresh opportunities and problems, for example, OECD meetings will cease to be small intimate affairs and will gradually become large gatherings, like mini-UN General Assemblies. Thus, the nature of the work will change if only due to the number of participants.

THE RISE OF LOCALIZATION

The Westphalian System is being eroded by both forces running across national boundaries and by the evolution of localization. The historian Paul Kennedy argued that the current relocation of authority from the nation-state to smaller units is also chiefly driven by economic and technological developments.[21] The breakdown of borders across Europe because of the European Union, for example, permits the emergence (in many cases, the re-emergence) of regional economic zones, which had been barred by national customs and tariff systems. As new trading relationships develop, the former ones fade: Slovenia trades increasingly with Austria and less with Serbia; Alsace-Lorraine becomes more integrated with Baden-Wurttemberg than with Paris; and northern Italy develops closer links with Alpine states than with Calabria or Sicily. Individual American states, often frustrated by the lack of interest shown by the federal government, open their own missions in Tokyo and Brussels in order to conduct investment and trade diplomacy. Russian cities like St. Petersburg declare themselves free-trade zones in order to attract foreign investment.

A similar view comes from Wouter van Dieren, Director of the Institute for Environment and Systems Analysis in Amsterdam, who is skeptical that the Maastricht Treaty will create a real European Union.[22] It may, instead, just break up Western Europe into a lot of local regions. Europe could break up into dozens of regions, like Flanders and Wallonia, Northern Italy, Catalania, Carinthia, and the new, small countries of Eastern Europe.

In 1992, the Stanley Foundation convened a conference which looked at the changing global situation and its domestic U.S. implications.[23] The conference examined a regional trend in the Pacific Northwest. Regional economic interdependencies are often more important than political boundaries; for example, businesses in Seattle see Japan as a neighbor and valued trading partner, while regarding New York and the East Coast as distant. A further illustration is the regional economic community that has developed across the United States-Canadian border among five American states and two Canadian provinces without the approval of Washington, D.C. or Ottawa. Similar, albeit less organized, trends are visible in the southwestern United States.

Within the global process of urbanization, the world is becoming a planet of cities, which overshadow small nation-states.[24] In Latin America, for example, 75 percent of Brazilians live in urban areas, a third of Argentinians live in Buenos Aires, and Mexico City has a population of about 30 million (almost half of the country's population).

The United States is too large an economy to be dominated by any one city, but Los Angeles provides another challenge to the idea of the nation-state.[25] Los Angeles is the world's second largest Hispanic city, after Mexico City. British journalist Simon Winchester has noted Los Angeles's size: It will soon overtake New York to become America's largest city, the only city of the Western industrialized world still to be growing.[26] By 2010, Los Angeles will have 19 million people, and the total value of the region's output is currently growing each year by 3.5 percent. John McDonnell, an Australian trade adviser, has pointed out that Los Angeles is now the fourth or fifth biggest economy in the world following only the United States as a whole, Japan, Germany, the United Kingdom.[27] Los Angeles has a bigger economy in terms of GDP than France or Italy.

In terms of economic size, Los Angeles would deserve to be an important UN member-country in its own right, its economy being even be larger than most nonpermanent members of the Security Council. But Los Angeles, under the current nation-state system will not get that right.

This is in contrast with the UN's 184th member-nation which joined the organization in July 1993. Andorra, on the Pyrenes between France and Spain, has a population of about 47,000 people, living in an area of 453 square kilometers. In due course, it will be eligible for election for a two-year term on the UN Security Council.

A CHANGED ROLE FOR NATIONAL GOVERNMENTS

Although national governments will not disappear in the new global era, they will have to adjust to a new role. This applies particularly in national economic policy. In business, there is a distinction between rule makers, corporations which set the lead in a particular market, and the rule takers, corporations which have to follow the lead of the rule makers.[28] While governments in the twentieth century were the rule makers of national economic policy, they now are moving into the role of rule takers, as other entities gradually set the running. In short, governments are losing control over the macro-development of their economies and are being obliged to focus on the micro-development.

The essence of the change is the end of the Keynesian Revolution.[29] The British economist John Maynard Keynes (1883–1946), responding to the Great Depression of the early 1930s, said that the government should intervene in the economy. The Keynesian breakthrough involved not so much argument for public works programs, as President Roosevelt was doing, but persuasion that Western governments must acknowledge the economy to be a government responsibility which should not be left solely to the market. Therefore, he argued that during a recession, governments should put money into circulation to stimulate economic activity, such as through tax cuts and public works programs, and, during an economic boom, increase taxation to prevent inflation.

But beginning in the 1970s, a new generation of economists came along who believed that Keynesian thinking no longer worked and that it was necessary to reduce the government intervention in the economy.[30] They preferred free trade, deregulation, privatization. When the U.S. Republicans were in power, the Conservatives had the upper hand in the United Kingdom and Labor in Australia and New Zealand. But the policies were very similar. Different party labels did not mean much.

Therefore, Western governments are now focusing on the detailed (micro) operations of the economy and other aspects of life for two reasons. First, they are losing control over the macro-development of the national economies. This is not a sudden transition; it is a process of evolution. Alan Wolfe, professor of sociology at the City University of New York has argued that the economy is not a sphere of activity separate from the state.[31] Instead, it has become so integrated with the state that, as far as diplomacy is concerned, it is impossible to tell where political considerations end and economic ones begin. The fact that capital has become internationalized, causing individual states, including those of the United States, to have circumscribed autonomy is not the product of insufficient will or poor political judgment on the part of capitalists. It is a structural feature of modern capitalism. There is no longer room for states to maneuver independently of their economic circumstances. Thus, governments regulate what they can now regulate, not necessarily what they could have controlled in the golden age of the Westphalian System and Keynesian economics.

Second, governments are expected to be more involved in matters in which they traditionally have had only a small, even nonexistent, role. As rule takers, so to speak, governments are having to be respond to the pressures from NGOs, ensuring, for example, that businesses do not pollute the environment, do hire more women, and do hire more people from minority groups, especially for senior positions. Thus, many of the new regulations affecting business are concerned with environmental protection, hiring and firing practices, and occupational health and safety.

To conclude, governments are buffeted by NGOs and transnational corporations. Forced into some activities, such as the creation of human rights policies, they are being forced out of others, such as the macro-management of their national economies.

EROSION OF THE DISTINCTION BETWEEN DOMESTIC AND FOREIGN POLICIES

Globalization is resulting in an erosion of the Westphalian distinction between domestic and foreign policies. Many domestic policies have foreign policy implications and many foreign policies have domestic implications.

This section begins with a long-standing example of this problem: the imposition of trade sanctions on countries. A country is obliged to weigh up its foreign political obligations with its domestic financial ones. The section ends with a study of the rise of global policy.

The Problem of Sanctions

British politician Richard Crossman recorded in his diary the dilemma confronting his country's government on what to do about British trade with the U.S.S.R. following the Soviet August 1968 invasion of Czechoslovakia.[32] The United States, even before the invasion, had tried to stop the sale of computers. The U.K. Ministry of Technology wanted all trade to go ahead; the Ministry of Defense wanted it stopped; and the Foreign Office was trying to remain on good terms with everyone. But the British computers contained American components, so the government could not afford to antagonize the United States. If the United Kingdom tried to sell British computers to the U.S.S.R. against the U.S. wishes, British computer production could have stopped altogether because there were quite a number of processes in their manufacture for which the British were dependent on the Americans.

Australia was faced with a similar dilemma in August 1990, following Iraq's invasion of Kuwait and the resulting international sanctions against Iraq. Especially for agricultural goods, Iraq had been a good customer for Australia. The Australian government decided to take part in the trade boycott and to deploy a small naval presence in the Gulf, thereby causing problems for Australia's exporters. Some U.S. politicians referred to Saddam Hussein as a brutal dictator, but to many Australian farmers he was a good customer.

Finally, there was the plight of Elian Gonzalez in 2000, the six-year-old Cuban shipwreck survivor. His mother died in the escape from Cuba; his father, who lived in Cuba, wanted him back. With the backing of the Clinton Administration but without Al Gore and George Bush who were both seeking the Cuban vote in Florida for the presidential election, he was returned to his relatives in Cuba. American sanctions against Cuba are an example of how a tail can wag a dog. The 678,000 Cuban Americans in Florida constitute a powerful lobby. No American presidential candidate can ever afford to be seen as "soft" on Castro. President Clinton wooed that community for votes in the 1992 and 1996 elections.

In fact, sanctions against Cuba have been one of the greatest failures in modern U.S. foreign policy. First, they were imposed when Castro came to power four decades ago. Castro is still there as one of the world's longest serving heads of state. He has survived in office longer than the nine U.S. presidents who have been in office during this same period. Second, the sanctions were designed to help stimulate domestic opposition to Castro. While there is some domestic opposition, it obviously is not effective. Instead, the sanctions give Castro the excuse periodically to crack down on dissenters.

Third, the legislative basis of the sanctions is contrary to international law. For example, the 1996 Helms-Burton Act allows suits to be filed in U.S. courts against any corporation from any part of the world that is doing business in Cuba. This is contrary to the U.S. obligations under the World Trade Organization on free trade.

Finally, the United States is flouting the UN; this is a broader issue. There is a mechanism for sanctions under international law: the UN Security Council. However, the United States could not get such a policy of sanctions through the Security Council. Therefore, the nation is going its own way. The largest single debtor to the UN, the United States has politicians such as Jesse Helms not only authoring the current sanctions policy, but also blocking the U.S. dues to the UN. Such heavy debt weakens U.S. standing in the UN. The nation's bullying of Cuba erodes its credibility in foreign policy. The sanctions policy only makes sense in terms of domestic American politics and the need to get the conservative vote.

The Rise of Global Policy

In science there is the so-called butterfly effect of chaos theory, which deals with the interrelatedness of issues. In theory, a butterfly fluttering its wings over New York will have implications for the weather over London. A Colombian peasant, to take one of the earlier case studies, cultivates cocaine to earn a living, and this shipment creates problems for the New York police. Another example involves how U.S. hostility toward the UN providing contraception in developing countries has been shaped by recent American presidents wishing to retain support at home from conservative Christian groups opposed to contraception and abortion.

Political scientist Walter Jones provided an example of this complexity in the context of US–Indonesian relations.[33] He gave the example of the way in which Indonesians might welcome the factory construction by U.S. corporations because factories create jobs, attract technology, provide export products for earning foreign exchange, and generate public revenue. All these would contribute to Indonesia's economic and social development as well as domestic tranquility. If any party lost in this arrangement, it would be the unemployed American worker whose job may have gone to Indonesia along with the decision to build there rather than in Atlanta or Chicago. The U.S. Government, for its part, would enjoy some gains and sustained some loses. On the positive side, corporate income would rise and, with it, its federal tax bill. On the negative side, the import of the company's Indonesian-produced goods would contribute to the balance of payments deficit, and individual income taxes are lost. This process would help remove Indonesia from the list of capital-starved Third World countries dependent on American and other support. On balance, then, although the United States would not entirely benefit by this arrangement, in the simultaneous pursuit of wealth and power the advantages seem roughly reciprocal to both countries. However, the unemployed American workers would find little consolation learning that their poverty is assisting U.S. foreign policy.

This complexity is exacerbated by the movement of people around the world and their exercising their rights to get involved in politics, especially via NGOs. These trends have been obvious for some years in the United States, with lobbies coming from Americans with Irish Catholic, Jewish, Arab, noncommunist Chinese, and Cuban backgrounds.

To conclude, an alternative approach to this characteristic of globalization is not to discuss a domestic foreign policy or foreign domestic policy. Rather, we need to note the evolution of a new form of policy: global policy, which has both domestic and foreign components. The shapers of such a form of policy are no longer only national governments. As price takers, governments influence and are influenced by such global actors as transnational corporations, inter-governmental organizations, and NGOs.

IMPORTANCE OF NEW TECHNOLOGY

"Technology," according to U.S. historian Daniel Boorstin, "is the natural foe of nationalism."[34] Technology is an important driving force in the globalization process.

This is all the more the case with the world passing through a new technological revolution.[35] New technologies include micro-robotics, miniature robots built from atomic particles which among other things could unclog sclerotic arteries; machine translation, telephone switches and other devices that will provide real-time translation between people conversing in different languages; digital highways into the home that will offer instant access to the world's store of knowledge and entertainment; urban underground automated distribution systems that will reduce traffic congestion; "virtual" meetings rooms which will save people the wear and tear of air travel; and satellite-based personal communicators that will allow one to "phone home" from anywhere on the planet. In addition, technologies will provide machines capable of emotion, inference, and learning which will interact with human beings in entirely new ways; biomimetic materials which will duplicate the properties of materials found in the living world; and bio-remediation, custom designed organisms that will help clean up the earth's environment.

It is now necessary to examine the leading examples of the impact of new technology on globalization. The main influences on globalization include the growth of functional co-operation, the mass media's erosion of national borders, the rise of consumerism, and the dual nature of the new global culture.

FUNCTIONAL COOPERATION

Functional cooperation means that specialists cooperate together, across national lines and out of the political spotlight, to work for a greater goal. The development of European railways is a good example of this working together, not least because rail travel crossing borders is something that is taken for granted. The Paris-based International Union of Railways has coordinated the development of an extensive railway network across Europe. With the thousands of railways crossing national borders each year, each has to operate according to synchronized timetables. Railway timetables now have to be coordinated with ship and air traffic. Not only do people cross borders, but also so do goods. Among the treaties governing the transport of such goods for over a century, the most recent is the 1980 Convention Concerning International Carriage by Rail. The European railway industry was one of the world's pioneers in international commercial arbitration, with a treaty in 1890 setting out how disputes were to be resolved by a central office, the Convention international sur le transport des marchandises par chemins de fer.

A similar process has been underway in the European airport industry.[36] Unlike in the United States where the Federal Aviation Administration has standardized hardware and software, Europe has no central authority to oblige countries to work together. The greatest technical challenge is gaining compatibility among the computers and radars of the many countries, so that air traffic and radar data can flow seamlessly across borders. This challenge is complicated by the desire of the former Eastern European bloc countries to join the system, but their infrastructure is not as advanced as that of the 23 existing members of the European Organization for the Safety of Air Navigation, called Eurocontrol. Additionally, air transport in all countries has more defense implications than the present rail transport system; so Eurocontrol has lagged behind the progress made by the International Union of Railways. However, growing air traffic is providing a major incentive for countries to finalize Eurocontrol arrangements for harmonizing the compatibility of computers and radars.

The final example of so-called cooperation is the Internet. The Internet was conceived in 1964 as a computer network that had thousands of links but no governing authority; messages traveled randomly. This was a response to worries during the Cold War about the threat of a surprise nuclear attack on the United States. If the U.S. surface was attacked and telephone lines destroyed, the senior officers would need a system that could not be disrupted. Thus Internet evolved. It has just kept growing.

To sum up, on the one hand, the world is going through a period of great change which seems so chaotic with so many armed conflicts underway. On the other hand, technological progress has made possible daily activities that would have been inconceivable only half a century ago. For example, it is possible to dial direct and without a local operator to almost every person in the world who has a telephone. The world's telephone numbering system has thus been standardized and coordinated. This, in turn, is linked to the major charge cards so that a person in a foreign airport, without local currency, can make a telephone call via a public telephone, that can first access that person's charge card account in his or her own country and then clear that card-holder to make a telephone call. Another example, is that a person in, say, Sydney can make an airline booking on a domestic flight across the United States or many other countries. Technology is thus helping to erode national boundaries and national political differences.

THE MASS MEDIA'S EROSION OF NATIONAL BORDERS

"Melbourne—Manchester—Manhattan—the middle of the MacDonnell Ranges—it's all going to be the same," according to media magnate Rupert Murdoch.[37] Anyone in the world who is able to go to a computer will be able to exchange messages with anyone else in the world, get information, news and entertainment, work and play, at minimal cost—and at no marginal cost for distance. What this means, at the very least, is that whole new audiences and markets are being created.

Communications technology erodes the power that national governments have over what their citizens hear, read, or watch—and their ability to communicate with the outside world. The control of information is a standard theme in many events in history. The rise of printing assisted the Protestant Reformation as European Christians were able to access copies of the Bible in their own languages Ever since that time, governments have tried to censor information and issue propaganda while generals have tried to distort the accounts of their battles. Some novels are based on this theme, such as George Orwell's *1984* in which the bending of truth is overt and Aldous Huxley's *Brave New World* in which the media makes people into comfortable consumers.

A casualty in the global reach of communications technology is national control over the mass media. The British Broadcasting Corporation, the world's pioneer in radio and television which remains highly regarded for its news coverage, is one such casualty. Pauline Webb, former head of BBC religious broadcasting, wrote about the somber, high-minded era of the early days of radio in Britain, when broadcasting was regarded as a medium of education rather than entertainment.[38] One of the most popular programs was known as *The Brains Trust.* Its content consisted mainly of answers to listeners' questions, which in those days were more often philosophical than political in emphasis. The resident panel included two erudite academics who, partly because of their eccentricities and partly because of their prodigious scholarship, became household radio personalities, communicating high culture, as it were, to the common people.

Although the BBC still maintained its tradition of high-brow broadcasting in the late 1950s, a new generation of consumers were emerging who would undermine it. Children born after World War II who had access to crystal sets and radios wanted something more exciting. Thus, they tuned to Radio Luxembourg based in the minute central European country of the same name, which broadcast to the United Kingdom pop music and cheery conversations. Radio Caroline was established off the east coast of the United Kingdom on what was called a pirate ship beyond British maritime jurisdiction. The BBC surrendered. Changing some of its programming, it introduced Radio One. With the BBC changing its standards (some might say, lowering them), the precedent was set for other countries to follow the BBC's example.

The biggest change has come, however, in television broadcasting. For example, in June 1989, the Chinese student demonstrators at Tianamen Square held placards explaining their views in English, which is hardly used in China. The students did not want to communicate with their fellow Chinese but immediately with foreigners who were watching on television. Cable News Network (CNN) has since become a standard force in television, especially during crises such as the 1990–1991 Gulf War.[39]

Television can also set the political agenda, irrespective of whether or not governments are willing to get involved, as with Somalia in 1992. It was only after the media steadily bombarded Western sensibilities with images of starving Somali children that the United States and other governments stopped dithering and began to act. Two years later in 1994, public response to the television also prompted the international response to helping the survivors of the Rwanda massacre.

Although conservative Islamic countries have endeavored to restrict outside nonIslamic influences, they are having more difficulty in the era of satellite broadcasting. Malaysia, for example, has strict regulations on pornography, and the sale of it is banned in Malaysia. However, the country's rapidly growing middle-class can afford satellite dishes that draw down, among other things, pornography from satellite television. Similarly, Christian evangelism is banned in some Middle Eastern countries. One measure of control that some of these governments try to exercise is access to satellite dishes, since such dishes are essential to pick up the transmissions. However, it is only a matter of time until the broadcasting will be done directly into television antennas, so that television will be as available as radio is today.

CONSUMERISM

The Global Middle Class

A major force behind the global communications revolution is consumerism. Chapter 1 noted the contribution that the thirst for western consumer goods had on the Soviet citizens' desire to end the Cold War.

A consignment of that civilization reached Russia in 1992, with a 249-part television series *The Rich Also Cry* made in 1979. The series was about Mariana, portrayed by Mexican actress Veronica Castro, who wept her way through poverty, wealth, wedded bliss, and marital woe. Although Mariana was not happy, the low-budget drama had 200-million people, 70 percent of the former Soviet Union, reaching for their hankies in sympathy and breaking all viewing records. The stars live like every woman dreams of living, explained a middle-aged school teacher: "They don't have to wash the dishes, wash clothes or cook; their lives are devoted to their emotions."[40] The luxury drawing these viewers was the free time in which to feel emotions.

Advertising is also a very important part of the consumer revolution. The U.S. economist John Kenneth Galbraith has complained about the way in which people, especially economics students, are encouraged to believe that "the consumer is in command."[41] In fact, the consumer is being manipulated by business. It is to this end that advertising and merchandizing in all their cost and diversity are directed; consumer wants are shaped to the financial interests of the firm.

Western cigarette companies, having a hard time in the more health-conscious West, see Eastern Europe as a new market for their products. Brands pushed in these countries include Marlboro, replete with cowboys from the American wild west, and the even more manipulative, specially created brand, Go West. The latter's advertisements encourage consumers to "Go West," which is the dream of eastern European smokers. Another sign of western civilization is the McDonald's hamburger. In 1992, McDonald's captured (after a 14 year campaign) the heart (or stomach) of the world's leading food country: it became France's largest single restaurateur.[42]

The amount of possessions a person needs to live on this planet is small, as many religious communities have shown for thousands of years. But modern economics, which is based on growth, requires the cultivation of unlimited wants; this fostering of material desires is done through changing fashions and the manipulation of popular taste. If the thirst for consumption ceased, the modern economy would slow down.

Thus, modern national governments are in a dilemma. On the one hand, their citizens want the good things in life, and improved global communications mean that they see others enjoying the good things. If governments try to deny the citizens what they want, the citizens will become unruly. On the other hand, as governments give what is desired, their control over people declines as they become locked into global consumer tastes manufactured by the global corporations.

The Global Underclass

Another problem for governments is that many citizens are not able to enjoy these good life-style things. Of the six billion people on earth, about half have neither cash nor credit to buy much of anything. A majority of people on the planet are at most window-shoppers. Many of those window-shoppers will be only too well aware of what they are missing out on because they do have access to radio and television, both of which show them how foreign tourists live in their areas.

Thus, there is a new global underclass developing. As national boundaries lose much of their significance, different consumption patterns are splitting the world in new ways. There is a Global North that now embraces city blocks and affluent suburbs in and around Manila, Mexico City, Santiago, and Nairobi. A Global South that now claims stretches of Los Angeles, Chicago and London.

These people will become increasingly resentful at the way in which they are missing out on the good things of life. They will either try harder, as through force, to get those good things; or they will oppose their fellow citizens who are enjoying material things, as through the reactions against globalization, to be examined later.

THE DUAL NATURE OF THE NEW GLOBAL CULTURE

There are serious implications arising from the creation of this new global culture. At first sight, the situation seems gloomy. For example, people becoming richer tend to eat more beef even though this meat consumption has some grave consequences for the environment.[43]

Additionally, while some technologically deterministic commentators applaud the development of the information superhighway, it is worth recalling that most Africans will be pedestrians on that highway because they lack access to that technology. Indeed, New York City alone has a more extensive telephone system than any African country.

Not just a time of limitless financial opportunities for the Rupert Murdochs of this world, the new era offers technology with some useful purposes. Not everyone is glued to entertainment on a television set. The 1993 Stanley Foundation Conference, for example, noted that some Americans are being drawn into global relationships, partly through global NGOs and partly through alternative sources of information.[44] Through churches, schools, professional associations, and cultural exchanges, Americans are being drawn into a vast array of transnational relationships. As these human networks proliferate, they greatly increase American sensitivity to foreign events. In the past, people have responded to information as conveyed by the press after a filtering by officials and experts. In the modern global village, individuals and private groups with their own global contacts are themselves often the source of the information that reaches traditional news purveyors.

An Australian example of this progress is the usefulness of the Internet to groups wanting an end to rainforest logging in Third World countries. As recently as the late 1980s, it took a Danish group eight months to organize worldwide protests over the Indonesian destruction of rainforest. John Seed, of Lismore's Rainforest Information Centre in New South Wales, says that when the Malaysian government was accused in November 1993 of breaking an anti-logging blockade in Sarawak, "demonstrations were held outside Malaysian consulates in Australia and the US the next day."[45]

The new era is not one of either/or but, rather, both/and: it is an era of multiple options. It is an era of far greater complexity than the one now ending. Thus, many people will no doubt sit at home watching entertaining television programs and ordering their goods through telemarketing. However, other people will be active in areas like human rights and environmental NGOs; these people will try to create a globalization from below to challenge the one from above being inflicted by the transnational corporations.

THE REACTION AGAINST GLOBALIZATION

Globalization is a modernizing and destabilizing influence. There is a tendency among some economic commentators, who endorse the process, to see it as an apolitical process without any cultural consequences. Nevertheless, some people feel threatened by change and the influx of foreign influences. Feeling off balance, they often look to political or religious leaders for answers. Nostalgia for the past, when life seemed less hurried, more ordered and less threatening, also can seem like a remedy. That golden era appears all the more golden, the further people move away from it, as time and change whisk them along.

The reaction against globalization is the least tangible of the characteristics examined in this chapter. There is obviously something going on in several countries. At this early stage, however, it is not possible to identify fully what the unease is about. It is impossible to untangle fully the threads which combine into a rope consisting of globalization, religious fundamentalism, political extremism, resentment by poor people at their poverty, and sheer opportunism as well as greed by some political and religious leaders who are looking for new causes to champion for their own private purposes. In short, although there is apparently both a religious and a religiously motivated political backlash against globalization, the precise chain of causation is not always clear.

THE REACTION AGAINST WORLD TRADE

The "Battle of Seattle" in late 1999 and the demonstrations throughout 2000 and 2001, including the loss of life in Genoa, had various participants with different agendas. But a common concern about the rise of corporate power and the weakness of national governments to respond was common to all. As this book has argued, governments are no longer the masters of their economic destinies. Transnational corporations are now the main global economic force.

Transnational corporations have eroded the notion of a national economy; there is now only a global one. About half of what is called international trade is actually trade conducted within different components of the same corporations. The pace of global economic change is increasing. World trade is growing faster than national economies. In other words, countries are doing more trade with each other as the years go by—and are doing so at a faster rate than their own national economic growth. Traditional national firms which have been iconic household names are being bought up by foreign investors.

In developed countries, the idea of a having a job for life has gone. While some unemployed middle-aged people, usually men, fear that they will never have a full-time job again,some young people fear that they will never get a full-time job at all. Those with jobs are working longer hours. Many young people fear that they will not be able to enjoy the same high standard of living of their parents when they enter the work force. Meanwhile, the heads of corporations are being paid very large salaries, apparently irrespective of how well the corporations actually perform. The rich are getting richer, and the poor are getting nowhere.

With some justification, globalization and transnational corporations are being held responsible for this troubling state of affairs. There is a call for the
return to protectionism, high tariffs, and Keynesian economics with a high
level of government involvement in the economy.

The remarkable thing about this trend is that is occurring at a time of a
growing global economy. A decade of economic growth has not won over all
people in developed countries because there have been too many casualties of
change. The warning to transnational corporations is that if there is a global
economic recession, they will have difficulty maintaining support among conventional politicians for free trade.

The problem for the protesters is that globalization has gone so far so quickly
that it is difficult to see how the process can be reversed. For example, re-
nationalization of utilities is unlikely in western European countries because
governments no longer have the money to buy back the shares of the privatized
corporations.

THE POLITICS OF ANGER

At the other end of the political spectrum are the nationalistic politicians
who tap into public disquiet in other ways.

First, people feel taken by surprise by all that is going on. As noted in chapter
1, the mass media give people what they want to watch, rather than what they
need to know. For example, television news programs are brisk, brief, colorful,
laden with emotion, short of facts, and not analytical about underlying trends.
Although the process of globalization has been publicly underway for some
decades, the process has been ignored by the mass media in preference to sports,
sex, and entertainment. Now the full force of globalization is striking home,
and there is an anger and confusion among people. They have been unprepared
for change. The voters are looking for someone to blame.

Second, there is a lack of political leadership from conventional politicians.
Politics has become a branch of the television entertainment industry: colorful,
superficial, and diverting. Politics have become a form of sport in which discussion is not so much based upon ideas as upon winners. Political parties
follow the opinion polls. Finding out what voters are concerned about, the
parties replay fears back to their constituents; the periodic law and order scares
are one good example. Reinforcing old fears, the political parties fail to provide
new ideas.

Politicians tell people what they want to hear, rather than what they need
to know. What people have needed to know is that the process of globalization
is underway, traditional ideas on the role of national government have to
change, and that the capacity for any government to do much to slow global
change is limited. But these issues have been avoided in the interests of more
trivial matters.

Meanwhile, politicians are digging their graves with their own tongues. The sarcasm and personal abuse of each other is adding to public skepticism about the entire electoral process. "Whoever you vote for, a politician always wins" sums up the cynicism about the political process felt by many people in developed countries. For example, only about half of the eligible voters actually vote in U.S. presidential elections. Australia is the only country governed under the Westminster model that compels citizens to vote and imposes fines for not voting. Even in Australia, however, opinion polls show that about 20 percent would not bother to vote if they were given the choice; the cynicism is highest among younger people.

The lack of conventional political leadership has created a political vacuum into which unconventional leaders have moved: Patrick Buchanan in the United States, Jorge Haider in Austria, Jean Le Pen in France, and Pauline Hanson in Australia. With the exception of Haider, who had a brief flirtation with national power in late 1999 through early 2000, all these politicians have remained on the margin of politics. They have a problem mobilizing supporters because those supporters are so alienated by the conventional political process that their expectations for any politician are low. This alienation reinforces an earlier claim in this book: Globalization has changed the role of governments and reduced their significance.

POST-MULTICULTURALISM?

The rise of globalization has fostered a rise of localization. One manifestation of this is the concern about the loss of local identity. As the world becomes a global village, each culture absorbs elements from other cultures so that its own individuality disappears. There is a loss of cultural diversity.

Thus, I suggest there is a tension between two groups: those who are holding onto their culture and those who are not. On the one hand, there are people who wish to hold onto their local culture and so live in a mono-cultural, or at least multicultural local society. On the other hand, the process of globalization leads to a form of post-multiculturalism in which the differences are more based on economics than culture. For example, middle-class consumers in each nation-state have similar worldviews with each other, rather than with their respective under-classes.

Language is one of the essential keys to cultural and personal identity. People construct their identities in the house of their language. In Africa, for example, when the term "tribe" is used as a synonym for "ethnic group," it is essentially referring to a linguistic group. The hundreds of ethnic groups, Igbos, Yorubas, Efiks, and others, in Nigeria are distinguished among along language lines.

By the same token, "linguicide," or the death of a language, is an important part of imperialism. For example, when Indonesia invaded East Timor in 1975, it banned the use of the indigenous language Tetum and insisted on its own language being used. Similarly, the Turkish Government is waging a war against the Kurds living within Turkey's boundaries. One component of that campaign is to stop parents from giving their children Kurdish names. An indication of a language's impending death is when it is no longer spoken by children. When the chords of linguistic transmission across the generations are cut, the language dies with the older people.

In Europe, the Westphalian System contributed to the death of local languages as nation-states required a national language as a unifying factor. Now that a global society is emerging, there is a need for a global language. Although Spanish is the most widely spoken language, English is most popular among the global middle class. While Spanish is more related to the world's poorer areas, English is spoken by wealthier people and is the language of international science. Thus, the English language has overtaken French as the language of the elites, such as diplomatists. English also is the language spoken in cyberspace; by contrast, only 1.2 percent of the world's websites use French.[46]

Languages are dying at a faster rate today than at any other time in human history. There are currently about 7,000 languages being spoken around the world. It is estimated that only about 10 percent of them will still be used in a century's time. Indeed, it is estimated that languages are dying at the rate of one per day.

RELIGIOUS FUNDAMENTALISM[47]

In the 1960s, it was a widespread Western view that politics had broken away from religion. Therefore, as societies became more modernized and industrialized, the impact of religion apparently would be reduced to the private sphere and individual morality, not politics. But this has not happened. Instead, there has been a resurgence of religious belief. There has been the revenge of God.[48]

This section argues that globalization has led to a rise of religious fundamentalism. Religious fundamentalism defines people by what divides them. It focuses on the differences in humankind, rather than what unites them. This fundamentalism is often partly motivated by a form of xenophobia, against either strangers of another country or of another religion, and a loss of members to other causes, perhaps more secular ones.

Thus, at first sight, some of the foregoing four characteristics of globalization could inflame religious fundamentalists. But, on closer inspection, the chain of causation is not quite so clear; there may be other motives involved, which enable leaders to exploit the fear of globalization for their own purposes. Here are examples taken from two of the world's main faiths, Hinduism and Islam.[49]

Hinduism

There is the campaign against "foreign influences" in India. The Hindu fundamentalist party, Rashtriya Swayamsevak Sangh (RSS), the grass roots organization to which the governing Bharatiya Janata Party (BJP) is linked, is leading a campaign against Coke and Pepsi as part of a larger movement to boycott the sale of foreign goods in India. RSS officials claim that Coke and Pepsi are "the most visible symbols of the multinational invasion of this country."[50] The RSS campaign is called "Swadeshi," which is a term borrowed from the movement launched by Mahatma Gandhi against British-made goods during India's freedom struggle. The use of this term exemplifies political opportunism because RSS has otherwise little love for Ghandi. A RSS member assassinated Gandhi in 1947 because the fundamentalist organization claimed that he was too close to the Moslem minority. But Swadeshi is a useful slogan since it taps into a tribal memory of Hindus and enables the RSS to exploit Hindu fears about Indian Moslems.[51]

The RSS is tapping into the concerns that Indians have about the globalization of their country. India is, for example, the largest maker of movies, much larger than Hollywood. But film-makers have to operate under strict censorship rules. Explicit sex scenes are forbidden; the camera moves off the lovers and looks at moving bushes. Pirated western sex videos, however, are gaining in popularity: Indians prefer to see Madonna full frontal rather than just moving bushes. Indian parents not only feel that they are losing control over the viewing habits of their children, but also that their children are reciting television advertising tunes more easily then nursery rhymes.

Until 1992, foreign transnational corporations were not allowed to control more than 40 percent of a domestic Indian enterprise; now they may acquire as much as 51 percent and, with special government permission, even 100 percent. One of the victims of the new era has been Parle, India's leading soft-drink company. Ironically it had been the Parle chairman Ramesh Chauhan who encouraged the government to expel Coca-Cola in 1977 for refusing to reveal the secret formula and to decrease the American company's ownership from 100 to 40 percent. India sought a "transfer of technology": the Coca-Cola formula. The corporation refused to divulge its formula and was expelled. India then produced its own Cola. As the middle-class has expanded, it now wants to drink the real thing, the global middle-class soft drink. So Coca-Cola is back in India—and on its own terms. Realizing that he could not win against Coca-Cola, Chauhan decided to get out of the soft drink business. In September 1993, Coca-Cola bought Parle.

This is a facet of the anxiety about the pace of change. Political cohesion is a delicate balancing act between the different religious and ethnic groups as well as the powerful trade unions and employers. Further, the cohesion demands balance among the underlying tensions of a majority Hindu society in which the ancient system of caste, which ascribes one's social rank at birth, is being challenged by the poorest and least powerful. Supporters of India's economic reforms can already point to a string of successful joint ventures with foreign companies and a corresponding increase in productivity and quality in local industry. But just as new modern industries are thriving, so are outdated industries dying and killing many jobs in a country with no welfare safety net.

Meanwhile, increased economy activity is worsening environmental problems as more cars pour onto the roads, more coal is burnt to produce electricity, and more factories discharge pollutants into the air and waterways.

Islam

Islam seems to be on a winning streak. Moslems have beaten the United States in Iran in 1979 and the Soviet Union in Afghanistan since 1979. Having driven Israel out of southern Lebanon, they also have seen Osama bin Laden's skill in destroying the World Trade Towers on September 11, 2001. In the resurgence of Islam since 1945, Moslems have come to represent about 18.5 percent of the world's population while Islam has become the world's second largest religious group after Christianity. It is one of the world's fastest growing religions.

But many Moslems are missing out on economic growth. Years ago, many of the leaders opposing governments in north Africa and the Middle East would have been communist; now they are Islamic. Communism has failed. Moslems have seen the collapse of the U.S.S.R. and its Eastern European allies. They have also derived little benefit from the quasi-socialistic regimes in places like Egypt and Turkey; these regimes are large, inefficient bureaucracies, which cannot cope with rapid urbanization and population growth.

Poor Moslems in developing countries are skeptical of the newly found Eastern European passion for the market system of economics. They can see in Western countries how the rich get richer and the poor more numerous. They are looking for a third way, and Islamic leaders are promising them a better future. Governments in developing countries need to provide a better option, or young, poor, unemployed Moslems will support the Islamic leaders in the hope of getting a better life. This will make life difficult for governments in Islamic countries. For example, the conflict in Algeria has cost about 90,000 lives. The conflict has been a great shock because Algeria was long seen as one of the most modern Islamic states. However, beneath the veneer of a modernizing state, there were pressures building up from Islam groups which saw the modernization process as eroding what they perceived as the basic ideas of Islam.

French political scientist Mahmoud Hussein explained the dual upheaval undergone by Islamic societies. First, there is their entry into the global market system of economics, whose pace of change is disrupting internal balances and hierarchies. Second, there is the advent of the autonomous individual into the political life of these societies, which is in place of the traditional feudal chiefs governing an hierarchical society. These developments are tending to increase the fragility of the national fabric, the psychic instability of individuals, and the unpredictability of events.[52]

Algerian governments, for example, have sought the improved status of women. But in a 1989 speech, Abassi Madani, a leader of the Islamic Salvation

Front (FIS), said a female should emerge from home only three times: "when she is born, when she is married, and when she goes to the cemetery."[53] The FIS has also opposed foreign investment in Algeria and the foreign mass media. Drawing its support from the poorer sections of the country, the FIS exploited their various resentments. The Algerian government annulled the election won by the FIS in 1991 on the grounds that the organization was pledged to scrap the democratic constitution and introduce a theocratic constitution, which would have the country governed by Islamic religious leaders. This annulment paved the way for the violent response by the now-banned FIS and the military's harsh crackdown.

The final issue to be examined is the way that some Islamic religious leaders have been angry about writers critical of some aspects of Islam, or at least the way that it is practiced. How critical these writers are as opposed to how politically convenient it may be to mobilize hatred against them is not possible to tell. After all, Moslems have a right to be suspicious of western ambitions because they have been colonized by western countries. Additionally, some Moslems are appalled by the low morality, the sex and greed, reflected in popular culture of the West.

British writer Salman Rushdie, author of *Satanic Verses*, was issued a death sentence by the late Ayatollah Khomeini in 1989. Bangladeshi author Taslima Nasrin, in 1994, fled her country for western Europe in order to escape legal charges in respect to her writing. Both episodes have globalization implications. First, in neither case would the mobs calling for the deaths of the writers be familiar with the writings; in particular, *Satanic Verses* is extremely allusive and opaque. But religious leaders have been able to arouse the mobs into great frenzies—they have used modern communications technology to do so. If books can become global property, so can the techniques to oppose them.

Second, the reactions to *Satanic Verses* show how people can think globally and act locally, albeit wrongly in my view. *Time* magazine in July 1993 put death toll related to the *Satanic Verses* at near 60: More than 20 Pakistanis and Bangladeshis were killed in riots in 1989; in July 1991, the Japanese translator was stabbed to death in Tokyo; in July 1993, 36 people were killed in a Turkish hotel blaze when Islamic radicals tried to kill the person who had made a translation of parts of the book. Many other people have been wounded, such as the Italian translator of the book, who was stabbed in July 1991 but managed to live.

Finally, the Rushdie case contains several ironies. A British subject living in London, the author has been sentenced to death by an Iranian leader, who has since died and so apparently the death sentence cannot be revoked. Rushdie is being protected by British police. However, since the British government is anxious to expand trade with Iran, it minimizes the furor over his death sentence. Rushdie has been helped by some NGOs that have been keeping his fate in the public eye, notably the International Committee for the Defence of

Salman Rushdie and his Publishers, which is housed at the Article 19 (freedom of information) NGO in London.

THE FUTURE BELONGS TO GLOBALIZATION

Because the new era is one of multiple options, it is possible that the process of globalization will coexist with people reacting against that process. At least, as with September 11, a nation might use a negative reaction for its own purposes.

Overall, however, the future belongs to globalization. First, the process has moved too far too fast to be stopped. Indeed, governments have been too slow to react to what was happening, such as the rise of transnational corporations.

Second, the religious and political extremists may try to arouse the mobs, but their kids want Big Macs, Coke, jeans, and Madonna videos. This is the problem the BBC encountered in the 1950s. However much an aesthete may be appalled at popular tastes, the fact is the tastes are popular. If people have large disposable incomes, they will want to spend on what they want; what a high-minded central committee or academic elite deem is good for them is not the preference.

Finally, the fanaticism that underpins much of the populist reaction against globalization cannot be maintained. The ethnic nationalism, for example, in the Balkans is not a good basis for maintaining a nation-state. The nationalist fervor is wonderful to get people to charge ahead in military campaigns. But at some point people feel the need to get married, have children, plant and harvest crops, and build schools as well as roads. Although the hostility of a campaign like that of the Bosnian Serbs is easy to mobilize for military purposes, it will eventually dwindle away as more domestic concerns take over.

"War is to men," according to Mussolini, "what maternity is to women."[54] Ironically, while the history books, mass media, and the public statues record the wars, the human race is continued by women. But, then, most of these records of war have been created by men reporting on male activities. History is his-story.

However, globalization is not a general riding across the world on a stallion. Globalization is embracing the world, partly as people seek a better material standard of life. It is enveloping the world in the ordinary everyday and practical matters. These practicalities are usually ignored by the mass media, so the pace and impact of globalization do not receive the attention they deserve.

GLOBALIZATION AND GLOBAL GOVERNANCE

What will be the future of the Westphalian System in the new global era? It is a sign of the times that no one can say—and one does not even know whom to ask. In the Westphalian era, one would have looked to a national leader to provide a sense of direction. But that is no longer the case. If an alien came from outer space and said, "Take me to your leader," to whom would one take the it? The President of the United States? The President of Russia? The UN Secretary General? Bill Gates? Rupert Murdoch?

In terms of influence, political leaders are often overshadowed by some of the leaders of transnational corporations. But such CEOs usually prefer to avoid direct partisan involvement in political issues, which could damage business prospects. Therefore, there is a leadership vacuum at the global level: Hence this book attends to both order and disorder.

How can we proceed in a time of confusion? This book ends with a business technique for thinking about the future (scenario planning) and the recommendation that it be used for preparing plans for global governance.

NOTES

1. Ranjit Kumar and Barbara Murck, *Our Common Ground: Managing Human-Planet Relationships,* Toronto: John Wiley, 1992, pp. 22–23.

2. See: William McNeill, *Plagues and Peoples,* Oxford: Basil Blackwell, 1977.

3. "The Red Cross Global Annual Appeal," *Weekly News of the International Red Cross and Red Crescent Movement* (Melbourne), December 11, 2000, p. 1.

4. Rachel Sacks, "Beyond Our Borders," *Development Bulletin* (Canberra), April 1999, p. 80.

5. Chris Beyrer, *War in the Blood: Sex, Politics and AIDS in Southeast Asia,* London: Zed, 1998.

6. "The Killers All Around" *Time,* September 12, 1994, pp. 60–61.

7. Jonathan Mann, "Globalism in Health" *Pacific Research* (Canberra), May 1993, p. 9.

8. "A Deadly Comeback" *Newsweek,* May 18, 1993, pp. 62–63.

9. See: Laurie Garrett, *The Coming Plague: Newly Emerging Diseases in a World Out of Balance,* New York: Farrar, Straus, Giroux, 1994.

10. Richard Preston, *The Hot Zone,* Sydney: Doubleday, 1994, p. 301.

11. For an introduction, see: Karen Litfin, *Ozone Discourses: Science and Politics in Global Environmental Co-operation,* New York: Columbia University Press, 1995; Ian Rowlands, *The Politics of Global Atmospheric Change,* New York: Manchester University Press, 1995.

12. Sir John Browne as quoted in Paul Hawken et al., *Natural Capitalism: The Next Industrial Revolution,* London: Earthscan, 1999, p. 241.

13. Clare Breidenich et al., "The Kyoto Protocol to the United Nations Framework Convention on Climate Change," *American Journal of International Law,* April 1998, pp. 315–331.

14. See: Keith Suter, *The History of the Development of the Law of the Sea,* Sydney: World Wide Fund for Nature Australia, 1994.

15. Andrew Fisher, "Voracious Visitor" *The Bulletin* (Sydney), August 31, 1993, p. 18.

16. "Hidden Dangers of Ballast Water" *Australian Environment Review* (Sydney), May 1994, p. 20.

17. Laszlo Somlyody, "Water Resources in a Changing World" *Options* (Vienna), Summer 1994, p. 4.

18. See: John Bulloch and Adel Darwish, *Water Wars: Coming Conflicts in the Middle East*, London: Victor Gollancz, 1993.

19. See: Arthur Westing (Editor) *Global Resources and International Conflict*, Oxford: Oxford University Press, 1986.

20. *The State of the World's Children 2002*, New York: UNICEF, 2001, p. 65.

21. Paul Kennedy, *Preparing for the Twenty-First Century*, London: Harper Collins, 1993, p. 132.

22. Wouter van Dieren, *The Erasmus Lecture 1993: The New Feudality and the Environmental Crisis*, Amsterdam: Institute for Environment and Systems Analysis, October 1993, p. 11.

23. *Global Changes and Domestic Transformations: New Possibilities for American Foreign Policy*, Muscatine, IA: The Stanley Foundation, 1992, p. 9.

24. A pioneer in looking at the importance of cities as economic actors is Jane Jacobs; see: *Cities and the Wealth of Nations: Principles of Economic Life*, New York: Random House, 1985; *Death and Life of Great American Cities*, New York: Random House; *Economy of Cities*, New York: Random House, 1970.

25. See: David Rieff, *Los Angeles: Capital of the Third World*, London: Jonathan Cape, 1992.

26. Simon Winchester, *Pacific Rising*, New York: Prentice Hall, 1991, pp. 410–411.

27. John McDonnell, "Development and the Trade Culture" in Ted Vandeloo (Editor) *Global Partnership in Development*, Melbourne: World Vision, 1989, p. 110.

28. Gary Hamel and CK Prahalad, *Competing for the Future*, Boston: Harvard Business School Press, 1994, p. 1.

29. See: Robert Lekachman, *The Age of Keynes: A Biographical Study*, London: Penguin, 1966; Michael Stewart, *Keynes and After*, London: Penguin, 1967.

30. A key advocate was Milton Friedman; see: Milton Friedman and Rose Friedman *Free to Choose: A Personal Statement*, Melbourne: Macmillan, 1979.

31. Alan Wolfe, "Crackpot Moralism, Neo-Realism, and US Foreign Policy," *World Policy Journal* (New York), Spring 1986, p 264.

32. Richard Crossman, *The Diaries of a Cabinet Minister Volume III*, London: Hamish Hamilton, 1977, p. 289.

33. Walter Jones, *The Logic of International Relations*, New York: Harper Collins, 1991, pp. 419–420.

34. Quoted in John Curtis Perry, "Asia's Telectronic Highway," *Foreign Policy* (New York), Summer 1985, p. 41.

35. For an introduction, see: Ray Kurzweil, *The Age of Spiritual Machines: When Computers Exceed Human Intelligence*, Sydney: Allen & Unwin, 1999; Michael Zey *Seizing the Future*, New York: Simon & Schuster, 1994.

36. Bruce Nordwall, "Europe Updates Air Traffic Control System," *Aviation Week and Space Technology*, May 4, 1992, pp. 58–60.

37. Rupert Murdoch as quoted in Brian Cummins, "Networking Beats 'Big Brother' in Infotech Gold Rush," *Insight* (Canberra), November 7, 1994, p. 15.

38. Pauline Webb, "Communication and Culture—Sharing the Inheritance," *Media Development* (London), April 1990, p. 15.

39. I do several radio programs each week in Australia. It is notable that radio stations have CNN running in the stations; CNN not only helps sets political priorities, but also shapes what fellow members of the mass media will regard as important that day.

40. Soviet woman as quoted in "The Russians Also Cry," *Time*, September 14, 1992, p. 66.

41. John Kenneth Galbraith, *The Culture of Contentment*, Boston: Houghton Mifflin, 1992, p. 134.

42. "Les Arches de Triomphe," *Time*, February 22, 1993, p. 14.

43. See: Jeremy Rifkin, *Beyond Beef: The Rise and Fall of the Cattle Culture*, London: Viking, 1992.

44. *Global Changes and Domestic Transformations: Southern California's Emerging Role*, Muscatine, IA: The Stanley Foundation, 1993, p. 7.

45. James Button, "Around the World in Eighty Seconds," *Time*, December 13, 1993, p. 56.

46. "Le Cyber Challenge," *The Economist* (London), March 11, 2000, p. 61.

47. For further information, see: Bronislaw Misztal and Anson Shupe, (Editors) *Religion and Politics in Comparative Perspective: Revival of Religious Fundamentalism in East and West*, Westport, CT: Praeger, 1992.

48. Gilles Kepel, *The Revenge of God: The Resurgence of Islam, Christianity and Judaism in the Modern World*, Oxford: Polity, 1993.

49. Orthodox Jews in Israel have also been active in opposing some products and the advertising there of because they believe them to be contrary to the spirit of the Torah; see: "Pepsi no Match for Rabbis," *The Australian*, June 5, 1993 p. 9; "Dinosaurs No Yo-Go for Strict Jews," *The Sydney Morning Herald*, August 14, 1993, p. 17.

50. "Hindu Boycott Hits Coke and Pepsi," *The Sydney Morning Herald*, July 9 1994, p 19.

51. Debesh Bhattacharya, "Crisis In India," *Current Affairs Bulletin* (Sydney), February 1993, p. 29.

52. Mahmoud Hussein, "Behind the Veil of Fundamentalism," *UNESCO Courier* (Paris), December 1994, pp. 26–27.

53. Abassi Madoni as quoted in "The Second Battle of Algiers," *Time*, January 9, 1995, p. 16.

54. Mussolini as quoted in "Is Fascism Returning to Europe?" *Media Development* (London), September 1992, p. 1.

6

Thinking About the Future: The Value of Scenario Planning

INTRODUCTION

The previous chapters have dealt with the rise and erosion of the nation-state as the basic building block of global politics and economics. A theme of the survey has been that people have been taken by surprise with events, especially the rise of globalization; this has resulted in the politics of anger.

It is worth recalling the extent of the political changes through which the world has passed in less than a century. Here, then, are some other instances in which there have been major changes in world affairs:

On June 28, 1914, Austrian Archduke Franz Ferdinand was assassinated in Sarajevo; because this was not seen as a major issue for western European governments, politicians went ahead with their summer vacation arrangements during July—but were at war with each other in August.

In the late nineteenth century, Karl Marx had predicted that the industrialized country Germany would be the first one to turn communist in the inexorable movement toward communism; actually the first country to do so was Russia, a backward agricultural society in 1917 which leapfrogged the series of steps laid down by Marxist theory.

The League of Nations was created at the end of World War I. This was then the most ambitious attempt to get governments (including traditional opponents like the UK and France, France and Germany) to work together to maintain international peace and security.

The League of Nations was effectively dead by 1938; within seven years, the United Nations emerged, full of hope and with a much larger agenda.

Although the U.S. army was smaller than the Greek one in 1940, within five years the United States had largely shrugged off its tradition of isolationism to become the world's most important military power.

In 1941, British Prime Minister Winston Churchill said that he had not become the "King's first minister in order to preside over the liquidation of the British Empire"— but within two decades most of the empire had achieved independence or was on the way to doing so.

In 1974, U.S. officials in Saigon were still confident that South Vietnam could continue its independent existence; (I was there speaking to them at the time). But the United States was forced out of the country in a humiliating defeat on April 30, 1975, and North Vietnam won the conflict.

In 1979, the Shah of Iran, who was modernizing his country, was overthrown and replaced by conservative Islamic clerics. These clerics, among other things, detained U.S. diplomats for a year.

In 1983, President Reagan, with a long history of hostility to communism, spoke of the U.S.S.R. as the "evil empire"—but four years later he negotiated the first ever U.S.-Soviet nuclear disarmament agreement (on intermediate nuclear forces).

In 1991 the US-led coalition defeated Iraq's Saddam Hussein in his occupation of Kuwait—but he was still in power a decade later (by which time all the political leaders who had opposed him were out of office).

On September 11, 2001, the most effective aerial hijacking in aviation history (in terms of the number of aircraft taken over) resulted in the destruction of the two World Trade Center Towers in New York and part of the Pentagon.

The list could go on. In each case, politicians and commentators were taken by surprise by the turn of events. By contrast, the process of globalization has been evolving with less drama over a longer period of time. Not a secret, the process has had no sinister force at work, despite what some anti-globalization protesters and conspiracy theorists may claim. But the process has still taken most politicians and commentators off guard. Globalization has not been a surprise, of course, for people working in transnational corporations because they have seen the process at work each day.

The challenge, then, for politicians and commentators is to recognize the need to take a long view of global change and to have contingency plans in place. Thus, this chapter examines scenario planning. This anticipation of the future helps us to rethink our worldviews. Encouraging us to think about the future differently, scenario planning liberates us from our prison of perception. Scenario planning is a business management technique that can help us to think about the future of globalization and enable us to be better prepared for it. Even though the future cannot be predicted with any precision, we can be sure that it will be different in many ways from the present. We are living in a period of rapid change. Many things taken for granted are changing. But some things remain the same. The challenge is to be prepared for the changes and continuations, and this requires a significant investment in time and resources.

This book is particularly about two sets of worldviews: the Westphalian system and the future evolution of globalization.

The rest of this chapter examines the scenario planning process in more detail. While chapter 7 introduces four worldviews for the possible evolution of globalization and the final chapter offers some ideas on how to cope with the new era.

SCENARIO PLANNING

Scenario planning is a technique to help us prepare for the future. The technique is not so much about predicting the future (since that is impossible) as about providing new ways of thinking about the future. The key issue is how we view the present and the future. This is called our "mental model" or "worldview." A "worldview" is a set of presuppositions, or assumptions, which we hold, consciously or unconsciously, about the basic make-up of our world. Filtering out some information, a worldview focuses on other information. What may be obvious to some people is not necessarily obvious to others.

Another name for worldview is "paradigm," as popularized by Thomas Kuhn in 1962.[1] He set out to investigate the reluctance of scientists to scrap old theories when new information was eroding the validity of those theories. He argued that when scientists had accepted a theory as satisfactory, they were deeply unwilling to admit that there was anything wrong with it and defended it against the onslaught on new information. Kuhn himself preferred the term to be used to explain the process of change in the natural and physical sciences. But the term has also become very popular in the social sciences because it is so useful.[2]

While people can look at the same object or event at the same time, they actually see different objects or events. We are prisoners of our perceptions. Our assumption is that there is only one way of looking at the world: "How could they have been so stupid to have done that?" This is a common reaction when looking back upon an event. But to the people involved at the time, it did not appear stupid; they were prisoners of their perceptions. It seemed quite rational to them. Humans will not believe what does not fit in with their plans or suit their own way of thinking.

One value of scenario planning is its speed and flexibility. At a time of rapid change, waiting until a trend has been validated before it becomes the basis of action is unwise. It may be too late. The window of opportunity may have closed, or the problem has become too large.

Second, the technique keeps an organization alert to change. Change often begins at the margins, rather than at the top. Therefore, any person at any level in an organization may be the first to detect a new development that could affect the organization. Thus, the completed scenarios have to become living documents known to all staff within an organization—and not a detailed but largely unread strategic plan gathering dust on a book shelf.

Third, scenario planning is not so much about forecasting the future as in making sure that an organization has contingency plans in place to cope with any eventuality. Therefore, the document is more one of narrative than tables and graphs. The narratives need to be well written and memorable. They should be easily absorbed so that they become second nature to the staff. The staff then becomes alert to the possibility of change—and the risks of not making changes in time.

An example of this process was the work done in the early 1980s by Clem Sunter on the future of apartheid and South Africa. The work was commissioned by Anglo American, the largest South African company. It had concerns about the future viability of apartheid, not just on ethical grounds but on practical ones. A growing shortage of skilled white managers meant that African managers were being appointed to supervise staff, some of whom were white. This was contrary to the apartheid policy. Sunter gave a series of public talks about two scenarios: "High Road" and "Low Road." Under the "High Road scenario," Nelson Mandela (then the world's longest serving political prisoner) would be released, a multiracial South Africa created, and Mandela elected President to steer South Africa on a new path. This shocked many white audiences, who said that this would never happen; Mandela would rot in prison. Sunter then explained the "Low Road" which would entail an increasingly violent South Africa, in which the whites could not keep winning because of being outnumbered and surrounded by Africans, not least in their own households as cheap labor. In short, whites could be murdered in their sleep. At this point, white audiences would ask for more information about the "High Road." These talks helped white South Africans change their worldviews to accept the 1990 release of Nelson Mandela by President Frederik de Klerk, who in due course became Vice President to President Mandela.[3]

Finally, scenario planning encourages interdisciplinary co-operation. It is not the preserve of any one particular academic discipline. It draws on a variety of them. It thus gets away from the tyranny of academic disciplines by encouraging a holistic approach to (in this book's example) world events.

THE EVOLUTION OF SCENARIO PLANNING

The Practice of Scenario Planning

Scenario planning began after World War II as a method for military planning, particularly within the U.S. Air Force. The intention was to imagine what the U.S. opponents might do. Although military thinkers have been doing this for millennia, the attempt to make this process more systematic and less intuitive was new. This was an outgrowth of Operations Research (OR), pioneered by the United Kingdom and United States in World War II, in which scientific techniques were used, for example, to deploy radar, bombers, and convoys more cost-effectively.[4]

The most well known example from that era was the work of Herman Kahn, who examined how a nuclear war could begin. The United States and U.S.S.R. were building nuclear weapons, but there had been little public debate as to exactly how such weapons could be used in a conflict. Kahn "thought the unthinkable": how World War III could come about. His books sold well, and phrases such as "thinking about the unthinkable" and "escalation" entered the popular vocabulary.[5] The books also helped trigger the anti-nuclear movement because people could now see that a nuclear war was not a distant possibility but could actually take place, maybe over a local dispute in the then divided city of Berlin.

Within the civilian sector, the person most credited with developing scenario planning was Pierre Wack.[6] He began working at Royal Dutch/Shell in 1960s London in the newly formed department called Group Planning, probably the world's first strategic planning unit in a transnational corporation. He encouraged Royal Dutch/Shell to think about the unthinkable: A dramatic increase in the price of oil was one possible scenario. This was contrary to the worldview of the entire oil industry, not just Royal Dutch/Shell; the post World War II economic boom was based partly on cheap oil. Wack was told by the corporation's directors that any government trying to increase the price of oil would be removed by the U.S. government.

However, Wack persisted and encouraged Shell to have contingency plans in place for an eventual oil price rise. He had no way of predicting the 1973 Arab-Israeli conflict, with the resulting use of oil as a weapon by the Organization of Petroleum Exporting Countries (OPEC). Unable to predict the cause, his persistence nevertheless ensured that Royal Dutch/Shell could cope with the effect, a dramatic increase in the price of oil. His corporation was the only oil company thus prepared. Previously regarded as the least profitable of the leading oil companies, Royal Dutch/Shell now outperformed its rivals. Group Planning has since become a good training place for a number of people who have applied their scenario planning skills, not least in books.[7] (One of Wack's projects in retirement was being part of the team that developed the "High Road" and "Low Road" scenarios in South Africa.)

Scenario planning has now become an accepted management tool in transnational corporations. It is also being used by nongovernmental organizations, for example, the Global Scenario Group convened by the Stockholm Environmental Institute as an independent, international, and interdisciplinary body to examine the requirements for sustainability at global and regional levels.[8] Also worth mentioning is the Washington D.C.-based Millennium Project of the American Council for the United Nations University; the project is a global participatory futures research think tank of futurists, scholars, business planners, and policy makers who work for international organizations, governments, corporations, NGOs, and universities. Its website contains many scenarios.[9]

Not Used in Politics

Unfortunately, the tool has not been used much in government.[10] Even the South African High and Low Road example involved changing public worldviews before letting that change flow through into the political system. In chapter 1 we encountered Peter Schwartz, one of the Royal Dutch/Shell team who went on to create his own scenario planning company, Global Business

Network.[11, 12] That chapter recalled his failure in 1984 to encourage the Reagan Administration to have a contingency plan to cope with a possible Soviet surrender without one shot. Thus, the United States was take by surprise by the Soviet surrender under its new leader Mikhail Gorbachev who came to power in 1985. In the early 1990s, the United States did not know how to make the most of its victory—or how to provide a safety net for the transition of the U.S.S.R. from enemy to friend. While America had spent trillions of dollars on defense against the U.S.S.R. and had a variety of plans on how to destroy it, not one plan existed on how to help the country shift to democracy and a market economy.[13]

By the same token, the U.S. official view did not give enough attention to detecting signs of change within the Soviet Union as it shifted into a post-Cold War posture. Since the official view saw the U.S.S.R. as the principal enemy, American intelligence and diplomatic services were not looking for any Soviet officials who could emerge as potential allies. No such era was likely to emerge, and it would be a waste of time looking for signs of one. However, change often begins at the margins. The United States was blind to those changes.[14]

Most mainstream politicians in the large political parties in democracies deal with the here and now immediate issues. They seem almost temperamentally unable to cope with events that could occur on the other side of an election. Such events are too far away. There is also the risk that long-term projections may contain implications that would counter their current worldviews. Preferring to stay in their comfort zones, many mainstream politicians are often taken by surprise.

For example, a 1984 U.S. contingency plan to cope with a Soviet surrender would presumably have had to include a reduction in American military expenditure, a conversion of some military employment to civilian work, and preparations for providing foreign aid to the U.S.S.R. to ease its transition into a modern industrial state with some semblance of democracy. Such a contingency plan would certainly have run counter to the Reagan Administration's prevailing worldview of the Soviet Union as the "evil empire." But that is what ought to have been done. The world would be a different place now if such a plan had been created and then implemented in due course.

THE PROCESS OF SCENARIO PLANNING: AN INTRODUCTION

This chapter ends with a brief statement on why scenario planning is used in business and how a scenario planning project is undertaken. The next chapter simply sets out four worldviews on the future of the Westphalian system in the era of globalization. Owing to a lack of space, chapter 7 does not cover the entire process but alerts the reader to how scenario planning makes the eroding nation-state and globalization thinkable.

Scenario planning is the development of a number of stories which describe quite different but plausible futures. It is important to develop scenarios that are mutually exclusive, with each scenario highlighting different facets of the possible future situation. Each collection of stories should be plausible, compelling, and relevant. Scenarios describe possible futures and interpret them They are not predictions or extrapolations of current trends.

Scenario planning is used in business, first, because it helps people to think about the future. The mere act of scenario planning obliges people to lift their eyes beyond the immediate tasks occupying their thoughts most of the time. Second, scenario planning helps people think specifically about how they make decisions. Many decisions are determined by factors at the sub-conscious level. Perceptions, rather than explicit, conscious thinking, do the thinking. Scenario planning makes those perceptions more explicit. Third, scenarios do not predict what is going to happen, but they do help people to better understand today what may happen tomorrow. Fourth, it helps people make better decisions about what they ought to do or avoid doing. The end result is not an accurate picture of tomorrow but better decisions about the future. Fifth, the process is a learning experience. It encourages people to go into a subject in more depth so that they will get to know what they did not know. People get a better feel for what might be beyond their immediate perception. Finally, scenario planning reduces the risk of being taken by surprise.

There is no one set recipe for scenario planning. Most scenario planning runs along the following steps:

1. Work out the basic issue. Scenario planning is done in response to the perception that there is some kind of problem to be solved. It is important that the right problem be identified. (In the following chapter, the problem is taken to be the ways in which the erosion of the nation-state and the process of globalization could evolve.)

2. Understand the organization that has commissioned the scenario planning. How does the organization perceive its business? Why has it decided that particular problem is to be investigated? What is the "official perception" of the future, namely the party line laid down by the board or CEO? How do those people see that future changing? What are their hopes and fears? What is the organization's future strategy? What are its stated values? Are they implemented in practice? Who are the stakeholders?

3. Work out the driving forces. The forces can be broadly grouped into five areas: Social; Technological; Environmental; Economic; and Political.

4. Rank the driving forces in order of importance. Many of the driving forces will be of interest to the scenario planning project, but some will be more important than others. Also look for factors about which there is uncertainty.

5. Work out the scenario logic. The drivers are then used as the axes along which the eventual scenarios will differ. There should be at least two scenarios. The maximum number is best kept at four because it gets a bit too complicated to go beyond that number in terms of recalling the scenarios and making use

of them. The scenarios are (up to) four different worlds. The task is not to pick winners and decide which is the most likely—that will become obvious in due course.

Conversations with those who are called "remarkable people" may be useful here. These are people who are outside the current scenario planning project and have different perceptions from what the scenario planning team may be thinking. Acknowledged experts in a particular field, these people are not specialized in the area under examination for the scenario planning project. Remarkable people help guard against group think and narrow perceptions. They can also suggest new matters to examine.

6. Make the scenarios come alive. Each scenario needs to be compelling. There has to be sufficient detail in each story to make it easy to follow. A scenario may be uncomfortable, but it needs to be believable. Each scenario should have a memorable name. People need to live within each scenario and become fully familiar with it. They will then be well positioned to gauge which of the scenarios is coming into play and have the contingency plans ready. If the scenarios are commissioned by a large organization, they should be discussed at the various levels of it so that staff can think through what each scenario means for their own area of work. Since the scenarios may represent a new world for staff, it is necessary to get their reactions. Change often begins at the margins and so junior staff may be placed best to detect it first. (The heads of companies, who may have a psychological bias in maintaining the known status quo may be less adept at detecting change.)

7. Identify the Leading Indicators. The future will determine which scenario was "right" in the sense that it was closest to what actually happened. It is important to have indications as quickly as possible about which scenario is coming into play. An initial source of the indicators are the driving forces. Each axis will have a "high" and "low" end; therefore, the indicators can be drawn from the way in which ends of the axes start to come into play. For example, in the next chapter one axis is the strength/weakness of the nation-state; Indicators can be based on seeing how nation-states thrive or collapse in the coming years.

8. Work out the Implications of the Scenarios. We now return to the original problem identified by the organization. What do the scenarios mean for the organization? What are the implications for the organization's current strategy? What contingency plans need to be in place? What are the options for the stakeholders?

It is now necessary to see how the essence of this technique can be applied to the future of the nation-state and globalization. Understanding will be helped by the creation of four worldviews.

NOTES

1. Thomas Kuhn, *The Structure of Scientific Revolutions*, Chicago: University of Chicago Press, 1962.

2. For example, there are conflicting paradigms among some historians on what actually defines history. According to one paradigm, history is primarily, often entirely, narrative: "What happened?" "How did it happen?" Now there is a paradigm by which history should be more analytic: "Why did it happen?" See: Gertrude Himmelfarb, *The New History and the Old: Critical Essays and Reappraisals*, Cambridge: Harvard University Press, 1987, p. 34.

3. In August 2001, I was a member of a seminar with Nobel Peace Prize Winners in Taiwan, and Frederik de Klerk acknowledged that the Sunter talks helped prepare the ground for his policy changes.

4. See: Agatha Hughes and Thomas Hughes (Editors), *Systems, Experts and Computers: Systems Approach in Management and Engineering, World War II and After*, Cambridge: MIT Press, 2001.

5. Herman Kahn, *Thinking About the Unthinkable*, New York: Horizon, 1962; Herman Kahn *On Escalation: Metaphors and Scenarios*, New York: Hudson Institute, 1965.

6. Pierre Wack, *Scenarios: The Gentle Art of Re-Perceiving (One Thing or Two Learned While Developing Planning Scenarios for Royal Dutch/Shell)*, Cambridge: Harvard Business School, 1984.

7. For example: Kees van der Heijden, *Scenarios: The Art of Strategic Conversation*, New York: Wiley, 1996.

8. P. Raskin et al. *Bending the Curve: Toward Global Sustainability*, Stockholm: Stockholm Environment Institute, 1998.

9. *www.geocities.com/~acunu*

10. For example, aged care is a major issue in Australia, but the national and state governments are reluctant to look at the long-term future of aged care; they prefer to deal with only immediate issues. The first use of scenario planning for Australian aged care has been conducted by a nongovernmental organization, which is one of the country's main providers of aged care: Keith Suter and Steve England, *Alternative Futures for Aged Care*, Sydney: Uniting Church in Australia, 2001.

11. Peter Schwartz *The Art of the Long View: Planning for the Future in an Uncertain World*, New York: Doubleday, 1991.

12. *www.gbn.com*

13. See: Peter Pringle and William Arkin, *SIOP: Single Integrated Operational Plan: Nuclear War from the Inside*, London: Sphere, 1983.

14. To her credit, the British Prime Minister Margaret Thatcher was quicker off the mark. In 1984, as a rising young Soviet minister, Gorbachev traveled to London where he and Raisa handled the British media and politicians very well. Mrs. Thatcher said, "I like Mr. Gorbachev. We can do business together." Donald Morrison (Editor) *Mikhail S Gorbachev: An Intimate Biography*, New York: Time, 1988, p. 129.

7

Four Worldviews on Globalization

INTRODUCTION

The purpose of this chapter is to explore four worldviews. What will be the next stage of the Westphalian System? As with all work in scenario planning, the purpose is to encourage thinking "outside the square" rather than to advocate a particular point of view. The task is not to pick a winning forecast; the future will determine that. Instead, the task is to create a set of worldviews, which in broad terms cover all the eventualities that could emerge. Thus, this chapter contains points of view that are contrary to my own thinking and values but need to be included so as to provide a broad range of worldviews.[1] Additionally, it is in the nature of worldviews that a piece of information could be used in two or more worldviews; viewed from more than one perspective, that information can be used in more than one worldview.

The four worldviews are drawn from the intersection of two axes. In determining the driving forces of change, I have opted for "strength/weakness of the nation-state" and "strength/weakness of international social cohesion," that is, level of international cooperation. This gives four quadrants which then become four worldviews:

1. Strong nation-state/weak international social cohesion (national governments remain in control of their destiny and are unwilling to work together on common problems): "Steady State." This is based on seeing the current global order, with all its problems, as the best that can be devised.

2. Strong nation-state/strong international social cohesion (national governments, while they remain in control of their destiny, are willing to work together on common problems and this evolves gradually into some form of global governance): "World State." This is based on there being no purely national solutions to transnational problems, and so governments have to work together through some form of global governance to solve common problems.

3. Weak nation-state/strong international social cohesion (national governments lose control over their countries and there is a willingness to have transnational corporations fill the vacuum): "Earth Inc." With the decline of the

nation-state, the only organizations capably of driving the pace of change are transnational corporations, which then knit the world together into one market as they fill the governmental vacuum.

4. Weak nation-state/weak international social cohesion (national governments lose control over their countries and there is no organization to fill the vacuum and so there is increasing chaos): "Wild State." This is the "nightmare" scenario: nation-states fall apart, "failed states" increase, masses of people move around, and environmental and health problems increase.

These are worldviews. They are not fully fleshed-out scenarios, with indicators and contingency plans drawn up. Such a project would be beyond this chapter's scope. Instead, the intention is to stimulate debate over the type of world that we are likely to confront in the hope that (as dealt with in the next chapter), there can be more attention to global governance.

1. STEADY STATE

Introduction

This worldview argues that despite the talk of global change and all it involves, the basic nation-state structure will remain. Although the structure may have problems, it is the best within the range of options. Instead of talking about a post-Westphalian order, it would be better for scholars to spend time on working out how the current order can be strengthened. This worldview is composed of three elements.

National Sovereignty

National sovereignty is here to stay. There may be some erosion of it. But even that may be in itself an exercise of national sovereignty: Governments are willing to surrender some sovereignty over an issue. But they do so because it is in the national interest. Surrendering a bit of national sovereignty consolidates overall national sovereignty. For example, governments will work together through an environmental treaty because it is of benefit to their own citizens.

More generally, however, governments are not willing to surrender national sovereignty. There has been little progress in establishing nonpartisan, not self-interested standards of behavior among governments. All forms of international cooperation are viewed from each government's point of view.

Regrettable, this self-interest is nevertheless a fact of political life. All politics is local; foreigners don't vote in national elections. For example, all western countries are now troubled by the mass movement of peoples into their them. While some countries are more at risk for this kind of migration than others, they are all concerned with it. For example, an unpopular government in Australia scored a surprise victory in the 2001 national election because it tapped into Australian fears of being swamped by asylum seekers; this government took elaborate steps to deter these would-be migrants from trying to reach Australia. Perhaps breaching Australia's international refugee treaty obligations, the deterrence won the government the election.[2] As long as some countries are extremely wealthy and others extremely poor, national boundaries, even in the future, will have to remain in place to restrict the movement of peoples. It is unlikely that this gap between rich and poor will disappear for many decades to come, if ever, given the nature of the international economic system. Therefore, national border protection will remain very important.

There is also the particular role of the United States. The nation is still responsible for about a quarter of global economic production as well as a great deal of scientific research and development. The United States is the world's only super power. All talk of global governance will get nowhere if the United States itself is not involved; it is too big to ignore. At present, there is no possibility of a global-minded presidential candidate ever getting elected. The last, and probably only, such serious candidate was Henry Wallace, who was Vice President in President Roosevelt's third term but dropped for the fourth one in favor of the less colorful Harry Truman. Wallace, as an independent candidate, called himself a "progressive capitalist" who advocated a greater U.S. involvement in international affairs than was acceptable at the time. Defeated in 1948, the scare campaign against him was of far greater intensity than any characterizing current election campaigns; he received only 1.2 million votes.[3] This concern with national sovereignty is not simply a western one. Developing countries also have a strong determination to maintain national sovereignty. Having fought hard for their independence from colonial masters, they are now troubled by threats of tribalism, fragmentation, and the erosion of national unity by cultural diversity and foreign influences. These countries are not going to surrender their national sovereignty for fear of being swamped by a fresh form of imperialism. At least their problems are ones of their own making.

Meanwhile there is no guarantee that the under-privileged—wherever they live—will be any better off under any other form of global governance. As long as there is a split between labor and capital, the nation-state will continue to be needed to safeguard the rights of workers. While capital is mobile, workers are not. Transnational corporations can move money and jobs around the globe, but workers cannot suddenly move from one country to another. National governments may not now be very effective in the face of transnational corporations, but workers have them. In contrast, transnational corporations make profits and do not look after the workers. While a corporation is accountable to its owners/stockholders, who may not necessarily reside in the countries where a corporation operates, governments are accountable to voters.

Similarly, if the affairs of a nation-state are mismanaged, on whom do the people vent their anger other than their government? In every country, the people look to their their various governments to provide the stability essential for the common benefit, national defense, law and order, social services, health care, education and public transport. They also look to the government for the preservation of national identity and all that that entails. Again, the systems of democracy may not be much—but they are something. There is nothing else to do this work.

This preference to retain national sovereignty is not a desire to return to the world order, for example, of the 1930s with its isolationism, feeble League of Nations with a limited membership, and competing trade blocs. The current situation shows that it is possible to have a world order based on respect for national sovereignty without a return to the risks of the 1930s. The problem with the advocates of globalization is that they tend to polarize the possibilities between some form of global governance or an era like the 1930s, with the inherent risks of another world war. In fact, maintaining a middle course between both extremes is possible, and governments are managing to do that at present.

Finally, it is important to remember the limits of what any country, even the United States, can achieve outside its own borders. Much of the current global governance discussion is based on inflated thoughts about what can be achieved. As Henry Kissinger has warned, the UN should not be over-rated on what it can do, the United States is not in a position to introduce genuine democratic reforms in Russia, and the United States should not have a "one size fits all" approach to the international protection of human rights.[4]

Similarly, although some change has occurred in, for example, the international protection of human rights, little consistency yet exists in it. The notion of "domestic jurisdiction" has been eroded, and there have been attempts, a few successful, to try people overseas for war crimes, such as the trials relating to former Yugoslavia. However, there is no reliable, standard system for such trials. While inconsistent measures are too often applied during the trials, some war crimes situations are ignored, and others pursued. All governments—in the pursuit of national sovereignty—have a policy of selective indignation: They criticize some alleged human rights violations (of their enemies) and ignore others (of their allies).

Reluctance to Change

There is a reluctance to change to some form of global governance. This can be seen at all levels of societies in which people may express their opinions freely.

First, there is no public groundswell in favor of global governance; people do not see themselves as world citizens. Even when drawn together in massive international events, such as the 2000 Sydney Olympics which was the largest

peacetime event in world history, they still retain their senses of national loyalties. This does not necessarily mean that they are violent towards other people, simply that they have a sense of national pride and a feeling of being
distinct from others. Paralleling this nationalism, little progress has been made
in gaining support for a common international auxiliary language, such as
Esperanto.

Meanwhile, very few mainstream nongovernmental organizations have
global governance as a key campaign issue. Recognizing that such a project is
too big, they prefer to stick to their own core business whether it be the environment, nuclear disarmament, the status of women in developing countries,
or another issue.

On the contrary, talk of global governance or world government only scares
most folk. They have enough difficulty trying to influence politicians at the
national level; they fear that they would stand very little chance of influencing
politicians at the international level. Besides, people are voting more often but
enjoying it less. Voter turnout in most western countries is now at a low level.
Even the eastern European countries, which have had only a decade or so of
free elections, are already experiencing low voter turnout. There is a widespread
cynicism about politicians. Who ever you vote for, a politician always wins.

Second, the various global governance groups themselves cannot work
within a single organization.[5] The bewildering variety of NGOs shows their
lack of ability to work together. If they cannot work together, what hope is
there that they can unite the world? Taken together, NGOs have a very small
membership, and usually an aging one. NGOs are obviously failing to capture
the public imagination, especially that of younger people.

Third, there is no sense of long-term vision in politics. People are far more
concerned about what is in it for them now. They have little concern about
subsequent generations, or even other people overseas. Paul Kennedy has argued that political leaders in many countries now find it hard to call on their
voters for sacrifices even for immediate purposes, such as increasing foreign
aid, abolishing farm support, or accepting drastic changes to their lifestyle to
fend off global warming.[6]

Information does not necessarily lead to action. Although optimists have
argued that learning about the problems of other people and the planet will
propel people into mass action, it has not. In fact, we now have an information
blizzard. Feeling overwhelmed by all the information, people are more para-
lyzed than mobilized. Further, people increasingly get the media they want. In
western societies, it is no longer possible for a high-minded person, such as
Lord Reith of the BBC, to decide that people should have what they need,
rather than what they want.[7] The public prefers to be entertained rather than
informed.[8]

Bystanders do not have obligations. Indeed, instead of being mobilized
by information about overseas problems, people tend to become even more

determined not to share their possessions with others. What they have, they hold. Instead of developing some form of global consciousness, the information adds to the fears that people have about other countries and hence their support for conservative politicians who promise to reduce foreign aid and refuse asylum seekers.

Fourth, much of global governance discussion is based on the wrong assumption: that there is some form of progress in political affairs. Science and technology obviously change in major ways, not all of which necessarily benefit humankind. However, there is not the same pattern at work in politics. Human nature never changes. A reader of Edward Gibbon's *The History of the Decline and Fall of the Roman Empire* (or, more likely these days, a person who has seen the award-winning move *Gladiator*) would see that politicians and their ambitions do not change much from one millennium to the next. Indeed, journalist Robert Kaplan, who has referred to the "disturbing freshness" of the Gibbon book, can see similarities between the declining Roman Empire and the United States today.[9]

Meanwhile, the twentieth century began with a war in the Balkans and ended with one. Half a millennium ago, Europeans were troubled by militant Islam, as it sought to get a toehold in Spain and in Eastern Europe; there are similar concerns now. No progress is evident in the peace process in the Middle East, an area with severe conflicts for thousands of years. In African countries, most citizens are poorer now than they would have been half a century ago when there were still European colonies.

Although war is terrible, it has its uses. The American Civil War ended slavery and preserved the Union. World War II ended militarism in Germany, Italy and Japan. The Korean War stopped the North Korean annexation of South Korea. The resistance of the East Timorese 1975–1999 forced the Indonesian invaders out of their territory; nothing else, certainly not UN resolutions was going to move them.

Fifth, most warnings in the name of global security have proved to be false alarms. Apparently created to encourage global governance, these warnings are over-statements of problems. The world can survive without the global governance remedy. Doom-laden Y2K predictions over a global computer crisis erupting on January 1, 2000, make up perhaps the most well known recent example of false warnings. Another example comes from the world's biggest business best-seller book in 1967: *The American Challenge* by Jean-Jacques Servan-Schreiber, a French journalist.[10] He predicted that by 1985 or 1990, the world's economy would be owned and run by a dozen or so huge American transnational corporations, whose plants would produce about 90 percent of the world's manufactured goods. Although the United States remains the world's biggest economy, the global economy in fact is not controlled by a dozen American corporations. Many of the corporations now flourishing are not based in the United States. Another false alarm came on May 9, 1969 from the UN Secretary-General, the late U. Thant:

I do not wish to seem over-dramatic, but I can only conclude from the information that is available to me as Secretary-General that the members of the United Nations have perhaps ten years left in which to subordinate their ancient quarrels and launch a global partnership to curb the arms race, to improve the human environment, to defuse the population explosion, and to supply the required momentum to world development efforts.[11]

Only a little progress has been made along these lines. But the world is still here over three decades later. Correct in one way according to the times, the UN Secretary-General was overly dramatic.

By the same token but from the other end of the political spectrum, fears about some form of business world government have not materialized either. For example, the creation of the Trilateral Commission by banker David Rockefeller in the 1970s gave rise to various fears from a group of business people and politicians running the world. One of Rockefeller's colleagues in that venture was the political scientist Zbigniew Brzezinski. He was later one of the 25 Trilateralists, including President Carter, to serve in that Administration (1976–1980). Despite all the alarms, the Carter Administration did not somehow implement the policies (whatever they were) of the Trilateral Commission and indeed left little mark on the U.S. political culture.[12] (Ironically, Carter has been a very influential ex-President, with pioneering work in international conflict resolution; however, that skill did not evidently come from his being involved with the Trilateral Commission.

Finally, life goes on. The United States is recovering from the September 11 attacks in much the same way as the Europeans recovered from World War II. Although people get shocked about certain events, the effect is absorbed in the ongoing flow of life. Humans are very resilient; the survivors recover from wars, plagues, famines, and more. This is a good facet of the unchanging nature of humans.

THERE IS NO ALTERNATIVE TO THE SYSTEM OF NATION-STATES

The Failure of Existing Organizations

Most obviously, the League of Nations failed and the UN has had only limited success. By being one of the authors of the League of Nations, President Woodrow Wilson sought a transformation of the international political system.[13] He wanted to move from a balance of power to a system of collective security in which an attack on one country would be seen as an attack on all. Wilson also wanted an end to militarism and imperialism. Possessing strong belief in the power of public opinion to influence recalcitrant governments, he certainly did not lack vision. However, Wilson could not even convince his own Congress to share that vision; the nation returned to a policy of isolationism.

While the UN has not collapsed, it is achieving less than its architects presumably hoped for in 1945; the world is beset with conflicts right now. Additionally, as was noted in chapter 4, there is much talk of UN reform. Yet no substantive change has been made to the UN Charter since its creation in 1945.

At the regional level, only the European Union shows much sign of progress. There are some free trade agreements, such as the North American Free Trade Agreement, but no other ambitious political unions as such. South America's largest trading block consisting of Argentina, Brazil, Paraguay, and Uruguay (Mercosur) has not grown in the way intended when it was created in March 1991. Mercosur has not, for example, become a customs union with a common external tariff; Member countries still have their own tariff arrangements when trading outside the Mercosur zone, which includes the bulk of their trade.[14] Of course, even the EU has its problems. It lacks a common foreign and defense policy. Additionally, there is concern about the lack of democracy and transparency within the EU bureaucracy. That a flourishing EU could have tensions with the United States over trade, military affairs, environmental protection, and the need to protect European culture from the Hollywood onslaught gives rise to further unease.[15] In short, a world of regional intergovernmental arrangements will not be without its own problems.

The Failure of Grand Proposals

Even modest versions of grand schemes have gone nowhere. One example of the failure to implement even modest reforms comes from Al Gore, the Democratic Candidate in the 2000 U.S. presidential election. In 1992, the then Senator Al Gore had written *Earth in the Balance: Forging a New Common Purpose*.[16] Although he became Vice President in that same year, very little of the book's many recommendations were implemented in the eight years of the Clinton Administration (1992–2000). Indeed, many of Gore's criticisms of the Reagan and Bush administrations, 1980–1988 and 1992–2000 respectively, could almost as easily be applied to the Clinton years. For example, Gore discusses the Bush administration's poor performance at the 1992 UN Conference on Environment and Development. However, there were few environmental successes for the Clinton Administration. The United States did not, for example, make much progress in reducing its greenhouse gases.

It is important to note that Vice President Gore was one of the closest advisers to the President. While most vice presidents have been ignored by their presidents, President Clinton gave Gore a large role. Despite all this status, very few of the book's ideas were implemented.

First, this is not an era for grand plans. Gore had discussed the need for a Global Marshall Plan in which countries would work with each other to protect the environment. But nothing contained in the book was introduced by the Clinton Administration. This is an era of cynicism, small government, low taxes, individualism, and electoral self-interest. Second, many members of Congress did not believe that the United States had any responsibility to assist other countries or the global environment. The people who created the original Marshall Plan in the late 1940s had seen the need for international co-operation to defeat Hitler. They had become afraid of the new communist threat from Moscow. They wanted to learn the lessons of history and the dangers of the United States being isolationist in the 1920s and 1930s. But many members of the current Congress have not been overseas as tourists—let alone as soldiers. The United States is in a new wave of isolationism as it reduces its role in international cooperation. For example, the original Marshall Plan meant that the country gave foreign aid worth 2.0 percent of its GNP per year; now the United States gives 0.10 percent of its GNP, and mostly to Israel and Egypt. Given this isolation from other nations and the globe, most members of Congress certainly are not willing to support grand schemes to help the environment.

Finally, the U.S. Government, like all governments, has little influence on international environmental policy. Americans themselves as consumers have significantly damaged the global environment, but their government has little influence on global environmental policy. Indeed, most decisions now affecting the environment are made outside national governments, such as those relating to the consumer demands created and satisfied by transnational corporations. Even within the UN, the UN Environment Program is a very small organization with a smaller budget than the international budget of Greenpeace. Therefore, there was little foreign government support for the grand plans set out by Al Gore.

A second example of modest reform failing occurred in the inefficacy of the Brandt Report.[17] The late Willy Brandt, former Chancellor of West Germany, was invited in 1977 by Robert McNamara, then President of the World Bank, to chair an inquiry on ways of assisting developing countries. The late Katherine Graham of *The Washington Post* and *Newsweek* was one of the 16 distinguished commissioners, and she wrote about the Commission's workings in her autobiography.[18] McNamara had hoped that she would use her media connections to get publicity for the report in the United States. In the end, not only did the report fail to have much political impact anywhere in the world, but also Graham was unable to get her own media outlets to give it much coverage. They did not think it important enough. She had implored her editors to devote a cover story of *Newsweek* to Third World issues—and it was the worst-selling issue of the year.

A final example concerns the international control of atomic energy. This was first raised in the 1946 Baruch Plan from theUnited States, which envisaged the creation of an international atomic development authority. The managerial control of all atomic energy activities potentially dangerous to world security as well as the power to control, inspect, and license all other atomic activities would have been among the functions of this body. The U.S.S.R., which was secretly developing its own atomic weapons, opposed it. The eventual International Atomic Energy Agency (IAEA) was a much more modest version of this proposal. A similar scheme for general and complete disarmament, the McCloy-Zorin Plan in1960, also failed. The recent disarmament treaties, while welcome, are a long way from the vision of the 1960 joint United States-U.S.S.R. proposal.[19] There is a failure by governments to take a risk for peace.

The Failure to Learn from History

American world governance activists also make too much of the "miracle at Philadelphia" in 1787, when the current U.S. Constitution was created.[20] Although the 1776 Articles of Confederation sufficed for the 13 colonies to win the war, the articles could not cope with the problems of peace. In 1783, the 13 sovereign American governments thought that they could retain their sovereignty and still be at peace with each other. This is a bit like the world today, and there were the same sorts of problems, on a much smaller scale, as the world has today. For example, border disputes broke out between Pennsylvania and New Jersey; Connecticut and Massachusetts could not agree on the acquisition of western territories; the currency fluctuated; and in December 1786, Captain Daniel Shays, a Continental Army veteran, led a rebellion to disrupt the Massachusetts Supreme Court. In 1787, the 13 states agreed to forego some of their sovereignty in the interest of creating a central government.

However, American global governance activists misread the applicability of their history to the rest of the world. They argue that because the Framers of the Constitution could create a document that has worn well for over two centuries, then some sort of international constitutional convention could also create an international constitution.[21] Although the Constitution has worn well, it in fact has not been without problems, such as the vote-counting problems in the November 2000 presidential election and the long-running legislative gridlock between the congressional and executive branches.

It also is important to note that the 1787 document was written by a group of white, property-owning, middle-class males with many similar outlooks. That such a document could be produced today is not clear. For example, the failure of the Equal Rights Amendment (ERA) shows that the U.S. political culture is now much more diverse. Similarly, the Canadians have not been able to agree on how their Constitution should be amended to accommodate Quebec and French-speaking interests, and the Australians have not been able to agree on whether their country should become a republic.

Finally, fearing a tyranny of the majority as well as an autocratic leader, the Framers in 1787 created the Supreme Court as an elite institution with powers to check the congressional and executive branches. Indeed, it seems that they wanted to put the legal system above party politics. Thus, the Court could hand down the *Brown v. Brown* school-desegregation decision in 1954, well ahead of local public opinion. Democracy evidently has its limits. This point of view cuts across all the NGO advocacy for some form of "global democracy."[22]

Too Big a Challenge

Finally, there are too many questions to be solved; the list is overwhelming. How would the form of global governance be created? Why would national governments want to give up their power? How would the leader be selected? Where would the world government be based? What is to stop the creation of a world dictatorship? How would the voting take place? Would China and India dominate proceedings by virtue of their population sizes? Would the United States do so because of its economic muscle? Given that voters are already cynical about national elections, why would they want to vote in an international election? How would it be financed? What happens if some countries refuse to join? What happens if a country wants to leave? Could there be a global civil war because some countries want to secede? What if there is corruption among the leadership? What is to be done to arrest an aggressive national leader who is protected by the country's armed forces? How would aggressive fanatical political or religious movements be handled? Would the world government have nuclear weapons and other weapons of mass destruction to keep member countries in order?

To conclude, it is better to stick with what we have. It may not be perfect, but it is too risky gambling on an alternative to the nation-state.

2. THE WORLD STATE

Introduction

This worldview argues that this is the first time in history that people have been confronted with the need to organize and manage the world as a totality. Beginning at the time of World War I, world history could be described as a single, protracted experiment in global governance. Underlying all the conflicts and upheavals, there has been a basic question: How is humanity to govern itself? While the problems are a long way from being solved, there is no choice but to continue the quest because the world as a whole, not just its parts, has to be managed. The world is now too interdependent, with one part affecting others, to try to operate on a piece-by-piece basis. For example, a nuclear disaster, such as the one at Chernobyl, has immediate and long-range implications for other countries.

Therefore, there is a need for some form of world government. The tendency among NGO advocates is now to talk more about "governance" because it is less threatening to the general public than "world government." Also, it may well be that its eventual form will have to be different from existing notions of national "government" and so the term "world government" is misleading because of the connotations of "government" at the national level.

The New Era

The Pace of Change

We are living in a new era. For example, there is no effective defense against modern methods of mass destruction. Therefore, no country is able to protect its citizens adequately merely through an increase in its military strength. Even though some progress has been made in reducing the number of U.S. and Soviet/Russian nuclear missiles, there are still enough in existence to destroy the world. Meanwhile, being the world's most powerful country did not protect the United States on September 11, 2001, from being attacked by the misuse of civilian airliners full of highly explosive aviation gas.

Therefore, the world order of nation-states cannot continue as per the Steady State worldview. Some problems are getting worse. This book has already identified many of them and so there is no need to repeat them in detail: warfare, transnational crime, environmental degradation, violations of human rights, plagues as well as diseases, poverty, illiteracy, and ethnic tensions. There are no national solutions to transnational problems.

Finally, predicting the long-term impact of technology on uniting the globe is impossible. In August 1971, the British writer Arthur C. Clarke, particularly well known for *2001*, told U.S. Secretary of State William Rogers, "You have just signed a first draft of the Articles of Federation of the United States of Earth."[23] The State Department signing ceremony was for an international agreement involving 80 countries on six continents, which would create an intergovernmental partnership for telecommunications. Soon after World War II, Clarke had proposed that countries create an international network of communications satellites to facilitate international civilian communications. Another distinguished guest at the signing ceremony was former First Lady Mamie Eisenhower. The first voice ever beamed to Earth from a communications satellite was that of her husband President Dwight Eisenhower in December 1958, just over a decade after Clarke's seminal essay was published. Now people use mobile telephones to ring around the globe and think nothing of it. This is a technology that we take for granted.

Clarke in his comments at the ceremony emphasized the impact of technology on uniting the United States. Recalling the way in which the railroad and the telegraph had brought the nation together in the nineteenth century, he looked forward to the impact of international telecommunications in creating a Federation of the United States of Earth. But such a federation will require skill, and there is a need to avoid complacency. Speaking at a World Telecommunications Day ceremony on May 17, 1983, Clarke recalled the comments of the Chief Engineer of the British Post Office, who was not impressed when he heard about Alexander Graham Bell's invention of the telephone; the telegraph system was fine for the British. "The Americans," the Chief Engineer said, "have need of the telephone—but we do not. We have plenty of messenger boys."[24]

An example of the importance of global communications came in 1990 with the attempted coup against Gorbachev.[25] The U.S. government had first realized that something was underway when its spy satellites showed that all telephone traffic from Gorbachev's Black Sea villa had ceased. The plotters had cut the lines. But the plotters in Moscow had overlooked Gorbachev's ability to stay in touch with events by listening to the BBC and Radio Liberty as both reported on the resistance in Moscow led by Boris Yeltsin. The plotters had also failed to control the Moscow media, which broadcast its own reports of the defiant Yeltsin atop a Soviet tank. Private computer users in Russia were also busy sending and receiving messages of the attempted coup. The attempted coup quickly collapsed.

An indicator of the speed of change is Moore's Law. Gordon Moore, a founder of Intel, observed in 1965 that computer power doubles about every two years and halves in price. This helps explain the way in which consumers are forever being obliged to upgrade their computers; this is not a conspiracy by the IT corporations to have built-in obsolescence. As with most other technological developments, the impact of Moore's Law is simply absorbed by most people without thinking about it. People see its impact all around them, including in something as basic as the special effects in movies, some of which could not have been produced as recently as five years previously. The Human Genome Project, the largest scientific project in history, has been mapping the DNA structure; the scientists have been calculating on Moore's Law assisting them. When the project began, it would have taken many decades to complete it on the computer technology then available. By the use of Moore's Law, however, the scientists predicted a completion date of 2003, which was largely met ahead of schedule in 2001.

Moore's Law cuts out by the year 2020. By about that time, the silicon circuits will have reached the end of their era and there will be a new basis for circuits, with computers designing the next era. Of course, also by that time computers will be very different from what they are now. Neil Gershenfeld, of the MIT Media Lab in Boston, has speculated that computer technology will pervade everything; we will be wearing computers in the fabric of our clothes everyday, and information will be everywhere all the time.[26] By that time, we may have also bridged the gap between humans and computers so that the computers will be "thinking" like humans.

Given this pace of change, it is impossible to predict what the impact could be on global governance, or many other forms of human endeavor. A Steady State mentality is not the right one with which to view the world because the computer world in itself is not in a steady state.

Different Routes to World Unity

Just how the world evolves to a different form of governance is not yet clear. There are three ways of trying to get countries united:

Federalist approach: the deliberate decision by national governments to transfer certain powers (such as maintaining armed forces) to a world government while retaining other powers (such as establishing laws concerning ownership of property) for themselves.

Functionalist approach: the creation of more global agencies (such as the World Health Organization) to handle a particular function (such as health) because experts can cooperate in a less politically-charged environment, and eventually the globe will be covered by a network of such agencies.

Populist Approach: the creation of a grass-roots people's movement to establish a democratic world government directly responsible to the people of the world, and in the meantime to generate ideas for world government and a groundswell in favor of it.

There is a chicken and egg dilemma. We cannot discuss world government because we have no world community to support it. Indeed, the discussion of world government may even retard the development of world community because of its evil overtones and associations with Orwellian Big Brother which, in turn, retards the movement towards world government. On the other hand, that cautious approach may over-emphasize the state of perfection which the world community must achieve before world government can be considered. The way to promote world community is to have world government. But since private citizens cannot establish a world government, the next best thing to promote world community is to talk about global governance. World discussion of world government may have some chance of uniting it. The consideration of what is necessary to unite the world and the discussion of a common problem of overwhelming importance could lead to a growing sense of community among all peoples.

An important reason for talking about world government is to clarify what it would be. Should a world government aim at limited measures designed to maintain what is called security, or is security itself dependent on the pursuit of broader purposes? Should a world state be federal or unitary, or should it, perhaps, contain the best features of each? What should be the relation of the world government to the citizens of extant states? What taxing powers should the world state have, and what order of military forces, if any? This list of questions can be prolonged indefinitely, and there are countless possible answers to each of them. Consequently, many global governance activists prefer to campaign on all three of the above approaches simultaneously. For example, they deal with the need for governments to work together at the political (federal) level and on common problems (functional approach) and the importance of people being involved in the campaign for world government. This may seem a bewildering range of activities and views. But it is clear from the *Federalist Papers* that the Framers of the U.S. Constitution also had a great deal of discussion on what a national government would look like.

The Long View

It is necessary to view the quest for global governance as a very long term project, in which some progress has been made. What may seem impossible at one point may be possible later on. Indeed, it is worth noting that Henry Wallace, the presidential candidate who was too imaginative for voters in 1948, had other policies which have since been accepted: an end to racial segregation, the vote for 18-year-olds, equal rights for women, and home rule for the District of Columbia. In a sense, many of his policies did win in the end.

Besides the experiments with the League of Nations and UN, there has been much progress in the virtual abolition of the international slave trade, the prohibition of slavery within many countries, and the eradication of some diseases, such as small pox. Each of these projects took time. For example, the British campaign to abolish the slave trade began with an NGO formed in 1783. The House of Lords, which then had more power than today, was dominated by plantation owners and so supported the slave trade. Slavery also was supported by a variety of other financial interests in England, such as the major port cities of Bristol and Liverpool. Some church leaders also argued that slavery was permitted by the Bible. Undeterred, William Wilberforce in 1787 first introduced the idea of abolition into the House of Commons, which was less influenced by the financial interests. Opinion began to change about 1792. Owing to the Napoleonic wars, the actual abolition did not take place until 1807, by which time England had control over the seas and could implement its policy of stopping the slave-carrying vessels. Therefore, with time, progress is possible.

There has also been the development of functional cooperation; specialists get together out of the political spotlight to devise methods of cooperation on particular functions. One of these is the standardization of national telephone systems so that people can telephone around the world.

Human affairs are not static. It is not only possible to improve human behavior, but also possible for people to be more cooperative. Dueling is now rare, when once in Europe and the United States it was a normal way among men to settle disputes. However, violence and war are not necessarily the norm in human affairs; some societies have no tradition of either. A learned behavior, warfare demands training. As the UNESCO Seville Statement has argued, war is not inherited from our animal ancestors and not genetically programmed into human nature. While a human does not have a "violent brain," battles do not arise from "instinct" or any single motivation.[27] Therefore, life is not necessarily the struggle of the most violent but may be the struggle of the more cooperative. As chapter 3 showed, there has been some progress in reducing the use of war as an instrument of national policy. Warfare between countries is now very rare. France and Germany, for example, have now gone for over half a century without a war, and it seems highly unlikely that these two traditional enemies will ever go to war with each other again. This does not mean that they have become permanent friends, only that they have developed less violent ways of settling disputes, such as through the European Union and the International Court of Justice.

This change can also be seen in the evolution of international law. Traditionally, international law was relegated to only a small area of relations among countries. However, today many domestic activities have regional and even global impacts; so there has a rapid expansion of international law to cope with these problems. The domain of international law has expanded to encompass matters usually thought to be within domestic jurisdiction, such as environmental law and economic law. The international rule of law will not come all at once. Instead, the field is evolving opportunistically and by piecemeal, like the common law in England, the United States, and some British Commonwealth countries.

There has also been the rise of interest in what is called cosmopolitan democracy, which refers to a system whereby citizens (and not merely governments) are able to manage and participate in the global community.[28] This is globalization from below, via the people and not imposed upon them by institutions.[29] Indeed, Jody Williams, who won the Nobel Peace Prize, led her international campaign to ban landmines from a farmhouse in Vermont. As with Wilberforce two centuries earlier, her point of view resonated with the mood of the times. Her advantage was the speed and low cost of electronic communications.

Meanwhile, recalling the slow evolution of democracy in western countries provides a good analogy for global governance. Not springing fully fledged upon citizens, democracy was granted a gradual accretion of power by the people. Even something as basic as the right to vote evolved over the centuries. It began with only adult, white male property owners, a minority in eighteenth century America, and now includes all adult U.S. citizens. As with democracy, the progress in global governance will be slow but irreversible.

Finally, a lesson of history is to be learned from the protracted unification of Italy in 1815–1870 and two key statements from the Prime Minister during that time. In 1861, Mr D'Azeglio remarked "Italy is now made, now we must make Italians."[30] Thus, we first create institutions that then change public attitudes. He also warned that "[t]o make an Italy out of Italians, one must not be in a hurry."[31] The same could be said about Earthlings.

Living by Hope and Not by Fear

Finally, it is better to live by hope than by fear. The Steady State worldview is based on fear. During the Cold War, the U.S. and U.S.S.R. each based international policy on fear, becoming mired in nuclear deterrence and the very expensive arms race.

First, we need to have optimism. Long recognized as an important American quality, optimism characterized the 55 delegates who met at the 1787 Philadelphia convention. Instead of looking for a problem in every opportunity, it is important to look for an opportunity in every problem. How can the current set of global problems be used to forge a better form of global governance? How can the tragedy of September 11 be used to create a better world order?

Second, it is necessary to step out in faith. Many problems of governance, at any level of society, have been around for centuries, if not millennia. For example, one of the basic political theory books is Plato's *Republic* which, over two millennia ago, raised issues still not satisfactorily resolved.[32] But people have not become too discouraged. Instead of waiting for a solution to be produced on paper, people have moved pragmatically forward in the hope of being able to find a solution. If they had waited for a perfect solution, there would not have been much progress in the intervening two millennia.

Third, humanity's quest has been assisted by some pioneer writers. World government writers Edith Wynner and Georgia Lloyd in 1949 did a chronological survey of proposals for world government. The first proposal in 1306, by the French jurist and politician Pierre Dubois, recommended the absolute dictatorship of one monarch to wage a war that would unify Christianity by force, make the Pope supreme ruler, and France the police.[33] There has been no shortage of ideas from lawyers and others. There are already many in circulation. There is no need to reinvent the wheel.

Fourth, when it is recalled just how much is achieved by the UN with so little money, we wonder what could be achieved if it had a very large budget. The UN has a budget just a bit larger than the state of Virginia. If its budget equaled that of California, even more progress could be made. Rather than the UN failing the world, the world has failed the organization by not providing it with sufficient resources to do its job.

Fifth, not too much should be made of cultural homogeneity. As the historian Gertrude Himmelfarb has pointed out, "national identity does not imply national homogeneity."[34] A country can become distinctive precisely because its population, as in the United States and Australia, has been drawn from a variety of other countries. It is that heterogeneity that helps make national identity. By the same token, there can be global governance based on heterogeneity. The invention of the orchestra did not mean the end of violins. Therefore, it is not necessary to wait for all people to somehow be the same before we can start talking of global governance.

Finally, there is a gradual movement of human consciousness from the tribe to the nation-state and now to the global community. This process has been largely due to the improvements in transport and communications. As Arthur C. Clarke foreshadowed, some additional major changes are soon to occur. It would be better to spend time trying to work out how they can be used to advantage global governance.

3. EARTH INC.

Introduction

This worldview argues that the nation-state will continue in its erosion and that transnational corporations will have an even greater say in how the world is run because they will fill the global governance vacuum. National govern-ments will not necessarily disappear any more than local governments vanished with the rise of national ones. Still, national governments will need to get used to the way that the Westphalian era is over and that corporations are the major player in world affairs. The challenge then is to devise some form of global governance based on the realities of corporation power as well as the need for corporations to assume greater responsibilities for the economic and social life of the countries in which they operate.

Money Is the Measure of All Things

Money is now the measure of all things: This new era maybe began in 1776 with the publication of Adam Smith's *The Wealth of Nations*, which saw the rise of modern capitalism.[35] The market, rather than government involvement or religious dictates, has increasingly set the pace for economic activities. In political terms, this is the classical liberal movement. It began in eighteenth century Europe as a reaction against the control of the government by the king, church, and landed gentry, particularly the way that such control stifled personal enterprise in the emerging Industrial Revolution. People like Adam Smith were the revolutionaries of their day. His *The Wealth of Nations* was coincidentally published in the year of the U.S. Declaration of Independence.

Although the early liberals were not necessarily atheists, they did question some of the basic fundamental Biblical principles about the importance of com-munity over the importance of the individual.

Some of those Biblical principles were set out by the British church leader William Temple (later Archbishop of Canterbury) in the early 1940s in his critique of capitalism.[36] Temple said that the Judeo-Christian ethic holds that the earth—the land—belongs to God, with all people enjoying the use of it. Ensuring that all members of the community shared in the enjoyment of some portion of the land was important. There was to be no proletariat. There were thus to be rights of property. But these rights were shared by all and were subject to the over-ruling consideration that God alone had ultimate ownership of the earth, the families to whom land was allotted being His stewards. The Law of Jubilee, by which alienated land reverted to its proper family every 50 years so that the permanent accumulation of a large estate in a single hand became impossible, rested on this basic principle of divine ownership. In short, the church saw the individual not merely as an individual but as part of a community with rights and duties vis-a-vis that community. As such, the in-dividual was not only to avoid exploiting others, but also to help the destitute. This Judeo-Christian reasoning may be seen in many other religions.

While Adam Smith also saw individuals as part of the community, he doubted that government and religious dictates were the best way to ensure economic growth. His book *The Wealth of Nations* has been in print for over two centuries.[37] Few other nonfiction books can claim such a record. He was an advocate of the policy of laissez faire, both nationally and internationally. Smith argued for the free market, to give the greatest scope to the division of labor; for competition, to assert itself provided monopolistic positions were not supported by the State; and for unimpeded international commerce.

Smith placed emphasis on individuals being left free to pursue their own interests. Self-interest or selfishness guides people, as though by the influence of an invisible hand, to the exercise of the intelligence that maximizes productive effort and thus the public good. Private vice becomes a public virtue. Therefore, a free market—not government—is the best allocator of resources and the best promoter of the public good. Government should be as small as possible, with limited responsibilities. Thus, the individual should be left to maximize his own income and determine how that money is to be spent. Two centuries later, this is now the world's most popular economic philosophy.

Meanwhile, with money as the measure of all things, national identity ceases to be such a major issue except where it can be turned into a commodity, as in corporations manufacturing support for local or national sporting teams. People are principally consumers or aspiring consumers. They are consumed by their desires for consumption. Politics and patriotism are not as pleasurable as the latest fashion in clothes, music, or technology. People are consumers rather than citizens. That is their choice. They have a freedom to choose.

The Erosion of National Government Power

Western governments have been reducing their role in the economic life of their countries for some years; the vacuum has been filled by transnational corporations. The twentieth century may be seen as the rise and fall of government. While the century began with limited government involvement in the economy, the Great Depression of the 1930s followed by World War II resulted in far greater government intervention in the economy, as part of the Keynesian revolution.

The process of withdrawing from the Keynesian revolution began in the late 1970s. Robert Skidelsky's three volume biography of John Maynard Keynes records the rise of Keynesian economics and notes at the end of the third volume, the beginning of the retreat from such thinking. In 1976, the British Labor Prime Minister, James Callaghan, announced the end of the era: "The option of spending our way out of recession no longer exists."[38] The process was greatly accelerated by the Conservative leader Margaret Thatcher, who was first elected in 1979.

As if to emphasize the irrelevance of party labels, the policies were principally introduced by conservative governments in the United States (Reagan) and United Kingdom (Thatcher) but by Labor governments in Australia and New Zealand. Successors of these leaders have maintained the policy of less government intervention. In the U.S.S.R., Gorbachev also decided to reduce government intervention in the economy and introduced "perestroika," or restructuring. In his 1997 Inaugural Address, President Clinton virtually said that government was irrelevant: "And once again, we have resolved for our time a great debate over the role of government. Today we can declare: Government is not the problem, and government is not the solution. We—the American people—are the solution."[39]

In the West, particularly outside the United States, this thinking has been manifested in terms of privatization and deregulation.

"Privatization" means selling off government assets, enterprises, and services to private entrepreneurs, in the expectation that they can run them more efficiently. This reduces the size of the public sector. Government ownership encourages relative inefficiency in two main ways. First, public enterprises are immune from the threat of takeover and can avoid the discipline of the financial markets. Second, these enterprises are more vulnerable than their private counterparts to political and industrial pressure. Privatization may lead to increased efficiency, but it also can mean less national government control over an industry if the shares are bought by foreigners. This helps pave the way for the erosion of national governmental control over some of the main institutions, such as transport and telephone utilities, in the economy.

Some of these bodies have national iconic value. They may carry the name of the country in their title but now actually have little to do with the country in terms of ownership. British Rail, for example, is partly owned by a French company. In 2000, the Ansett Australian airline, a private one, collapsed through poor management. It had been bought a few years earlier by Air New Zealand, and the New Zealand Government was held responsible by angry Australians for the collapse of this well known company. But Air New Zealand itself was sold off many years earlier to be largely owned by Singapore interests, as the New Zealand Prime Minister tried to explain during a rowdy meeting in Australia. Meanwhile, the Bank of New Zealand is owned by the National Australia Bank.

In popular language, deregulation means abolishing red tape. The assumption is that individuals and corporations could be more enterprising and productive if only they were freer to do so. A major example of this is the deregulation of the financial services sector, which includes permitting people to own gold bullion and to buy foreign currency. The other side of financial deregulation has been the control over government policies by financial markets. Even if they want to, governments cannot adopt policies to increase growth, reduce unemployment, and expand government if financial markets disapprove.

Transnational corporations have eroded the notion of a national economy; there is now only a global one. Kenichi Ohmae, a Japanese business consultant, has coined a new term: the Inter-Linked Economy (ILE) of the Triad (United States, Europe, and Japan), joined by the Asian "tigers" (such as Taiwan, Hong Kong, and Singapore).[40] The emergence of the ILE has created much confusion, particularly for those who are used to dealing with economic policies based on conventional economic statistics that compare one country against another. Their theories do not work any more. For example, if a government tightens the money supply by increasing interest rates, loans may come in from abroad and make the country's monetary policy nearly meaningless because cheaper funds flow in from elsewhere in the ILE. For all practical purposes, the ILE has made obsolete the traditional instruments of central bankers, interest rate and money supply.

These trends help explain the low voter turn out in Western elections: Voters think that the elections are increasingly irrelevant. A political party may come to office—but not necessarily to power. That power is held elsewhere.

Meanwhile, the triumph of corporate power continues. Not only has government risen and fallen in Western countries, but also communism has in Russia. Perestroika, or restructuring, had its origins in the failure of the Soviet system to deliver the goods. Gorbachev's impulse to change was not out of idealism but out of necessity. Given the failure of the U.S.S.R. centralized economic system, Gorbachev went to, in effect, the 1776 text book.

The Soviet State was founded in 1917. Its first leader, V.I. Lenin, did not arrive in power with a clear economic policy. Karl Marx, who had died three decades earlier, thought he had detected a pattern in history which meant that socialist revolutions would take place in industrialized societies and would be led by the factory workers. The process would roll along of its own accord. However, Lenin found himself running a Marxist state in a still largely rural society. Stalin, who took over from Lenin in 1924, had a model of economic development in which the consumer came last while heavy industry came first. The hope was that by initially giving priority to heavy industry and capital accumulation, the Soviet overall economic growth would be faster in the long run than if light industry had been stressed. Once the economic foundation had been created, economic planners theoretically would have been able to pay more attention to consumers. Soviet consumers were obliged to waited patiently for an abundant tomorrow—which never came.

When Gorbachev became the Soviet leader in 1985, he recognized that the U.S.S.R. was in deep trouble. Gorbachev became a glorious failure, loved in the West and hated in his own country. Ending the Cold War, he presided over the collapse of the Soviet Union. Fifteen new countries emerged from the U.S.S.R., many of them with disputed borders and ethnic rivalries. While Gorbachev and the U.S.S.R. have gone, economic reforms have brought few benefits to the ordinary Russian.

But there is no turning back now. A strong Russian ruler of the old Tsarist/ Soviet style could close off the borders, reintroduce the secret police, and keep out foreign investment. Even if it were possible to bring back such protections, such an isolated country could not keep out foreign media broadcasts. Further, the people would not get what they demanded, notably, western goods and services. Russia, without foreign investment and technological services, would remain a Third World economy producing resources for export, but no value-adding and few services. Thus, Russia has no choice but to go forward with the globalization of its economy and make the best of it.

Corporations Rule the World

There is a great deal of agreement among writers of different viewpoints about the growing power of transnational corporations. The disagreement involves whether this trend should be welcomed. On the one hand, some people view this power as a sinister force. David Korten, whose best-selling book *When Corporations Rule the World* lends itself to the above subheading, sees corporations as eroding local cultures, encouraging materialism, and looking after only people with money.[41] Another long-term critic of corporate power is Richard Barnet of the Washington, D.C. Institute of Policy Studies; he is worried about the power of corporations to influence government decision-making for their own benefits rather than the interests of the citizens.[42]

On the other hand, some writers have claimed the process is overall a good one. A rising tide lifts all boats. Kenichi Ohmae sees the world as borderless with national boundaries as simply "cartographic illusions" and with many opportunities for people who wish to take them. There is now a new "invisible continent" in which bold new corporations, such as Microsoft, Dell, and Cisco, can flourish.[43]

Meanwhile, journalist Thomas Friedman of *The New York Times* has written about a world of the efficient manufacture of the Lexus automobile which represents all the burgeoning global markets, financial institutions, and computer technologies with which people pursue higher living standards; the "olive tree" represents a person's traditionally rooted identity and home.[44] Friedman looks to an era in which the world can be made safe for corporations, consumers, and the flourishing of democracy. He is confident that the rooted identity interests can be preserved in an era of rapid modernization.

The modern capitalist economy creates more opportunities for more people than any other economic system. This system feeds upon itself so that more wealth creates more wealth. Supply creates its own demand, as consumers get introduced to goods and services they previously could not conceive of but now cannot live without.[45] Then this wealth trickles down to other areas, where economic growth can begin. Unlike our ancestors, we expect things to change, and we expect to have a better standard of living in the revolution of rising expectations. As this mindset is now taking hold in countries outside the western world, we can expect the twenty-first century to contain the world's greatest economic growth for the largest number of people. Citizens everywhere will achieve this wealth via transnational corporations, rather than government departments and their directives.

Not only is globalization good for people, but it also reduces the risk of international conflict. Why fight against people who could be your customers or are your suppliers? International conflicts are now very rare (if they take place at all) among countries with free trade. More colorfully, countries that have McDonald's fast food outlets do not fight each other: "the golden arches theory of conflict prevention."[46] There is nothing special about fast food as such. But its sale within a country indicates that the government of that country is a believer in free trade and that the citizens are too busy enjoying life to maintain old feuds and hatreds.

Thus, Earth Inc. both rests on increasing global social cohesion and contributes to it. It creates a virtuous spiral.

To conclude, with the down-sizing of governments, transnational corporations as well as businesses in general will become the major factors in determining the pace of change. Businessperson and environmentalist Paul Hawken has argued that business is not merely a reasonable agent for change but the only mechanism powerful enough to reverse global environmental, and social degradation.[47] Every commercial act in today's industrial society Hawken maintains, actually though perhaps not intentionally degrades the environment. What we need is a system in which the opposite is true: The everyday acts of work and production help the environment. His ideas include an intelligent product system that rents, and never sells, toxins. This product system also phases out all payroll and income taxes over two decades by adopting a broad base of green fees that will make it possible for companies to engage in sustainable production as they increase profitability, hire new staff, and become more competitive. In short, business can do better than government in saving the environment.

4. WILD STATE

Introduction

The previous worldviews are all too optimistic. They have focused too much on order, rather than disorder. Of the many sources of disorder in the world, this section will examine three. The Wild State worldview assumes both the continued erosion of the nation-state and the decline of international social cohesion; these trends mean that each nation-state will have to do its best with what is because nothing else will give much assistance.

Money Comes First

Transnational corporations are not a force for good. First, they are motivated only by money. They are out to make money for their owners/stock holders. Out for profit, these corporations do not improve the world unless money can be made from doing so. They are not really accountable to anyone, not even their own stockholders, many of which are pension funds only concerned about the rate of return and not how it is acquired.

The full extent of their evil may not be known for years. For example, Edwin Black, the son of Polish survivors, has examined IBM's role in the Holocaust. When Hitler came to power in 1933, a central Nazi goal was to identify and destroy Germany's Jewish community which had 600,000 members. This is the type of work that requires a computer which did not exist in those days. The closest technology was a Dehomag Hollerith machine for handling punch cards; the machine was owned by IBM in New York. Black argues that "IBM NY always understood—from the outset in 1933—that it was courting and doing business with the upper echelon of the Nazi Party."[48] Indeed,the company leveraged that connection to do business elsewhere in Nazi-dominated Europe. More recent unethical corporate actions remain to be seen. Just what deals are being made and what skullduggery is being committed by the present corporations will be discovered by historians. However, there is not enough research into corporate power; Indeed, as Page Smith argued, university research is being stifled partly by corporate power.[49]

Second, corporations have no allegiances and no loyalties. Thus, they can move production and service centers from one country to another looking for the best rate of return. They can also set one government off against another in a bidding war to attract the corporation to be based in that country. Thus, they get special "export zones," exemptions from labor and environmental regulations as well as favorable tax treatment. Meanwhile, China is undergoing the largest industrial revolution in world history. Its low-paid workers are producing cheap goods which flood foreign markets, undercutting the cost of goods made in those developed countries.

Third, because the corporations are mobile, they have created a race to the bottom. Manufacturers search the world, the single and borderless economy, for greater returns on investment, moving their assembly lines to low-wage countries. The globalization of industrial production is resulting in excess supplies of goods and labor, which in turn exert downward pressures on prices and wages.[50]

Fourth, since corporations also move in search of low-tax regimes, governments lack the funds for the supply of services. Along with the revolt against paying taxes by individuals comes a resistance by corporations to pay taxes. While this extra money in the hands of individuals and corporations has helped finance a vast consumer expansion over the past three decades or so, there also are shortages in essential services and infrastructure. No politician in the English-speaking world will get elected on a ticket of "vote for me and I will increase taxation."

Meanwhile, transnational corporations can legally pay the least amount of tax because they can afford to employ better lawyers and accountants than a national tax office, not to mention the small local businesses in a country. They know how to operate the system. This is linked to the rise of tax havens in exotic locations like the Caribbean island of Bermuda and the South Pacific

Cook Islands. Thus, major corporations register their loss-making operations in high taxation regimes, such as the United States and Australia, and their profitable ones offshore in tax havens. The lack of international social cohesion militates against governments working together to close these loop holes.

Thus, we get the what is called the rich state/poor nation paradox: A country may rate highly for economic development in aggregate terms while its own people may fare badly in terms of, for example, life expectancy. In terms of mortality rates, the United States ranks 158 on the UNICEF scale for deaths of children under five years old (U5MR), an apparently good ranking as Afghanistan, for example, scores as number one. However, the United States is the main economic power in the world. In contrast as one of the world's poorest countries, Cuba also ranks 158.[51]

Fifth, the pace of globalization has gone so far so fast that national governments no longer have much chance to resist the continued erosion of their control over their economies. For example, in the early 1990s, economist Robert Kuttner recommended that the U.S. government should do more to protect its own economy, such as by government intervention.[52] In these times, however, governments cannot pick winners; intervention will only lead to distortion in the economy, as already happens with Congressional pork-barreling to assist particular districts. Therefore, it is better that government keep out of the strategic management of the economy. The vacuum has been filled by corporations, which set the pace of economic change.

Finally, there is the fear that the world could be heading for another Great Depression. Particularly since 1991, the United States had enjoyed an era of optimism, economic growth, and strong sense of security. However, September 11 showed that perhaps the nation was overly confident. Like on December 7, 1941, and the attack on Pearl Harbor, national intelligence failed. In a deeper sense, the high level of optimism already had led to excessive consumer debt and unrealistic expectations about the unlimited, continued growth of the economy. It remains to be seen how the September 11 tragedy will reduce the American sense of optimism.

The global economy has three locomotives that pull the rest of the global economy: the United States, Western Europe (including the UK), and Japan; at least one of these powers must keep growing so as to haul world economy along. While the Japanese economy has been stalled since the early 1990s, the western European one remains in recession.[53] Now there is concern also about the United States. British writer Charles Leadbeater has recalled the fragility of the global economy: In 1999, it "was hanging by a thread," kept going by the "capacity of U.S. investors for collective self-delusion."[54] The high consumer confidence fed into the stock market's strong growth, which then fed back into consumers thinking that they had a lot of money to spend, which then fed back into the stock exchange, and so on.

This is a bubble economy. At some point the bubble will burst.

"The Coming Anarchy"

This phrase is from an article by Robert Kaplan in 1994, who had visited some failing nation-states such as Sierra Leone, which has become even more anarchic in the years since his visit. Kaplan talks about a "withering away of central government, the rise of tribal and regional domains, the unchecked spread of disease, and the growing pervasiveness of war."[55] This trend provides two components for this part of the scenario: increased chaos within nation-states and the reluctance of others to get involved.

Increased Chaos

The nation-state system is not coping with problems. Those of us who live in developed countries should not assume that what we see here is what is to be seen in the rest of the world.[56] A world made in the image on McDonald's and Coke is not necessarily one safe for democracy and the protection of human rights. We should not assume that the consumption of western goods leads inevitably to the rise of democracy. The Romans provided bread and circuses for the masses; they did not provide democracy.

While much favorable publicity is given to the Newly Industrialized Countries (NICs) and especially to East Asia, most developing countries have not met the targets laid down in the UN Development Decades, which began four decades ago. Indeed, in some African countries, people were economically better off under their European colonial rulers. In the early years of the decolonization process, such countries could claim that they were still subjects of colonialism, with their former colonial masters still running their economies. But the further they get from their dates of independence, the less that form of blaming has relevance.

There are various domestic obstacles to development. There is a capital shortage to sustain large investments in infrastructure (such as transport and developing new sources of energy) and the creation of new industries. In short, poor countries remain poor partly because they lack money for investment. Second, developing countries lack scientific and technological research and development facilities. Ninety-seven percent of all the world's scientists are in the developed western and former communist nations. Eighty percent of humankind have 3 percent of the world's scientists. Third, there is a shortage of skilled personnel to run complicated equipment. Fourth, developing countries are devoting a great deal of attention, in terms of money and skilled personnel, to running defense forces. Fifth, there is a lack of entrepreneurial skills. While business get up and go is taken for granted in developed countries, it takes a while for an entrepreneurial culture to evolve. Finally, many developing countries have corrupt rulers who acquire foreign aid funds to use them for their own purposes, rather than national development.

All of these factors will deter transnational corporations from risking their investments and their foreign-recruited staff in these countries. Thus, some of the current poor countries will fade into greater poverty and obscurity.

Despite the high level of military expenditure (or perhaps even because of it) national governments are losing their monopoly over organized violence. Hence the rise of so-called failed states. While Somalia has gone for a decade without any government, Sierra Leone's governing body has limited power usually only in the daylight hours, and Afghanistan acquired such a system, temporarily anyway, only through international intervention in late 2001. Instead, the pattern resembles one of warlords and bandits controlling fiefdoms. The world is slipping back into a pre-Westphalian era.

Incidentally, another echo of the pre-Westphalian era is the way in which the optimum economic unit in the world is increasingly the city-state.[57] This may be seen in many countries which are descending into anarchy, where central governments only control the big cities rather than all the countryside. For the first time in human history, there are as many people worldwide living in metropolitan settlements as in the rural sectors. Looking for a better life outside the rural sector, people have drifted into urban areas and cannot go back. Their children have no rural experience at all and so cannot go back, even if they wanted to. Therefore, big cities become the location for an underclass. The conditions of over-crowding, bad housing, poor sanitation, and malnutrition all contribute to the spread of diseases. Undercutting social stability, this trend of city-states augments the fragmentation of nation-states. The twenty-first century may well see the nation-state withering away.

Increased Reluctance to Intervene

Reduced international cohesion means that other countries are reluctant to intervene in the affairs of other countries. This may be seen in three ways: the UN's failure to mount operations, the lack of political will among governments to get involved, and the lack of public support in developed countries for such operations.

First, the UN was designed to fight Hitler, as a major threat to international peace and security who was opposed by many other countries. The UN was not designed to rush from one domestic trouble spot to another; it cannot cope with all the conflicts now underway, let alone those likely to occur in the future. For example, General Sir Michael Rose, one of the most experienced officers in low-intensity warfare in the British Army, has written an account of the chaos within the UN operation in Bosnia in the mid-1990s.[58] Even the UN force's title was misleading: "UNPROFOR: UN Protection Force"; it created public expectations well beyond the practical capabilities of any peacekeeping mission. This is just symptomatic of the UN's inability to keep up with the changing nature of the warfare state, not that any government is doing very well, either. The continuing UN operations in the Balkans have not increased the appetite of western governments to get involved in peacekeeping operations. If anything, the operations have reduced the appeal because so little seems to be achieved of a long-range nature. As British writer William

Shawcross has argued in his review of the operations throughout the 1990s, there is no clear formula for determining when the UN will intervene in a crisis or how.[59]

There is also the problem of paying for the operations. The European Union, with 375 million people to the American 280 million, spends only about 57 percent of what the United States does on the military. Additionally, there is a duplication of forces because each country has its own force. NATO calculates that the Europeans have only a tenth of the readily deployable forces available compared with the United States.[60] However, there would be political problems in creating one centralized European defense force on a uniform basis.

Finally, there is the basic question centered on whether the UN can rebuild a system of governance. In other words, if a country collapses and the UN sends in peacekeeping and humanitarian personnel, can the UN set up a valid government in that country? The system would be based on the nation-state which, particularly in Africa, has at most only shallow roots. Thus, even if the UN created a perfect military and civilian operation, it could not impose a stable nation-state system on a country with few traditions of a similar system. It will be interesting to see how the government in Afghanistan, created in December 2001, proceeds. The omens are not good.

The second group of concerns come from a lack of political will for governments to intervene. One of the international community's most controversial failures occurred in 1994 when Rwanda's ruling Hutus set out to eliminate the minority Tutsis. Within about 100 days, an estimated 800,000 Tutsis, out of an approximately 1.2 million, were killed. To kill that many people in so little time required more than just a spontaneous uprising; in comparison, this daily rate of death exceeded the Nazi genocide in World War II. *New Yorker* journalist Philip Gourevitch has examined why the international community ignored warnings about the looming massacre and did nothing as it proceeded. After all, the number of Tutsis killed far exceeded all the people killed in Bosnia, where the international community did eventually get involved.[61] Essentially, Rwanda was of no strategic interest to the United States. With U.S. Rangers recently killed in Somalia, the United States did not want to have another African war; in any case, the victims were black, and Rwanda had no oil. The issue was really one for France, with its own agenda for not wanting to protect human rights, to deal with; with the Cold War being over, the danger of communist mischief-making was not serious. Further, the international media were slow to see Rwanda as a story, and most Americans were more interested in the O.J. Simpson trial then underway.[62]

Perhaps Africa will be the world's first "failed continent."[63] The international community's failure in Rwanda is symptomatic of its overall neglect of Africa in the face of the continent's apparently insurmountable problems. There has been a decline in foreign aid. For example, Australia is the only developed country to have extensive experience with dry land farming as is common in Africa, but the country has few projects in Africa and very little demand by public opinion to increase help with farming. Since western countries prefer to provide aid to countries which have a potential for success (and thus buying some of their exports), the West gives little to Africa.

Finally, there is the role of public opinion in developed countries. Perhaps the notion of the global village, as coined by Marshall McLuhan three decades ago, was flawed. He was correct that the current communications revolution would enable people to learn more about the rest of the world, and we would feel like we were all living in one large village. However, the blizzard of information, particularly bad news, is so overwhelming that people do not want to help those in the community.

Some of the problem may come from the Western media. *Medecins Sans Frontieres* (MSF), created in 1971, is the world's largest independent organization for emergency medical aid. It is famous for bringing swift and direct aid to all populations affected by war and natural disaster, regardless of government consent. MSF is critical of the mass media haphazardly setting political priorities. Somewhat cynically, the media has described how to engineer an international event. First, pictures, and not words, turn an incident into an event, provided that the images be available in a continuous flow to be tapped several times a day for cumulative effect. Second, the conflict must be isolated if it is not to be ousted by a parallel conflict: A television news service cannot cover two African wars at once. Third, there must be a personality from the West, or a volunteer from a humanitarian organization, to "authenticate" the victim, channel the emotion generated, and provide distance as well as connection between the spectator and the victim. Although viewers cannot identify with dying Africans, they can identify with, say, a British entertainer who speaks on behalf of that person. Finally, there must be a victim who is spontaneously acceptable in her or his own right to viewers in the West: For example, the Iraqi Shi'ites stand no more chance of passing this test than do the Palestinians, regardless of the hardships they may be suffering.[64]

In case this sounds a bit cynical, it is worth recalling what we now know the truth about one of the most famous television scenes in the 1990–1991 Gulf War. Shortly before the U.S. Congress voted to go to war in 1990, a television report shook that nation: A girl (whose identity could not, for fear of reprisals, be revealed) sobbed during her report on the atrocities committed by Iraqi soldiers as they invaded Kuwait City. She described the wrecking of the hospital's pediatric departments including the destruction of incubators and infants left to die on the floor. This was great television. Unfortunately, it was not true. The interview was a fake, the interviewee was the daughter of the Kuwaiti ambassador in Washington, playing with talent an imaginary role. One of the leading U.S. communications agencies, financed by Kuwait, was behind this charade to ensure that Congress voted to go to war.[65] The popular movie *Wag the Dog* (which has been seen by many children in the West, even if their parents have not seen it) also captured the role of media manipulation in preparing the United States for a war.

Finally, assuming that the world heads into more problems, such as global economic downturn, western populations will argue that charity belongs at home. When there are so many issues to deal with at home as unemployment, crime, and family breakdown, they will not want their money spent overseas. They will not be sympathetic to their governments taking in more asylum seekers as people flee their own counties in search of a better life. This lack of support for foreign causes will be particularly acute if the U.S. "war against terrorism" goes sour and drags out.

DISASTERS AND CYCLES

Although chapter 5 examined some of the world's major environmental problems and suggested solutions, it is important to note that there is no guarantee that science will solve the problems or that humans will change their lifestyles in time. Not a guarantee, hope for solutions is based on rational human behavior; there is no guarantee that humans will always behave rationally. People often do act in ways that are contrary to their own interests, as shown by the number of people who smoke tobacco.

The irrationality of humans is not a new issue. The Reverend Thomas Robert Malthus (1766–1834) was one of the founders of economics. The first edition his *An Essay on the Principles of Population* (1798) was partly a reply to the prevailing optimism of the Enlightenment, whose writers argued that reason would solve the world's problems. Increased population, it was argued, would provide more hands to work and more consumers to buy goods and services. Malthus, by contrast, warned that extra people would result in increased conflict and shortages of food and living space. He warned that the rate of population growth was faster than the rate at which new sources of food could be developed.

Interest in Malthus declined during the nineteenth and early twentieth centuries. Land was colonized and cultivated as in the United States, Canada, and Australia. New forms of technology, such as railways, coal-fired/oil-fired ships, and refrigeration, enabled food to be transported long distances. Thus, Malthus's *Essay* left the public eye.

But Malthus died too early. In the latter part of the nineteenth century, the rate of global population began to accelerate. Paul Meyer of the Australian National University has set out both the figures and what he calls a "population paradox."[66] The global population rate increased to a rate of about 1 percent per year around 1940 and peaked at around 2.1 percent in the second half of the 1960s. The current rate is about 1.7 percent. However, that good news is offset by a paradox. The annual increments in global population (the numbers being added each year, about 80 million) are still increasing, even though the rate of growth has begun to decline. The earth's population momentum will carry on for at least another century.

Eighty percent of the world population is contained in developing countries. These countries are also the main ones for increased population growth. In contrast, the developed world, or North America, Europe, Japan, and Australia, has approached or gained zero population growth. To sum up, we are in a time of transition. In the past, there were high global birth and death rates; that is, people did not live long lives, and survival of the human race required high birth rates. The goal is to have low global birth and death rates, fewer people being born and each person living a long life. But since about 1970, we have a high birth rate and a low death rate due to advances in medicine. Thus, we might say that the world has death control but not birth control.

Of course, the controlling of death is weakened by sudden arrivals of major diseases. HIV/AIDS is an example of a disease suddenly hitting the human race. It is a disaster because it obliges governments to divert expenditure from other endeavors to caring for the victims, and many of the victims are in the prime of life and potential productivity. HIV/AIDS also contributes to the spread of other diseases, notably tuberculosis, because it erodes the immune system and so lowers resistance to other diseases.

Thus, humankind is destined to remain affected by cycles. Life is not a straight upward line of progress, with times getting better and better for more and more people. Instead, there are cycles. We see them everyday: morning and evening, sun and rain, joy and sorrow, booms and recessions. There is nothing new under the sun.

Similarly countries rise and fall. In 1850, the United Kingdom controlled the largest empire in world history. By 1950, it was the U.S.'s turn. It may well be somebody else's turn by 2050, probably China on current indications. Wealth and power have never remained permanently in any location.

For example, Russia is the first developed country to have declining life expectancy, and it is the first developed country to actually have a reduced population, as distinct from reduced population growth. The average life expectancy in 2000 was 65.9 years, down from 68.8 years in 1965.[67] Russians are giving up trying to live. They have seen their country descend from super power to beggar in only a few years.

Similarly empires have collapsed and have been followed by centuries of barbarism. For example, it took Western Europe centuries before its standard of living got back to the level enjoyed by free Romans during the highpoint of the empire. As we have noted, life for many Africans now is worse than it was in the late colonial era. There is no guarantee that life in the twenty-first century will be better than it was in the twentieth century for most people, in fact, it could be worse for all if diseases and environmental problems get out of control.

CONCLUSION

To conclude, the globe's future will be, in broad terms of global governance, along one of those four worldviews. It is possible for one worldview to dominate globally and for another to flourish in a particular area. The challenge is to attract more attention to the issue of global governance.

NOTES

1. I have been writing about the advantages of, in effect, the World State approach for over two decades; see, for example, Keith Suter, *A New International Order: Proposals for Making a Better World*, Sydney: World Association of World Federalists (Australian Branch), 1981.

2. Keith Suter, "Tampa to the Rescue," *The World Today* (London), October 2001, pp. 22–23.

3. See: John Culver and John Hyde, *American Dreamer: A Life of Henry A Wallace*, New York: Norton, 2000.

4. Henry Kissinger, *Does America Need a Foreign Policy? Toward a Diplomacy for the 21st Century*, New York: Simon & Schuster, 2001.

5. For example: Harold Bidmead, *The Parliament of Man: The Federation of the World*, Barnstaple, England: Patton, 1992; Commission on Global Governance *Our Global Neighborhood*, Oxford: Oxford University Press, 1995; Ronald Glossop, *Confronting War: An Examination of Humanity's Most Pressing Problem*, Jefferson, N.C.: McFarland, 1987; Christopher Hamer, *A Global Parliament: Principles of World Federation*, Sydney: Oyster Bay Books, 1998; Martin Polak, *A Short Path to World Peace*, Hilversum, Netherlands: Boer, 1960; Charlotte Waterlow, *The Hinge of History*, London: One World Trust, 1995.

6. Paul Kennedy, *The Rise and Fall of Great Powers*, London: Fontana, 1989, p. 121.

7. Ian McIntyre, *The Expense of Glory: A Life of John Reith*, London: Harper Collins, 1993, p. 209.

8. See: Robert McChesney, *Rich Media, Poor Democracy: Communication Politics in Dubious Times*, Urbana: University of Illinois Press, 1999.

9. Robert Kaplan, "And Now for the News," *The Atlantic Online*, March 1997: http://www.theatlantic.com/issues/97mar/decline/decline.htm

10. Jean-Jacques Servan-Schreiber, *The American Challenge*, London: Collins, 1967.

11. Thant as quoted in: Richard Falk, *The Endangered Planet*, New York: Vintage, 1972, p. 415.

12. For example: Holly Sklar (Editor), *Trilateralism: The Trilateral Commission and Elite Planning for World Management*, Boston: South End Press, 1980.

13. See: August Heckscher, *Woodrow Wilson*, New York: Scribner's, 1991; J.W. Schulte Nordholt, *Woodrow Wilson: A Life for World Peace*, University of California Press, 1991.

14. "Another Blow to Mercosur," *The Economist* (London), March 31 2001, pp. 35–36.

15. John Redwood, *Stars and Strife: The Coming Conflict Between the USA and the European Union*, London: Palgrave, 2001.

16. Al Gore, *Earth in the Balance: Forging a New Common Purpose*, London: Earthscan, 1992.

17. Report of the Independent Commission on International Development Issues, *North-South: A Program for Survival*, London: Pan, 1980.

18. Katherine Graham, *Personal History*, New York: Alfred Knopf, 1997, pp. 587–588.

19. See: Allan McKnight and Keith Suter, *The Forgotten Treaties: A Practical Plan for World Disarmament*, Melbourne: Law Council of Australia, 1983.

20. Catherine Drinker Bowen, *Miracle at Philadelphia: The Story of the Constitutional Convention*, Boston: Little, Brown & Co., 1966.

21. For example, Barbara Walker (Editor), *The World Federalist Bicentennial Reader*, Washington, D.C.: World Federalist Association, 1987; *A Constitution for the Federation of Earth*, Lakewood, CO: World Constitution and Parliament Association, 1987.

22. For example: Frank Barnaby (Editor), *Building a More Democratic United Nations*, London: Frank Cass, 1991.

23. Neil McAleer, *Odyssey: The Authorized Biography of Arthur C Clarke*, London: Victor Gollancz, 1992, p. 245.

24. Ibid, p. 313.

25. William Shawcross, *Rupert Murdoch*, London: Pan, 1993, p. 528.

26. Neil Gershenfeld, *When Things Start to Think*, London: Hodder & Stoughton, 1999, p. 179.

27. David Adams (Editor), *The Seville Statement on Violence: Preparing the Ground for the Constructing of Peace*, Paris: UNESCO, 1989.

28. For example: Daniel Archibugi and David Held (Editors), *Cosmopolitan Democracy: An Agenda for a New World Order*, Cambridge, MA: Polity Press, 1995.

29. See: Richard Falk, *On Humane Governance: Toward a New Global Politics*, Oxford: Polity Press, 1995.

30. Mr. D'Azeglio as quoted in: Andrina Stiles, *The Unification of Italy*, London: Hodder & Stoughton, 2001, p. 91.

31. Ibid, p. 107.

32. Plato, *The Republic*, London: Penguin, 1972.

33. Edith Wynner and Georgia Lloyd, *Searchlight on Peace Plans: Choose Your Road to World Government*, New York: Dutton, 1949, p. 31.

34. Gertrude Himmelfarb, *The New History and the Old: Critical Essays and Reappraisals*, Cambridge: Harvard University Press, 1987, p. 126.

35. Adam Smith, *The Wealth of Nations*, London: Penguin, 1983 (1776).

36. William Temple, *Christianity and Social Order*, London: SPCK, 1976 (1942), p. 48.

37. In fairness to Adam Smith, who did subscribe to Judeo-Christian ethics, Nobel Economics Prize winner Amartya Sen of Cambridge has argued that Smith would not approve of the way that his writing has been used in recent years to make a virtue out of selfishness and that he was a critic of corporate power; see: Amartya Sen, *Development as Freedom*, Oxford: Oxford University Press, 1999.

38. Callaghan as quoted in: Robert Skidelsky, *John Maynard Keynes: Fighting for Britain*, London: Macmillan, 2000, p. 508.

39. William Jefferson Clinton, *Text of President Clinton's Inaugural Address, January 21 1997*, Washington D.C.: U.S. Information Agency, p. 2.

40. Kenichi Ohmae, *The Borderless World*, London: Collins, 1990, p. xi.

41. David Korten, *When Corporations Rule the World*, London: Earthscan, 1996.

42. For example, Richard Barnet and John Cavanagh, *Global Dreams*, New York: Simon & Schuster, 1994.

43. Kenichi Ohmae, *The Invisible Continent*, London: Nicholas Brealey, 2001.

44. Thomas Friedman, *The Lexus and the Olive Tree*, New York: Farrar, Straus, Giroux, 1999, pp. 26–28.

45. See: Paul Zane Pilzer, *Unlimited Wealth*, New York: Crown, 1994.

46. Ibid, pp. 197–213.

47. Paul Hawken, *The Ecology of Commerce: A Declaration of Sustainability*, New York: Harper Business, 1993.

48. Edwin Black, *IBM and the Holocaust: The Strategic Alliance Between Nazi Germany and America's Most Powerful Corporation*, London: Little, Brown & Co., 2001, p. 9.

49. Page Smith, *Killing the Spirit: Higher Education in America*, New York: Viking, 1990.

50. See: William Greider, *One World, Ready or Not: The Manic Logic of Capitalism*, New York: Simon & Schuster, 1998.

51. *The State of the World's Children 2001*, New York: UNICEF, 2000, pp. 108, 111.

52. Robert Kuttner, *The End of Laissez-Faire: National Purpose and the Global Economy after the Cold War*, New York: Knopf, 1991.

53. There has even been speculation that a Tokyo earthquake could bring down the Japanese economy, and this would have grave consequences for the rest of the world; see: Peter Hadfield, *Sixty Seconds that will Change the World*, London: Sidgwick & Jackson, 1991.

54. Charles Leadbeater, *Living on Thin Air: The New Economy*, London: Penguin, 2000, p. 5.

55. Robert Kaplan, "The Coming Anarchy," *The Atlantic Monthly*, February 1994, p. 46.

56. Of course, it could be argued that the United States is not as well off as it would like to seem; see: Marc Miringoff and Marque-Luisa Miringoff, *The Social Health of the Nation: How America is Really Doing*, Oxford: Oxford University Press, 1999.

57. Much the same could be said about the United States, where Houston is now the fourth biggest city (bigger than Berlin with an economy larger than Hong Kong's), see: "The Blob That Ate East Texas," *The Economist*, June 23 2001, pp. 40–42.

58. Sir Michael Rose, *Fighting for Peace*, London: Harvill, 1998.

59. William Shawcross, *Deliver Us From Evil: Peacekeepers, Warlords and a World of Endless Conflict*, New York: Simon & Schuster, 2000.

60. "European Defence: If Only Words Were Guns." *The Economist*, November 24 2001, pp 51–52.

61. Philip Gourevitch, *We Wish to Inform You That Tomorrow We Will be Killed With Our Families: Stories from Rwanda*, London: Picador, 1999.

62. An equally depressing account is: Linda Melvern, *A People Betrayed: The Role of the West in Rwanda's Genocide*, London: Zed, 2000.

63. See: Keith Suter, "The Lost Continent: Has Africa Run Out of Hope?," *The Age* (Melbourne), January 27, 2001, p. 11.

64. Francoise Jean (Editor), *Life, Death and Aid: The Medecins Sans Frontieres Report on World Crisis Intervention*, London: Routledge, 1993, p. 150.

65. Ibid, p. 155.

66. Paul Meyer, "Population Paradoxes" *Development Studies Network Newsletter* (Canberra), July 1992, p. 19.

67. "Numbers," *Time*, December 18, 2000, p. 20.

8

Ready for Change

INTRODUCTION

"For years our tallest buildings were the fire towers. We had fires all of the time, we burned as a matter of habit" writes novelist E.L. Doctorow in *The Waterworks*[1] as he describes New York City in 1872 and the perpetual risk of fire. Gradually, the city was made safe by improved fire precautions, building regulations, and the removal of particularly flammable materials. Contingency planning greatly reduced the risk of fire. Changes were made and they paid off.

To survive, whether as individuals, companies or countries, it is necessary to adapt to change quickly and decisively. Not being able to predict the future, we need to have contingency plans to cope with eventualities. We need to avoid being taken by surprise. The previous two chapters have argued the case for greater use of scenario planning in addressing the future of the nation-state in the era of globalization.

This chapter is a recommendation to bring scenario planning in from the cold and use it to encourage more discussions and contingency planning for global governance.

LOOKING TO THE FUTURE

People should be encouraged to think more about the future because that is where they will be spending the rest of their lives. In particular, global governance requires more attention.

I know from my work in the Australian media that global governance has a high MEGO (My Eyes Glaze Over) rating. But at the systemic level, that is precisely what the September 11 tragedy and the U.S. response have been about. The problem is that editors assumed that the color and drama of the military response got better ratings than a discussion on global governance.

Similarly, politicians are not too keen on the subject either. Indeed, the Bush Administration has been contradictory. On the one hand, its pursuance of free trade is based on increased international social cohesion; on the other hand, its opposition to the International Criminal Court, Kyoto Protocol, Comprehensive Test Ban, and withdrawal from the Anti-Ballistic Missile Treaty all suggest reduced international social cohesion. Similarly, the United States has a tradition of defending the rule of law at home, notably via the pioneering Bill of Rights, but is now evidently opposing it overseas, such as not supporting the International Criminal Court.

Politicians can get away with these inconsistencies as long as they deal with one issue at a time. They lurch from one media headline to the next. A systemic discussion of global governance would encourage a more thoughtful examination of where a country stands in the world and what ought to be the basic foundations of its foreign policy.

This takes us back to the value of scenario planning in the context of global governance. First, the people and organizations that do deal explicitly with global governance, such as the various world government organizations, do so with an explicit agenda: They are advocating their solution. This is not a criticism of their work because that is why they exist. (I do the same work in my various world government capacities.) But scenario planning is more neutral. It does not argue that there is only one solution. Instead, it sets out the challenges that need to be addressed and helps people to work their own way through to a solution for themselves.

This was a value of the Clem Sunter work in South Africa. His company had problems with the apartheid regime. If the Sunter team had simply spoken out against apartheid, it would have been labeled in the public mind as a yet another anti-apartheid group. However, the Sunter team made the exercise more one of education than advocacy, encouraging white South Africans to work out for themselves the long-term consequences of their actions.

Second, it could be that we are in a better position than the people in 1648. No one suddenly got out of bed that year and said that a new world order was being created. Indeed, there was no guarantee that the Thirty Years War (1618–1648) was going to be the last major religious war in Europe. No one knew that three centuries were to pass before Europe again endured the same level of violence as it did between those years. Instead, that a new world order had in fact been created became obvious only as the decades rolled by. The term "Westphalian" itself does not seem to have entered the vocabulary of international lawyers until the twentieth century (and of course it is still not in the popular vocabulary).

However, we are in a position to learn from history. We are possibly at the first time in human history at which we can understand the process of change, benefit from an historical context, deliberately design a different world order, and work out the implications of doing so.

Finally, good ideas have no boundaries. As this book has shown, there are major challenges ahead, and at root they have implications for global governance. The widespread use of scenario planning in the interest of global governance could stimulate the necessary global debate and political will for changes that will create a safer world.

The Scenarios in the previous Chapter set out four worldviews. In a full scenario planning project, there would also be indicators to help detect which of the four scenarios is coming into play and some ideas for contingency plans to cope with that Scenario. In the interests of space, these have not been included. Indeed, even the four scenarios have themselves been somewhat abbreviated. However, it is hoped that enough has been done to indicate that international relations as a discipline could benefit from the greater use of scenario planning as a tool. It is also hoped that the book will stimulate greater attention to the future of global governance. As with the fire precautions in New York City just over a century ago, contingency planning pays off. If we can make security improvements at the city level we can also do so at the global level.

NOTE

1. E.L. Doctorow, *The Waterworks*, Melbourne: Pan Macmillan, 1994, p. 11.

Selected Bibliography

Archer, Clive. *International Organizations*. London: George Allen & Unwin, 1983.

Barnaby, Frank (ed.). *Building a More Democratic United Nations*. London: Frank Cass, 1991.

Bendiner, Elmer. *A Time for Angels: The Tragicomic History of the League of Nations*. London: Weidenfeld & Nicolson, 1975.

Black, Edwin. *IBM and the Holocaust: The Strategic Alliance Between Nazi Germany and America's Most Powerful Corporation*. London: Little, Brown, & Co., 2001.

Black, Maggie. *A Cause for Our Times: OXFAM, The First 50 years*. Oxford: Oxford University Press, 1992.

Boulding, Elise. *Building a Global Civic Culture: Education for an Interdependent World*. New York: Columbia University Teachers' College Press, 1988.

Bowen, Catherine Drinker. *Miracle at Philadelphia: The Story of the Constitutional Convention*. Boston: Little, Brown & Co., 1966.

Brierly, J.L. *The Law of Nations*, Oxford: Clarendon, 1963.

Brown, Lester. *Building a Sustainable Society*. New York: Norton, 1993.

Bull, Hedley, and Adam Watson (eds.). *The Expansion of International Society*. Oxford: Clarendon, 1985.

Cannon, Lou. *President Reagan: The Role of a Lifetime*. New York: Simon & Schuster, 1991.

Clairmonte, Frederick, and John Cavanagh. *Transnational Corporations and Global Markets: Changing Power Relations*. Sydney: Transnational Corporations Research Project, University of Sydney, 1984.

Claude, Innis. *Swords into Plowshares: The Problems and Progress of International Organization*. London: University of London Press, 1964.

Cullen, Robert. *Twilight of Empire: Inside the Crumbling Soviet Bloc*. London: The Bodley Head, 1991.

Davidson, Basil. *The Black Man's Burden: Africa and the Curse of the Nation-State*. London: James Carey, 1992.

———. *The Search for Africa: A History in the Making*. London: James Carey, 1994.

Evans, Gareth. *Co-operating for Peace: The Global Agenda for the 1990s and Beyond*. Sydney: Allen & Unwin, 1993.

Falk, Richard. *This Endangered Planet*. New York: Vintage, 1972.

———. *On Human Governance: Toward a New Global Politics*. Oxford: Polity Press, 1995.

Fawcett, J.E.S. *The Law of Nations*. London: Penguin, 1971.

Friedman, Thomas. *The Lexus and the Olive Tree.* New York: Farrar, Strauss, Giroux, 1999.

Galbraith, John Kenneth. *The Culture of Contentment.* Boston: Houghton-Mifflin, 1992.

George, Susan. *The Debt Boomerang: How Third World Debt Harms Us All.* Sydney: Pluto, 1992.

Gershenfeld, Neil. *When Things Start to Think.* London: Hodder & Stoughton, 1999.

Graham, Katherine. *Personal History.* New York: Alfred Knopf, 1997.

Greider, William. *One World, Ready or Not: The Manic Logic of Capitalism.* New York: Simon & Schuster, 1998.

Guyatt, Nicholas. *Another American Century? The United States and the World After 2000.* London: Zed, 2000.

Hawken, Paul. *The Ecology of Commerce: A Declaration of Sustainability.* New York: HarperBusiness, 1993.

Hawken, Paul, L. Hunter Lovins, and Amory Lovins. *Natural Capitalism: The Next Industrial Revolution,* London: Earthscan, 1999.

Higgins, Rosalyn. *The Development of International Law Through the Political Organs of the United Nations.* Oxford: Oxford University Press, 1963.

Himmelfarb, Gertrude. *The New History and the Old: Critical Essays and Reappraisals.* Cambridge: Harvard University Press, 1987.

Jacobs, Jane. *Cities and the Wealth of Nations: Principles of Economic Life.* New York: Random House, 1985.

James, David. *The Fall of the Russian Empire.* London: Granada, 1982.

Jean, Francoise (ed.). *Life, Death and Aid: The Medecins Sans Frontieres Report on World Crisis Intervention.* London: Routledge, 1993.

Johansen, Robert. *The National Interest and the Human Interest: An Analysis of US Foreign Policy.* Princeton, NJ: Princeton University Press, 1980.

Joyce, James Avery. *Broken Star—The Story of the League of Nations 1919–39.* Swansea: Christopher Davies, 1978.

Kahn, Herman. *On Escalation: Metaphors and Scenarios.* New York: Hudson Institute, 1965.

———. *Thinking About the Unthinkable.* New York: Horizon, 1962.

Kaldor, Mary. *The Baroque Arsenal.* London: Andre Deutsch, 1982.

Kennedy, Paul. *The Rise and Fall of Great Powers.* London: Fontana, 1989.

———. *Preparing for the Twenty-First Century.* London: HarperCollins, 1993.

Kinsman, Francis. *Millennium: Towards Tomorrow's Society.* London: W.H. Allen, 1990.

Kissinger, Henry. *Does America Need a Foreign Policy? Toward a Diplomacy for the 21st Century.* New York: Simon & Schuster, 2001.

Korten, David. *When Corporations Rule the World.* London: Earthscan, 1996.

Kuhn, Thomas. *The Structure of Scientific Revolutions.* Chicago: University of Chicago Press, 1962.

Kumar, Ranjit, and Barbara Murck. *Our Common Ground: Managing Human-Planet Relationships.* Toronto: John Wiley, 1992.

Kurzweil, Ray. *The Age of Spiritual Machines: When Computers Exceed Human Intelligence.* Sydney: Allen & Unwin, 1999.

Leadbeater, Charles. *Living on Thin Air: The New Economy.* London: Penguin, 2000.

Luard, Evan. *The Blunted Sword: The Erosion of Military Power in Modern World Politics*. London: Tauris, 1988.

Mead, Dana. *High Standards, Hard Choices: A CEO's Journey of Courage, Risk and Change*. New York: John Wiley, 2000.

Meadows, Dennis et al. *The Limits to Growth*. New York: Universe Books, 1972.

Medvedev, Zhores. *Nuclear Disaster in the Urals*. New York: Norton, 1979.

Melvern, Linda. *A People Betrayed: The Role of the West in Rwanda's Genocide*. London: Zed, 2000.

Mitrany, David. *The Functional Theory of Politics*. London: Martin Robertson, 1975.

Morrison, Donald (ed.). *Mikhail S. Gorbachev: An Intimate Biography*. New York: Time, 1988.

Nicolson, Harold. *Diplomacy*. Oxford: Oxford University Press, 1963.

Ohmae, Kenichi. *The Borderless World*. London: Collins, 1990.

O'Neill, Michael. *The Third America: The Emergence of the Non-Profit Sector in the United States*. San Francisco: Jossey-Bass, 1990.

Pakenham, Thomas. *The Scramble for Africa: The White Man's Conquest of the Dark Continent from 1876 to 1912*. London: Random House, 1991.

Pakenham, Valerie. *The Noonday Sun: Edwardians in the Tropics*. London: Methuen, 1985.

Preston, Richard. *The Hot Zone*. Sydney: Doubleday, 1994.

Redwood, John. *Stars and Strife: The Coming Conflict Between the USA and the European Union*. London: Palgrave, 2001.

Scheer, Robert. *With Enough Shovels: Reagan, Bush and Nuclear War*. New York: Random House, 1982.

Schwartz, Peter. *The Art of the Long View: Planning for the Future in an Uncertain World*. New York: Doubleday, 1991.

Seagrave, Sterling. *Lords of the Rim*. New York: Putnam, 1995.

Sen, Amartya. *Development as Freedom*. Oxford: Oxford University Press, 1999.

Servan-Schreiber, Jean-Jacques. *The World Challenge*. London: Collins, 1981.

Shawcross, William. *Deliver Us From Evil: Peacekeepers, Warlords and a World of Endless Conflict*. New York: Simon & Schuster, 2000.

Shoup, Laurence, and William Minter. *Imperial Brains Trust: The Council on Foreign Relations and United States Foreign Policy*. New York: Monthly Review Press, 1977.

Sklar, Holly (ed.). *Trilateralism: The Trilateral Commission and Elite Planning for World Management*. Boston: South End Press, 1980.

Smith, Hedrick. *The Russians*. London: Sphere, 1976.

Stonier, Tom. *The Wealth of Information*. London: Thames Methuen, 1983.

Summy, Ralph, and Michael Salla (eds.). *Why the Cold War Ended: A Range of Interpretations*. Westport, CT: Greenwood Press, 1995.

Suter, Keith. *Reshaping the Global Agenda: The United Nations at Forty*. Sydney: United Nations Association of Australia, 1986.

Thomson, David. *Europe Since Napoleon*. London: Penguin, 1970.

Toffler, Alvin. *Powershift*. New York: Bantam, 1990.

van der Heijden, Kees. *Scenarios: The Art of Strategic Conversation*. New York: Wiley, 1996.

Wack, Pierre. *Scenarios: The Gentle Art of Re-Perceiving (One Thing or Two Learned While Developing Planning Scenarios for Royal Dutch/ Shell)*. Cambridge: Harvard Business School, 1984.

Walker, Barbara (ed.). *The World Federalist Bicentennial Reader.* Washington, D.C.: World Federalist Association, 1987.

Ward, Geoffrey. *The West: An Illustrated History.* London: Weidenfeld & Nicolson, 1996.

Weizacker, Ernst von et al. *Factor 4: Doubling Wealth–Halving Resource Use: The New Report to the Club of the Rome.* London: Earthscan, 1997.

Willens, Harold. *The Trimtab Factor.* New York: Morrow, 1984.

Willetts, Peter (ed.). *The Conscience of the World: The Influence of Non-Governmental Organizations in the UN System.* London: Hurst, 1996.

Winchester, Simon. *Pacific Rising.* Upper Saddle River, NJ: Prentice-Hall, 1991.

Wiskemann, Elizabeth. *Europe of the Dictators 1919–1945.* London: Fontana, 1971.

World Commission on Environment and Development. *Our Common Future.* Oxford: Oxford University Press, 1987.

Yergin, Daniel. *Shattered Peace: The Origins of the Cold War and the National Security State.* London: Penguin, 1977.

Index

Acid rain, 123
Aerial hi-jacking, 54
Afghanistan, 47, 49, 61, 103
Africa as a "failed continent", 188
Algeria, 145–6
Allain, Annelies, 97
Amnesty International, 75
Andorra, 130
Antarctica, 11–12, 99, 121
Anti-Slavery International, 97–98
Apartheid, 128, 154, 196
Australia, 11–12, 23, 32, 37–8, 132

Bank of Credit and Commerce
   International (BCCI), 105–7
Barnet, Richard, 182
Berlin Conference (1884–5), 35, 38–9
Black, Edwin, 184
Brandt, Willy, 169
British nuclear tests, 38, 95
Brown, Lester, 13
Browne, John, 121
Brownlie, Ian, 18
Buchanan, Patrick, 3, 142
Bull, Hedley, 21
Bush, George, 41, 50, 126–7, 168
Bush, George W., 39, 61–2, 132

Calvocoressi, Peter, 36
Carrier, James, 71
Catholic Church, 18–19, 41, 97, 127, 177
Cavanagh, John, 68–9
Chernobyl nuclear disaster, 7, 171
China, 72, 107–8, 184, 191

Churchill, Winston, 62, 85, 151
Civil Society Organizations (CSOs), 92
Clairmonte, Frederick, 68–9
Clarke, Arthur C, 172, 177,
Climate change, 121–2
Clinton, William Jefferson (Bill), 39, 62,
   72, 84, 132, 168
Club of Rome, 12
Cold War, 2, 5–13, 51, 79, 85–6, 127–8
Common law, 176
Congress of Vienna (1815), 38, 41, 78
Consumerism, 5–6, 51, 71–4, 137–8
Conventional warfare, 44–6
Creveld, Martin van, 44–5
Crime, globalization of, 101–9
Crossman, Richard, 131
Cuba, 132, 185
Cullen, Robert, 12
Cultural Survival, 24–5

Decolonization, 34–6
Dieren, Wouter van, 129
Diseases, globalization of, 116–20
Doctorow, E.L., 195
Dulles, Allen, 27–8

"Earth Inc." (scenario), 161–2, 177–83
East Timor, 32, 34, 85–6, 142, 166
Ebola, 119–20
Environment movement, 1, 12–13
Equal Rights Amendment, 170
European Union, 90–2, 129, 168
Europeanization (of the globe), 2, 31–6
Evatt, H.V., 82

Falk, Richard, 23
Fawcett, James, 77
Foreign exchange, 76, 91
Foreign Terrorist Organizations (FTOs),
    55
Friedman, Thomas, 182
Functional co-operation, 11, 81, 134,
    174

Galbraith, John Kenneth, 42, 137
George, Susan, 104
Gershenfeld, Neil, 173
Global gladiators, 104
Global North, 138
Global policy, rise of, 133
Global South, 138
Globalization, 1–3; characteristics of,
    115–6
Gonzalez, Elian, 132
Gorbachev, Mikhail, 7–9, 50, 156, 173,
    179–80
Gore, Al, 132, 168
Goresky, Dorothy, 81
Graham, Katherine, 169
Greenpeace, 57, 75, 98–9
Group of 77 (G77), 127–8
Guerrilla warfare, 43–4, 47–50
Gurwin, Larry, 106–7

Haider, Jorge, 3, 142
Hanson, Pauline, 3, 142
Hawken, Paul, 183
Higgins, Rosalyn, 82
Hinduism, 143–5
Himmelfarb, Gertrude, 177
Hitler, Adolf, 22, 28, 56, 58, 58, 82, 184,
    187
HIV/AIDS, 116–8, 191
Hobbes, Thomas, 22
Holocaust, 22, 82, 184
Hussein, Mahmoud, 145
Hussein, Saddam, 50, 85, 132, 152

IBM (International Business Machines),
    184
India, 33, 36, 58, 75, 88
Indigenous peoples, 24–5, 36–8, 89, 142
Infant formula powdered milk, 96–7

Information technology, 6–7, 102, 134–5,
    173, 184
Inter-Linked Economy, 180–1
International Atomic Energy Agency
    (IAEA), 170
International Court of Justice, 80, 87, 94
International Criminal Court, 39, 62, 196
International Law Association, 53, 62
International Relations, study of, 67
International Maritime Organization, 11
International Telecommunications
    Organization, 11
International war, 49–50
Islam, 52, 75, 137, 145–7
Italian unification, 176

James, Alan, 26
Jones, Walter, 133
Johansen, Robert, 19
Johnston, Douglas, 94

Kahn, Herman, 154
Kaldor, Mary, 24
Kaplan, Robert, 166, 186
Kedourie, Elie, 27, 34–5
Kennedy, Paul, 8–9, 20, 165
Keynes, John Maynard, 130, 179
Kinsman, Francis, 73
Kissinger, Henry, 56, 64, 106, 164
Klerk, Frederick de, 154, 159
Korten, David, 182
Kuhn, Thomas, 153
Kumar, Ranjit, 115
Kuttner, Robert, 185
Kyoto Protocol, 122, 196

Laden, Osama bin, 61, 103
Leadbeater, Charles, 185
League of Nations, 27, 32, 58, 77–9, 151,
    164
Libya, 55–6, 61, 69
Lloyd, Georgia, 177
Localization, rise of, 128–30
Los Angeles, 129, 138
Luther, Martin, 18–9, 136

McCloy-Zorin Plan, 170
Macmillan, Harold, 33–4

Maier, Karl, 35
Malthus, Thomas, 190
Mandela, Nelson, 53, 128, 154
Mann, Jonathan, 118–9
Marshall Plan, 168–9
Mead, Dana, 51, 69
Medecins Sans Frontieres (MSF), 189
Media, 3–4, 8, 47–8, 75–6, 86–7, 135–7, 141, 188–9
Meyer, Paul, 190
Mitrany, David, 11
Moore's Law, 173
Murdoch, Rupert, 135, 139, 148
Murck, Barbara, 115
Myers, Norman, 13

Narcotic drugs, 102–5, 133
Nasrin, Taslima, 146
Nation, definition of, 23
Nation-State, characteristics of, 20–23
Natural Law, 21–2, 29
Nauru, 37–8, 41
New Zealand, 57
Nigeria, 35–6
Non-Governmental Organization (NGO), 92; characteristics of, 93–101
Nostalgia, 140
Nuclear warfare, 46–7

Ohmae, Kenichi, 70, 180–1
Organization for Economic Co-operation and Development (OECD), 128
Oxford Committee for Famine Relief (OXFAM), 94
Ozone layer, 122–3

Pakenham, Valerie, 42
Papua New Guinea, 32, 74
Paradigm, 153
Peace Movement, 1, 12, 95, 154–5
People smuggling, 107–8
Philadelphia Convention (1787), 170, 176
Pinochet, Augusto, 56
Politics of anger, 3, 141–2
Positivism, 22

Post-modern warfare, 50–2
Preston, Richard, 119–20

Reagan, Ronald, 6–9, 152, 156, 168, 179
Rogue states, 55–6
Romania, 12
Rose, Michael, 187
Ruthenia, 25–6
Rushdie, Salman, 146–7
Russia (since 1991), 51–2, 55, 182, 191
Rwanda, 188

Sampson, Cynthia, 94
Scenario planning, 9–10, 153–8, 196–7
Schumacher, E.F., 96,
Schwartz, Peter, 9, 155–6
Seattle (1999 demonstration), 1, 140
Secession, 52–3, 86
Seed, John, 139
Self-determination, 27–8, 32–8, 103–4
September 11 2001, 52–3, 61–2, 85, 101–3, 152
Servan-Schreiber, Jean-Jacques, 10, 69, 199
Seville Statement, 175
Sharman, Anne-Marie, 98
Shawcross, William, 187–8
Shelton, Dinah, 94
Smith, Adam, 178–9
Smith, Page, 184
Solzhenitsyn, Aleksandr, 6
Somalia, 49–50, 86, 187
Sovereignty, 22–3, 26–7, 103–4, 162–4
Soviet Union, 5–13, 151, 181–2
Stalin, Josef, 7, 56, 181
Stanley, Richard, 100
State, definition of, 25
"Steady State" (scenario), 161–71
Stonier, Tom, 43
Strange, Susan, 67
Subsidiarity, 91
Sunter, Clem, 154, 196

Tax havens, 184–5
Terrorism, 53–61
Temple, William, 178
Thant, U, 166–7
Thatcher, Margaret, 47–8, 50, 75, 179

Thirty Years War, 19, 196
Thomson, David, 39
Toffler, Alvin, 104
Transnational corporation, definition of, 68
Transnational corporations, power of 68–77
Transparency, 7–8, 14
Trilateral Commission, 167
Truell, Peter, 106–7
Tuberculosis, 119

Unemployment, 72, 133, 140
United Nations: domestic jurisdiction, 82–3, 86–7; reform of, 87–90
United Nations Conference on Environment and Development (UNCED), 12, 124, 126–7, 168
United Nations Economic and Social Council (ECOSOC), 81, 90
United Nations General Assembly, 79, 89
United Nations Peacekeeping operations, 77, 85–7, 187
United Nations Secretary-General, 81, 87–88, 166–7
United Nations Security Council, 79, 89
United Nations Trusteeship Council, 32, 80–1, 89
United States, 5–13, 20, 23–6, 32, 48, 61–2
Urals nuclear disaster, 7
Urquhart, Brian, 25

Vernon, Raymond, 71
Vietnam War, 47–8, 65, 152

Wack, Pierre, 155
Wag the Dog, 189
Wallace, Henry, 163, 175
Wallace, William, 21
Water, 123–5
Webb, Pauline, 136
Wells, HG, 77
Westphalia, Treaty of, 17–8
Westphalian System, definition of, 17
Westphalian worldview, 115–6
Wilberforce, William, 175
"Wild State" (scenario), 162, 183–91
Williams, Jody, 101, 176
Wilson, Woodrow, 27, 77–8, 80, 167
Winchester, Simon, 129
Wiskemann, Elizabeth, 58
Wolfe, Alan, 130
Women's movement, 1, 146
World government, 165
World Health Organization (WHO), 11, 81, 97
World Meteorological Organization (WMO), 11
"World State" (scenario) 161, 171–7
Worldview, 153
World Trade Organization (WTO), 1, 3, 132
Wynner, Edith, 177

Yugoslavia, 39, 50–2, 58, 78, 86, 151, 164

About the Author

KEITH SUTER is Senior Fellow, Global Business Network Australia, Chairperson of the Environment Committee of the Australian Institute of Company Directors, and Director of Studies, International Law Association (Australian Branch). Among his earlier books is *In Defense of Globalization* (2001).